Foundations of Language & Literature

Workbook

Renée H. Shea | John Golden | Tracy Scholz

bedford, freeman & worth
high school publishers

Manufactured in the United States of America.

1 2 3 4 5 6   25 24 23 22 21 20

For information, write: BFW Publishers, One New York Plaza, New York, NY 10004

ISBN 978-1-319-35852-5

Contents

Vocabulary
Chapter 5

Chapter 6

Chapter 8

Key Passages
Chapter 5

Chapter 6

The Veldt (p. 165)
Ray Bradbury

For each term in bold below, determine the meaning of the word in the context of the sentence, and then describe the effect of the word: how the author's word choice contributes to the meaning and tone of the sentence(s).

1. "They stood on the **thatched** floor of the nursery. It was forty feet across by forty feet long and thirty feet high; it had cost half again as much as the rest of the house." (par. 13)

Meaning:

Effect:

2. "Now, as George and Lydia Hadley stood in the center of the room, the walls began to purr and **recede** into crystalline distance, it seemed, and presently an African veldt appeared, in three dimensions, on all sides, in color reproduced to the final pebble and bit of straw." (par. 14)

Meaning:

Effect:

3. "Now the hidden odorophonics were beginning to blow a wind of odor at the two people in the middle of the baked **veldtland**." (par. 18)

Meaning:

Effect:

4. "The lions were coming. And again George Hadley was filled with admiration for the mechanical genius who had **conceived** this room." (par. 29)

Meaning:

Effect:

5. "A miracle of **efficiency** selling for an absurdly low price. Every home should have one." (par. 29)

Meaning:

Effect:

6. "Oh, occasionally they frightened you with their **clinical** accuracy, they startled you, gave you a twinge, but most of the time what fun for everyone, not only your own son and daughter,

but for yourself when you felt like a quick jaunt to a foreign land, a quick change of scenery. Well, here it was!" (par. 29)

Meaning:

Effect:

7. "Outside, in the hall, with the door slammed he was laughing and she was crying, and they both stood **appalled** at the other's reaction." (par. 34)

Meaning:

Effect:

8. "'They live for the nursery.' 'It's got to be locked, that's all there is to it.' 'All right.' **Reluctantly** he locked the huge door." (par. 46-48)

Meaning:

Effect:

9. "'If children are **neurotic** at all, a room like that –' 'It's supposed to help them work off their neuroses in a healthful way.' 'I'm starting to wonder.' He stared at the ceiling." (par. 131-133)

Meaning:

Effect:

10. "'I think we'd better get downstairs before those kids get **engrossed** with those damned beasts again.'" (par. 247)

Meaning:

Effect:

Reindeer Games (p. 176)
Sherman Alexie

For each term in bold below, determine the meaning of the word in the context of the sentence, and then describe the effect of the word: how the author's word choice contributes to the meaning and tone of the sentence(s).

1. "And I didn't want to get cut from the team. I didn't think I could live through that **humiliation**." (par. 1)

Meaning:

Effect:

2. "'You have to dream big to get big.' 'That's pretty dang **optimistic** for you, Dad.'" (par. 14- 15)

Meaning:

Effect:

3. "Twenty boys **puffed** up their chests. They knew they were good enough to make either the varsity or the junior varsity." (par. 31)

Meaning:

Effect:

4. "'You play with **dignity** and respect, and I'll treat you with dignity and respect, no matter what happens, okay?'" (par. 33)

Meaning:

Effect:

5. "After fifty laps, one guy quit, and since quitting is **contagious**, three other boys caught that disease and walked off the court, too." (par. 38)

Meaning:

Effect:

6. "This time, Roger tried to dribble down the court. And I played defense. I crouched down low, spread my arms and legs high and wide, and **gritted** my teeth." (par. 55)

Meaning:

Effect:

7. "When our bus pulled into the high school parking lot, we were greeted by some **rabid** elementary school kids." (par. 105)

Meaning:

Effect:

8. "They **pelted** our bus with snowballs. And some of those snowballs were filled with rocks." (par. 106)

Meaning:

Effect:

9. "And, then, as one, they all turned their backs on me. It was a fricking awesome display of **contempt**." (par. 128-129)

Meaning:

Effect:

10. "Bleeding and angry, I glared at the crowd. They **taunted** me as I walked into the locker room." (par. 156-157)

Meaning:

Effect:

Mirror Image (p. 184)

Lena Coakley

For each term in bold below, determine the meaning of the word in the context of the sentence, and then describe the effect of the word: how the author's word choice contributes to the meaning and tone of the sentence(s).

1. "The surprise and **disbelief** at seeing the reflection was a joke she played on herself over and over." (par. 1)

Meaning:

Effect:

2. "It was **disquieting**, however, to come upon a mirror without warning." (par. 2)

Meaning:

Effect:

3. "The human mind is incredibly **adaptable**. Her mother was always telling her that." (par. 4)

Meaning:

Effect:

4. "At first the world was nothing but a mush of dark images, **disconnected** voices and prickly feelings all over her skin." (par. 8)

Meaning:

Effect:

5. "When she finally learned, the tone was different, but the **inflections** and the slight Maritime accent were the same." (par. 8)

Meaning:

Effect:

6. "The doctors had taken the precaution of giving her a mild **sedative**. It made her feel like everything was happening to someone else, far away." (par. 24)

Meaning:

Effect:

7. "She held the silver mirror in one hand. With the other, she pulled at her face, squeezed it as if it were clay. Alice was **mesmerized** by the unfamiliar eyes, big and brown and dark." (par. 24)

Meaning:

Effect:

8. "Alice tried hard to swallow, tried hard not to let her face show any reaction to the cake, but the taste of the mocha forced her mouth into a **grimace**." (par. 57)

Meaning:

Effect:

9. "Sometimes things were **exquisitely** clear and sharp, although she wasn't wearing her contacts, and she hadn't yet learned to ignore her eyelashes which seemed longer and darker than they had been before." (par. 72)

Meaning:

Effect:

10. "'I'll tell her,' Mr. Jarred's voice began to **falter**, but he looked at her straight on, 'I'll tell her I looked into your eyes and that I didn't see my daughter.'" (par. 88)

Meaning:

Effect:

What, of This Goldfish, Would You Wish? (p. 192)
Etgar Keret

For each term in bold below, determine the meaning of the word in the context of the sentence, and then describe the effect of the word: how the author's word choice contributes to the meaning and tone of the sentence(s).

1. "Onto this shot he'd **superimpose** the subject's name, family situation, monthly income, and maybe even the party he'd voted for in the last election." (par. 2)

Meaning:

Effect:

2. "All that, combined with the three wishes, and maybe he'd end up with a **poignant** piece of social commentary, a **testament** to the massive rift between our dreams and the often compromised reality in which we live." (par. 2)

Meaning (poignant):

Meaning (testament):

Effect:

3. "With a little decent footage, he was sure he'd be able to sell it to Channel 8 or Discovery in a flash, either as a film or as a bunch of **vignettes**, little cinematic corners, each with that singular soul standing in a doorway, followed by three killer wishes, precious, every one." (par. 3)

Meaning:

Effect:

4. "A Holocaust survivor with a number on his arm asked very slowly, in a quiet voice—as if he'd been waiting for Yoni to come, as if it weren't an exercise at all—he'd been wondering (if this fish didn't mind), would it be possible for all the Nazis left living in the world to be held **accountable** for their crimes?" (par. 5)

Meaning:

Effect:

5. "Yonatan knew that if the project was going to have any weight, he'd have to get to everyone, to the unemployed, to the ultrareligious, to the Arabs and Ethiopians and American **expats**." (par. 8)

Meaning:

Effect:

6. "Maybe somewhere in that city some **<u>beleaguered</u>** Arab man would stand in his doorway and, looking through Yonatan and his camera, looking out into nothingness, just pause for a minute, nod his head, and wish for peace-that would be something to see." (par. 8)

Meaning:

Effect:

7. "His father had been a **<u>Zionist</u>**, which was pretty much an invitation for them to drop by any old time." (par. 9)

Meaning:

Effect:

8. "Until one day some kid with a ring in his ear, looking a little bit homosexual, comes knocking. Hard like that—**<u>rapping</u>** at his door. Just the way Sergei doesn't like." (par. 11)

Meaning:

Effect:

9. "He's already making his movie, running his camera without any permission, and from behind the camera he's still telling Sergei about his face, that it's full of feeling, that it's **<u>tender</u>**." (par. 13)

Meaning:

Effect:

10. "In his mind, he was less sure, and all kinds of thoughts about other things he could have done with that wish continued to **<u>gnaw</u>** at him, half driving him mad." (par. 31)

Meaning:

Effect:

The Cask of Amontillado (p. 198)
Edgar Allan Poe

For each term in bold below, determine the meaning of the word in the context of the sentence, and then describe the effect of the word: how the author's word choice contributes to the meaning and tone of the sentence(s).

1. "The thousand injuries of Fortunato I had borne as I best could, but when he **ventured** upon insult I vowed revenge." (par. 1)

Meaning:

Effect:

2. "I must not only punish but punish with **impunity**." (par. 1)

Meaning:

Effect:

3. "It must be understood that neither by word nor deed had I given Fortunato cause to doubt my good will. I continued, as was my wont, to smile in his face, and he did not perceive that my smile now was at the thought of his **immolation**." (par. 2)

Meaning:

Effect:

4. "He **accosted** me with excessive warmth, for he had been drinking much." (par. 4)

Meaning:

Effect:

5. "'My friend, no; I will not **impose** upon your good nature. I perceive you have an engagement. Luchresi—'" (par. 19)

Meaning:

Effect:

6. "There were no attendants at home; they had **absconded** to make merry in honour of the time." (par. 24)

Meaning:

Effect:

7. "We came at length to the foot of the descent, and stood together upon the damp ground of the **catacombs** of the Montresors." (par. 25)

Meaning:

Effect:

8. "He raised it to his lips with a **leer**. He paused and nodded to me familiarly, while his bells jingled." (par. 40)

Meaning:

Effect:

9. "His eyes flashed with a fierce light. He laughed and threw the bottle upwards with a **gesticulation** I did not understand." (par. 54)

Meaning:

Effect:

10. "In niche, and finding an instant he had reached the extremity of the niche, and finding his progress arrested by the rock, stood stupidly bewildered. A moment more and I had **fettered** him to the granite." (par. 71)

Meaning:

Effect:

The Most Dangerous Game (p. 212)
Richard Connell

For each term in bold below, determine the meaning of the word in the context of the sentence, and then describe the effect of the word: how the author's word choice contributes to the meaning and tone of the sentence(s).

1. "'The old charts call it 'Ship-Trap Island',' Whitney replied. 'A suggestive name, isn't it? Sailors have a curious **dread** of the place. I don't know why. Some **superstition**—'" (par. 3)

Meaning (dread):

Meaning (superstition):

Effect:

2. "'Can't see it,' remarked Rainsford, trying to peer through the dank tropical night that was **palpable** as it pressed its thick warm blackness in upon the yacht." (par. 4)

Meaning:

Effect:

3. "'One superstitious sailor can **taint** the whole ship's company with his fear.'" (par. 24)

Meaning:

Effect:

4. "'Sometimes I think evil is a **tangible** thing--with wave lengths, just as sound and light have.'" (par. 25)

Meaning:

Effect:

5. "He did not recognize the animal that made the sound; he did not try to; with fresh **vitality** he swam toward the sound." (par. 36)

Meaning:

Effect:

6. "Jagged crags appeared to jut up into the **opaqueness**; he forced himself upward, hand over hand." (par. 38)

Meaning:

Effect:

7. "**Bleak** darkness was blacking out the sea and jungle when Rainsford sighted the lights."
   (par. 45)

Meaning:

Effect:

8. "Half apologetically General Zaroff said, 'We do our best to preserve the **amenities** of
   civilization here. Please forgive any lapses.'" (par. 66)

Meaning:

Effect:

9. "Even so **zealous** a hunter as General Zaroff could not trace him there, he told himself; only
   the devil himself could follow that complicated trail through the jungle after dark. But
   perhaps the general was a devil—" (par. 171)

Meaning:

Effect:

10. "An **apprehensive** night crawled slowly by like a wounded snake and sleep did not visit
    Rainsford, although the silence of a dead world was on the jungle." (par. 172)

Meaning:

Effect:

Lelah (p. 228)

Angela Flournoy

For each term in bold below, determine the meaning of the word in the context of the sentence, and then describe the effect of the word: how the author's word choice contributes to the meaning and tone of the sentence(s).

1. "She'd always imagined the men who handled evictions as **menacing**-big muscles, loud mouths. These two were young and large, but soft looking, baby-faced. Like giant chocolate **cherubs**." (par. 2)

Meaning (menacing):

Meaning (cherub):

Effect:

2. "He had a plan ready if she snapped and started throwing dishes at him, if she called for backup-a brother or cousin to come beat him up-or if she tried to **barricade** herself in the bathroom." (par. 3)

Meaning:

Effect:

3. "She had anticipated a strange stare, or at least a **smirk**, as the valet helped her out of her overflowing car, but he hadn't seemed to notice. Or maybe she wasn't the only homeless gambler in Motor City tonight." (par. 18)

Meaning:

Effect:

4. "**Camaraderie** was appreciated, outright advice was not." (par. 19)

Meaning:

Effect:

5. "[A]t the **grievance** meeting HR brought up the money she'd borrowed going all the way back to Brenda. They claimed she'd borrowed more than five thousand dollars over the four years, but that didn't sound right to Lelah." (par. 21)

Meaning:

Effect:

6. "She never bet all inside, or all out; she spread her chips around the table, she never begged the dealer to let her play out her last chip, and she didn't make loud **proclamations**, speak directly to the little white ball as if it gave a damn about her, or beg the chips to behave any particular way." (par. 22)

Meaning:

Effect:

7. "It was awkward, being at a table but not playing at the table. You had to smile, look **indifferent** and simultaneously interested enough to justify taking up space." (par. 27)

Meaning:

Effect:

8. "'Like hell you can't,' the woman said. Then she leaned in closer, whispered, 'Roulette ain't a **spectator** sport.'" (par. 37)

Meaning:

Effect:

9. "There was a red convertible sitting on top of the Wheel of Fortune slots, and though she despised slots as an amateur, **vulgar** game, she imagined winning so much at a table that they gave the damn thing to her; just put a ramp over the front slots so she could climb up, drive her new Corvette down, and pick up the rest of her winnings at the cashier." (par. 42)

Meaning:

Effect:

10. "It wasn't to feel alive, but it also wasn't to feel numb. It was about knowing what to do **intuitively**, and thinking about one thing only, the possibility of winning, the possibility of walking away the victor, finally." (par. 48)

Meaning:

Effect:

Two Kinds (p. 237)

Amy Tan

For each term in bold below, determine the meaning of the word in the context of the sentence, and then describe the effect of the word: how the author's word choice contributes to the meaning and tone of the sentence(s).

1. "We didn't immediately pick the right kind of **prodigy**. At first my mother thought I could be a Chinese Shirley Temple." (par. 2)

Meaning:

Effect:

2. "Instead of getting big fat curls, I emerged with an uneven mass of crinkly black fuzz. My mother dragged me off to the bathroom and tried to wet down my hair. 'You look like a Negro Chinese,' she **lamented**, as if I had done this on purpose." (par. 3-4)

Meaning:

Effect:

3. "My mother and father would adore me. I would be beyond **reproach**." (par. 6)

Meaning:

Effect:

4. "She would look through them all, searching for stories about **remarkable** children." (par. 7)

Meaning:

Effect:

5. "And after seeing, once again, my mother's disappointed face, something inside me began to die. I hated the tests, the raised hopes and failed **expectations**." (par. 11)

Meaning:

Effect:

6. "The girl staring back at me was angry, powerful. She and I were the same. I had new

thoughts, **willful** thoughts - or rather, thoughts filled with lots of won'ts." (par. 12)

Meaning:

Effect:

7. "She seemed entranced by the music, a **frenzied** little piano piece with a mesmerizing quality, which alternated between quick, playful passages and teasing, lilting ones." (par. 15)

Meaning:

Effect:

8. "And right then I was determined to put a stop to her foolish **pride**." (par. 40)

Meaning:

Effect:

9. "But my mother's expression was what devastated me: a quiet, blank look that said she had lost everything. I felt the same way, and everybody seemed now to be coming up, like **gawkers** at the scene of an accident to see what parts were actually missing." (par. 53)

Meaning:

Effect:

10. "So I never found a way to ask her why she had hoped for something so large that failure was **inevitable**." (par. 69)

Meaning:

Effect:

from _Outliers_ (p. 250)

Malcolm Gladwell

For each term in bold below, determine the meaning of the word in the context of the sentence, and then describe the effect of the word: how the author's word choice contributes to the meaning and tone of the sentence(s).

1. "For almost a generation, psychologists around the world have been engaged in a **spirited** debate over a question that most of us would consider to have been settled years ago." (par. 1)

Meaning:

Effect:

2. "The question is this: is there such a thing as **innate** talent?" (par. 1)

Meaning:

Effect:

3. "In those first few years, everyone practiced roughly the same amount, about two or three hours a week. But when the students were around the age of eight, real differences started to **emerge**." (par. 3)

Meaning:

Effect:

4. "The students who would end up the best in their class began to practice more than everyone else: six hours a week by age nine, eight hours a week by age twelve, sixteen hours a week by age fourteen, and up and up, until by the age of twenty they were practicing-that is, purposefully and single-mindedly playing their instruments with the **intent** to get better-well over thirty hours a week." (par. 3)

Meaning:

Effect:

5. "In fact, by the age of twenty, the **elite** performers had each totaled ten thousand hours of practice." (par. 3)

Meaning:

Effect:

6. "The **striking** thing about Ericsson's study is that he and his colleagues couldn't find any 'naturals,' musicians who floated effortlessly to the top while practicing a fraction of the time their peers did. Nor could they find any "grinds," people who worked harder than everyone else, yet just didn't have what it takes to break the top ranks." (par. 5)

Meaning:

Effect:

7. "Their research suggests that once a musician has enough ability to get into a top music school, the thing that **distinguishes** one performer from another is how hard he or she works." (par. 5)

Meaning:

Effect:

8. "The idea that excellence at performing a complex task requires a **critical** minimum level of practice surfaces again and again in studies of expertise. In fact, researchers have settled on what they believe is the magic number for true expertise: ten thousand hours." (par. 6)

Meaning:

Effect:

9. "It seems that it takes the brain this long to **assimilate** all that it needs to know to achieve true mastery.'" (par. 7)

Meaning:

Effect:

10. "But to Ericsson and those who argue against the **primacy** of talent, that isn't surprising at all." (par. 11)

Meaning:

Effect:

from *Battle Hymn of the Tiger* (p. 253)
Amy Chua

For each term in bold below, determine the meaning of the word in the context of the sentence, and then describe the effect of the word: how the author's word choice contributes to the meaning and tone of the sentence(s).

1. "As an adult, I once did the same thing to Sophia, calling her garbage in English when she acted extremely disrespectfully toward me. When I mentioned that I had done this at a dinner party, I was immediately **ostracized**." (par. 3)

Meaning:

Effect:

2. "'Good point,' I **conceded**. 'No wonder it didn't work.' I was just trying to be **conciliatory**. In fact, it had worked great with Sophia." (par. 7-8)

Meaning (conceded):

Meaning (conciliatory):

Effect:

3. "(I also once heard a Western father toast his adult daughter by calling her 'beautiful and incredibly **competent**.' She later told me that made her feel like garbage.)" (par. 9)

Meaning:

Effect:

4. "They **assume** strength; not fragility, and as a result they behave very differently." (par. 11)

Meaning:

Effect:

5. "Other Western parents will sit their child down and express disapproval, but they will be careful not to make their child feel **inadequate** or insecure, and they will not call their child 'stupid,' 'worthless,' or 'a disgrace.'" (par. 11)

Meaning:

Effect:

6. "That's why the solution to substandard performance is always to **excoriate**, punish, and shame the child." (par. 12)

Meaning:

Effect:

7. "(And it's true that Chinese mothers get in the trenches, putting in long **grueling** hours personally tutoring, training, interrogating, and spying on their kids." (par. 13)

Meaning:

Effect:

8. "[My husband] Jed actually has the opposite view. 'Children don't choose their parents,' he once said to me. 'They don't even choose to be born. It's parents who **foist** life on their kids, so it's the parents' responsibility to provide for them. Kids don't owe their parents anything. Their duty will be to their own kids.' This strikes me as a terrible deal for the Western parent." (par. 13)

Meaning:

Effect:

9. "Every year, Jed's parents let him spend the entire summer having fun with his brother and sister at an **idyllic** place called Crystal Lake; Jed says those were some of the best times of his life, and we try to bring Sophia and Lulu to Crystal Lake when we can." (par. 17)

Meaning:

Effect:

10. "First; like many mothers, I did most of the parenting, so it made sense that my parenting style **prevailed**." (par. 19)

Meaning:

Effect:

How to Raise a Creative Child. Step One: Back Off (p. 259)
Adam Grant

For each term in bold below, determine the meaning of the word in the context of the sentence, and then describe the effect of the word: how the author's word choice contributes to the meaning and tone of the sentence(s).

1. "Their classmates shudder with **envy**; their parents rejoice at winning the lottery." (par. 1)

Meaning:

Effect:

2. "From its inception in 1942 until 1994, the search recognized more than 2000 **precocious** teenagers as finalists." (par. 2)

Meaning:

Effect:

3. "They **conform** to codified rules, rather than inventing their own." (par. 5)

Meaning:

Effect:

4. "Creativity may be hard to nurture, but it's easy to **thwart**." (par. 9)

Meaning:

Effect:

5. "Their children had freedom to sort out their own values and discover their own interests. And that set them up to **flourish** as creative adults." (par. 11)

Meaning:

Effect:

6. "They responded to the **intrinsic** motivation of their children." (par. 12)

Meaning:

Effect:

7. "Expert bridge players struggled more than **novices** to adapt when the rules were changed; expert accountants were worse than **novices** at applying a new tax law." (par. 16)

Meaning:

Effect:

8. "No one is forcing these **luminary** scientists to get involved in artistic hobbies." (par. 19)

Meaning:

Effect:

9. "[Albert Einstein's] mother enrolled him in violin lessons starting at age 5, but he wasn't **intrigued**." (par. 19)

Meaning:

Effect:

10. "You can't program a child to become creative. Try to engineer a certain kind of success, and the best you'll get is an **ambitious** robot." (par. 20)

Meaning:

Effect:

from *Drive* (p. 262)

Daniel Pink

For each term in bold below, determine the meaning of the word in the context of the sentence, and then describe the effect of the word: how the author's word choice contributes to the meaning and tone of the sentence(s).

1. "From this episode, Twain **extracts** a key motivational principle, namely "that Work consists of whatever a body is OBLIGED to do, and that Play consists of whatever a body is not obliged to do." (par. 3)

Meaning:

Effect:

2. "In other words, rewards can perform a weird sort of behavioral **alchemy**: They can transform an interesting task into a drudge." (par. 4)

Meaning:

Effect:

3. "Instead, they referred to the **counterintuitive** consequences of extrinsic incentives as 'the hidden costs of rewards.'" (par. 5)

Meaning:

Effect:

4. "Even two weeks later, those **alluring** prizes-so common in classrooms and cubicles-had turned play into work." (par. 8)

Meaning:

Effect:

5. "Only **contingent** rewards-if you do this, then you'll get that-had the negative effect." (par. 9)

Meaning:

Effect:

6. "These insights proved so **controversial**-after all, they called into question a standard practice of most companies and schools-that in 1999 Deci and two colleagues reanalyzed

nearly three decades of studies on the subject to confirm the findings." (par. 11)

Meaning:

Effect:

7. "Try to encourage a kid to learn math by paying her for each workbook page she completes-and she'll almost certainly become more **diligent** in the short term and lose interest in math in the long term." (par. 12)

Meaning:

Effect:

8. "Take an industrial designer who loves his work **arid** try to get him to do better by making his pay contingent on a hit product-and he'll almost certainly work like a maniac in the short term, but become less interested in his job in the long term." (par. 12)

Meaning:

Effect:

9. "Despite the work of a few skilled and passionate popularizers-in particular, Alfie Kahn, whose **prescient** 1993 book, Punished by Rewards, lays out a devastating indictment of extrinsic incentives-we persist in trying to motivate people this way." (par. 13)

Meaning:

Effect:

10. "Or perhaps there's a better reason. Even if those controlling "if-then" rewards activate the Sawyer Effect and **suffocate** the third drive, maybe they actually get people to perform better." (par. 14)

Meaning:

Effect:

from *Open* (p. 266)

Andre Agassi

For each term in bold below, determine the meaning of the word in the context of the sentence, and then describe the effect of the word: how the author's word choice contributes to the meaning and tone of the sentence(s).

1. "I keep begging myself to stop, and I keep playing, and this gap, this **contradiction** between what I want to do and what I actually do, feels like the core of my life." (par. 1)

Meaning:

Effect:

2. "My father has **deliberately** made the dragon fearsome." (par. 1)

Meaning:

Effect:

3. "He's given it an extra-long neck of aluminum tubing, and a narrow aluminum head, which **recoils** like a whip every time the dragon fires." (par. 1)

Meaning:

Effect:

4. "The trajectory makes the balls nearly impossible to return in a **conventional** way: I need to hit every ball on the rise, or else it will bounce over my head." (par. 2)

Meaning:

Effect:

5. "Every ball I send across the net joins the thousands that already cover the court. Not hundreds. Thousands. They roll toward me in **perpetual** waves." (par. 2)

Meaning:

Effect:

6. "But I take no pride in my reflexes, and I get no credit. It's what I'm supposed to do. Every hit

is expected, every miss a **crisis**." (par. 2)

Meaning:

Effect:

7. "He dislikes when I hit the ball wide, he yells when I hit a ball long, but when I **muff** a ball into the net, he foams at the mouth." (par. 3)

Meaning:

Effect:

8. "Never mind that I don't want to play Wimbledon. What I want isn't **relevant**." (par. 3)

Meaning:

Effect:

9. "The net is the biggest enemy, but thinking is the **cardinal** sin." (par. 4)

Meaning:

Effect:

10. "Or, with all his yelling, has he turned me into a thinker? Is my thinking about things other than tennis an act of **defiance**? I like to think so." (par. 4)

Meaning:

Effect:

Once Upon a Time (p. 271)
Nadine Gordimer

For each term in bold below, determine the meaning of the word in the context of the sentence, and then describe the effect of the word: how the author's word choice contributes to the meaning and tone of the sentence(s).

1. "I think of sending a postcard saying I don't accept that I "ought" to write anything. And then last night I woke up—or rather was awakened without knowing what had **<u>roused</u>** me." (par. 1)

Meaning:

Effect:

2. "There was no human weight pressing on the boards, the creaking was a buckling, an **<u>epicenter</u>** of stress." (par. 6)

Meaning:

Effect:

3. "The stope where the fall was could have been disused, dripping water from its ruptured veins; or men might now be **<u>interred</u>** there in the most profound of tombs." (par. 6)

Meaning:

Effect:

4. "They had a housemaid who was absolutely trustworthy and an **<u>itinerant</u>** gardener who was highly recommended by the neighbors. " (par. 8)

Meaning:

Effect:

5. "There were riots, but these were outside the city, where people of another color were **<u>quartered</u>**. These people were not allowed into the suburb except as reliable housemaids and gardeners, so there was nothing to fear, the husband told the wife." (par. 9)

Meaning:

Effect:

6. "The riots were **<u>suppressed</u>**, but there were many burglaries in the suburb and somebody's trusted housemaid was tied up and shut in a cupboard by thieves while she was in charge of

her employers' house." (par. 10)

Meaning:

Effect:

7. "The trusted housemaid of the man and wife and little boy was so upset by this misfortune befalling a friend left, as she herself often was, with responsibility for the possessions   of the man and his wife and the little boy that she **implored** her employers to have burglar bars attached to the doors and windows of the house, and an alarm system installed." (par. 10)

Meaning:

Effect:

8. "The husband said, 'She's right. Take **heed** of her advice. You only encourage them with your bread and tea.'" (par. 13)

Meaning:

Effect:

9. "It was the ugliest but the most honest in its suggestion of the pure concentration-camp style, no frills, all evident **efficacy**." (par. 15)

Meaning:

Effect:

10. "Placed the length of walls, it consisted of a continuous coil of stiff and shining metal **serrated** into jagged blades, so that there would be no way of climbing over it and no way through its tunnel without getting entangled in its fangs." (par. 15)

Meaning:

Effect:

Nemecia (p. 278)

Kirstin Valdez Quade

For each term in bold below, determine the meaning of the word in the context of the sentence, and then describe the effect of the word: how the author's word choice contributes to the meaning and tone of the sentence(s).

1. "Even in my white dress I look like a boy; my hair, which I have cut myself, is short and jagged. Nemecia's head is tilted; she looks out from under her eyelashes at the camera. My expression is **sullen**, guilty." (par. 1)

Meaning:

Effect:

2. "The doll sat on the bureau in our bedroom, its face round and **placidly** smiling behind its net of brown cracks, hands folded primly across white lace, a strange and terrifying mix of young and old." (par. 3)

Meaning:

Effect:

3. "Nemecia had an air of tragedy about her, which she **cultivated**." (par. 4)

Meaning:

Effect:

4. "When I think of Nemecia as she was then, I think of her eating. My cousin was **ravenous**." (par. 5)

Meaning:

Effect:

5. "She was **adept** at slicing and spooning, so her thefts weren't noticeable." (par. 6)

Meaning:

Effect:

6. "'I killed them,' Nemecia said into the darkness. She spoke as if **reciting**, and I didn't at first know if she was talking to me." (par. 10)

Meaning:

Effect:

7. "The next day, the world looked different; every adult I encountered was **diminished** now, made **frail** by Nemecia's secret." (par. 22)

Meaning (diminished):

Meaning (frail):

Effect:

8. "Hell, demons, flames—these were the horrors that I couldn't picture. Nemecia's fury, though—that was completely **plausible**." (par. 31)

Meaning:

Effect:

9. "Nemecia stopped seeing me, and, without her gaze, I became **indistinct** to myself." (par. 47)

Meaning:

Effect:

10. "Then I would stand, walk with grace to the front of the church, and there, before the altar, I'd speak with **eloquence** that people afterward would describe as unearthly." (par. 55)

Meaning:

Effect:

Story of an Hour (p. 292)

Kate Chopin

For each term in bold below, determine the meaning of the word in the context of the sentence, and then describe the effect of the word: how the author's word choice contributes to the meaning and tone of the sentence(s).

1. "Knowing that Mrs. Mallard was **afflicted** with a heart trouble, great care was taken to break to her as gently as possible the news of her husband's death." (par. 1)

Meaning:

Effect:

2. "She could see in the open square before her house the tops of trees that were all **aquiver** with the new spring life." (par. 5)

Meaning:

Effect:

3. "There was something coming to her and she was waiting for it, fearfully. What was it? She did not know; it was too subtle and **elusive** to name." (par. 9)

Meaning:

Effect:

4. "Now her bosom rose and fell **tumultuously**. She was beginning to recognize this thing that was approaching to possess her, and she was striving to beat it back with her will--as powerless as her two white slender hands would have been." (par. 10)

Meaning:

Effect:

5. "A clear and **exalted** perception enabled her to dismiss the suggestion as trivial." (par. 11)

Meaning:

Effect:

6. "There would be no powerful will bending hers in that blind **persistence** with which men and women believe they have a right to impose a private will upon a fellow-creature." (par. 12)

Meaning:

Effect:

7. "And yet she had loved him--sometimes. Often she had not. What did it matter! What could love, the unsolved mystery, count for in the face of this possession of **self- assertion** which she suddenly recognized as the strongest impulse of her being!" (par. 13)

Meaning:

Effect:

8. "No; she was drinking in a very **elixir** of life through that open window." (par. 16)

Meaning:

Effect:

9. "She arose at length and opened the door to her sister's **importunities**." (par. 18)

Meaning:

Effect:

10. "There was a feverish **triumph** in her eyes, and she carried herself unwittingly like a goddess of Victory." (par. 18)

Meaning:

Effect:

Name_____

Date_____Class_____

Why School Should Start Later in the Day (p. 349)

Lisa Lewis

For each term in bold below, determine the meaning of the word in the context of the sentence, and then describe the effect of the word: how the author's word choice contributes to the meaning and tone of the sentence(s).

1. "It's well known that teens who don't get at least eight hours of sleep a night face a **slew** of problems." (par. 1)

Meaning:

Effect:

2. "Many districts are reluctant to change their schedules because they see the shift as too expensive and **disruptive**." (par. 2)

Meaning:

Effect:

3. "Later start times can mean less missed school — absences dropped 15% in Bonneville County, Idaho, after it **instituted** such a change, according to a 2014 Children's National Medical Center report." (par. 3)

Meaning:

Effect:

4. "Another **potential** problem schools commonly raise is that later start times would lead to kids missing classes at the end of the day in order to attend sporting events, or that athletic participation rates would decline." (par. 6)

Meaning:

Effect:

5. "Two-thirds of the athletes who didn't meet this **threshold** got injured." (par. 7)

Meaning:

Effect:

6. "When they get behind the wheel, they **contribute** to what the National Highway Traffic Safety Administration calls the "extreme danger" of drowsy driving, which has an estimated

annual societal cost of $109 billion." (par. 9)

Meaning:

Effect:

7. "Beyond the obvious safety concerns, there's a **corresponding** hike in car insurance premiums, with a 2013 study by InsuranceQuotes.com finding that Californians' rates jump an average of 62% after just one claim." (par. 9)

Meaning:

Effect:

8. "The title of a 2014 report in the Journal of Youth and Adolescence says it all: 'Sleepless in Fairfax: The Difference One More Hour of Sleep Can Make for Teen Hopelessness, Suicidal **Ideation**, and Substance Use.'" (par. 11)

Meaning:

Effect:

9. "Districts **implemented** early starts for efficiency and cost-cutting reasons; tiered bus systems, for instance, led to staggered start times for elementary, middle and high schools — with high schools starting first." (par. 11)

Meaning:

Effect:

10. "At the time, the risks of teen sleep **deprivation** were not widely known." (par. 11)

Meaning:

Effect:

End the Gun Epidemic in America (p. 352)
New York Times Editorial Board

For each term in bold below, determine the meaning of the word in the context of the sentence, and then describe the effect of the word: how the author's word choice contributes to the meaning and tone of the sentence(s).

1. "All decent people feel sorrow and **righteous** fury about the latest slaughter of innocents, in California." (par. 1)

Meaning (dread):

Meaning (superstition):

Effect:

2. "The attention and anger of Americans should also be directed at the elected leaders whose job is to keep us safe but who place a higher premium on the money and political power of an industry dedicated to profiting from the **unfettered** spread of ever more powerful firearms." (par. 2)

Meaning:

Effect:

3. "It is a **moral** outrage and a national disgrace that civilians can legally purchase weapons designed specifically to kill people with brutal speed and efficiency." (par. 3)

Meaning:

Effect:

4. "These are weapons of war, barely modified and deliberately marketed as tools of macho **vigilantism** and even **insurrection**." (par. 3)

Meaning (vigilantism):

Meaning (insurrection):

Effect:

5. "America's elected leaders offer prayers for gun victims and then, **callously** and without fear of consequence, reject the most basic restrictions on weapons of mass killing, as they did on Thursday." (par. 3)

Meaning:

Effect:

6. "Opponents of gun control are saying, as they do after every killing, that no law can unfailingly **forestall** a specific criminal." (par. 4)

Meaning:

Effect:

7. "They point out that determined killers **obtained** weapons illegally in places like France, England and Norway that have strict gun laws." (par. 4)

Meaning:

Effect:

8. "Worse, politicians **abet** would-be killers by creating gun markets for them, and voters allow those politicians to keep their jobs." (par. 5)

Meaning:

Effect:

9. "It is not necessary to debate the **peculiar** wording of the Second Amendment." (par. 6)

Meaning:

Effect:

10. "What better time than during a presidential election to show, at long last, that our nation has **retained** its sense of decency?" (par. 8)

Meaning:

Effect:

History Shows the Folly of Disarming Lawful People (p. 354)

Thomas Sowell

For each term in bold below, determine the meaning of the word in the context of the sentence, and then describe the effect of the word: how the author's word choice contributes to the meaning and tone of the sentence(s).

1. "Sometimes someone **inadvertently** performs a public service by bringing an unbelievably stupid and dangerous idea to the surface, where it can be exposed for what it is." (par. 1)

Meaning:

Effect:

2. "Actually having to shoot someone is the **exception**, not the rule." (par. 5)

Meaning:

Effect:

3. "Yet The New York Times **conjures** up a vision of something like the gunfight at the OK Corral." (par. 5)

Meaning:

Effect:

4. "The fatal **fallacy** of gun control laws in general is the assumption that such laws actually control guns." (par. 7)

Meaning:

Effect:

5. "Mass shooters are often portrayed as '**irrational**' people engaged in 'senseless' acts." (par. 9)

Meaning:

Effect:

6. "But mass shooters are usually **rational** enough to attack schools, churches and other places where there is far less likelihood of someone being on the scene who is armed." (par. 9)

Meaning:

Effect:

7. "As with domestic gun control laws, the agreemets were followed by peaceful countries and ignored by **belligerent** countries that built up huge war machines, such as in Nazi Germany and imperial Japan." (par. 12)

Meaning:

Effect:

8. "The net result was that the belligerent countries had every **incentive** to start wars, and   that they inflicted devastating losses on the peaceful countries that had drastically curtailed their own military forces." (par. 13)

Meaning:

Effect:

9. "**Undaunted** by history, the same kind of thinking that had cheered international disarmament treaties in the 1920s and 1930s once again cheered Soviet-American disarmament agreements during the Cold War." (par. 15)

Meaning:

Effect:

10. "**Conversely**, there was hysteria when President Ronald Reagan began building up American military forces in the 1980s." (par. 16)

Meaning:

Effect:

Why Was Harambe the Gorilla in a Zoo in the First Place? (p. 357)
Marc Bekoff

For each term in bold below, determine the meaning of the word in the context of the sentence, and then describe the effect of the word: how the author's word choice contributes to the meaning and tone of the sentence(s).

1. "People are **keenly** interested in how and why nonhuman animals – animals – are used by humans in a wide variety of venues, in this case 'in the name of human entertainment.'" (par. 3)

Meaning:

Effect:

2. "While some might say Harambe had a 'good life' in the zoo, it doesn't come close to the life he would have had as a wild gorilla, with all its **attendant** risks." (par. 4)

Meaning:

Effect:

3. "When the boy fell into his home it was a trespass of sorts, and it's most likely Harambe was startled, perhaps feeling **vulnerable** and unprotected, and wondering what was going on." (par. 5)

Meaning:

Effect:

4. "Harmabe's hold on the child and his sheltering of the youngster are **indicators** of protection." (par. 6)

Meaning:

Effect:

5. "Along these lines, it's **essential** that the people who work with zoo-ed animals know their behavior in detail, and those people who know individuals the best—the caretakers who interact with certain individuals daily—be called in in emergency situations." (par. 7)

Meaning:

Effect:

6. "I like to ask people to use their companion animals to close the **empathy** gap because people get incredibly upset when a dog is harmed because they see dogs as **sentient**, feeling beings." (par. 8)

Meaning (empathy):

Meaning (sentient):

Effect:

7. "So, would you allow your dog to be put in a zoo? If not, then why Harambe and millions of other individuals who **languish** behind bars?" (par. 9)

Meaning:

Effect:

8. "Indeed, a recent study conducted by zoos themselves, showed that what people learn is very limited in **scope** in terms of what the new knowledge means in any practical sense." (par. 11)

Meaning:

Effect:

9. "Zoos also should be turned into **sanctuaries** for the animals themselves." (par. 12)

Meaning:

Effect:

10. I hope Harambe did not die in **vain**, and that this moment can be turned into a movement that is concerned with the **plight** of captive animals." (par. 15)

Meaning (vain):

Meaning (plight):

Effect:

Is It Immoral to Watch the Superbowl? (p. 362)

Steve Almond

For each term in bold below, determine the meaning of the word in the context of the sentence, and then describe the effect of the word: how the author's word choice contributes to the meaning and tone of the sentence(s).

1. "What I remember most of all is the thought that dogged me in the days afterward, as it became clear that a star player had been **rendered** quadriplegic on national television: Surely the game of football would now be outlawed." (par. 4)

Meaning:

Effect:

2. "The N.F.L. **juggernaut** rolled on, solidifying its place atop America's Athletic Industrial Complex." (par. 5)

Meaning:

Effect:

3. "Recently, though, medical research has confirmed that football can cause **catastrophic** brain injury — not as a rare and unintended consequence, but as a routine byproduct of how the game is played." (par. 6)

Meaning:

Effect:

4. "Never is this sponsorship more overt than next Sunday, for the Super Bowl has become an event of such magnitude that it ranks as a **secular** holiday at this point, as much a celebration of the sport's ability to draw multimillion-dollar ads as the contest itself." (par. 7)

Meaning:

Effect:

5. "I love the tension between the **ornate** structure of the game and its improvisatory chaos, and I love the way great players find opportunity, even a mystical kind of order, in the midst of that chaos." (par. 8)

Meaning:

Effect:

6. "The problem is that I can no longer indulge these pleasures without feeling **complicit**." (par. 9)

Meaning:

Effect:

7. "The autopsy confirmed that he had chronic traumatic encephalopathy, or C.T.E., the cause of the dementia that is increasingly **prevalent** among former players." (par. 10)

Meaning:

Effect:

8. "Now that the medical evidence is **incontrovertible**, it has sought to reduce high-speed collisions, fining defenders for helmet-to-helmet hits and other **flagrantly** violent play." (par. 11)

Meaning (incontrovertible):

Meaning (flagrantly):

Effect:

9. "The second argument is that players choose to **incur** the game's risks and are lavishly compensated for doing so." (par. 12)

Meaning:

Effect:

10. "Pro sports are, by definition, **monetized** arenas for hypermasculinity." (par. 14)

Meaning:

Effect:

The Paranoid Style of American Policing (p. 370)

Ta-Nehisi Coates

For each term in bold below, determine the meaning of the word in the context of the sentence, and then describe the effect of the word: how the author's word choice contributes to the meaning and tone of the sentence(s).

1. "And yet the notion that it is **permissible**, wise, moral, or advisable to kill such a person as a method of de-escalation, to kill because one was afraid, did not really exist among parents in my community." (par. 2)

Meaning:

Effect:

2. "When LeGrier attempted to break down his father's door, his father called the police, who apparently arrived to find the 19-year-old **wielding** a bat." (par. 8)

Meaning:

Effect:

3. "Interpreting this as a **lethal** threat, one of the officers shot and killed LeGrier and somehow managed to shoot and kill one of his neighbors, Bettie Jones." (par. 8)

Meaning:

Effect:

4. "By that logic, one might **surmise** that the police would be better able to mediate conflicts than community members." (par. 9)

Meaning:

Effect:

5. "**Legitimacy** is what is ultimately at stake here." (par. 11)

Meaning:

Effect:

6. "Asked about the possibility of an investigation, Melvin Jones, the brother of Bettie Jones, could **muster** no confidence." (par. 11)

Meaning:

Effect:

7. "When police can not **adhere** to the standards of the neighborhood, of citizens, or of parents, what are they beyond a bigger gun and a sharper sword?" (par. 12)

Meaning:

Effect:

8. "When Bettie Jones's brother displays zero confidence in an investigation into the killing of his sister, he is not being **cynical**." (par. 14)

Meaning:

Effect:

9. "He is **shrewdly** observing a government that executed4 a young man and sought to hide that fact from citizens." (par. 14)

Meaning:

Effect:

10. "A state that allows its agents to kill, to beat, to tase, without any real **sanction**, has ceased to govern and has commenced to simply rule." (par. 14)

Meaning:

Effect:

Labeling the Danger in Soda (p. 374)

Tina Rosenberg

For each term in bold below, determine the meaning of the word in the context of the sentence, and then describe the effect of the word: how the author's word choice contributes to the meaning and tone of the sentence(s).

1. "A 16-ounce Snapple Kiwi Strawberry — "Made from the Best Stuff on Earth," it **boasts** — has 12." (par. 2)

Meaning:

Effect:

2. "Britain's Conservative government put one in its just-released budget — largely because of the **indefatigable** work of the chef Jamie Oliver — although it wouldn't kick in for two years." (par. 4)

Meaning:

Effect:

3. "Another is that two groups have been **conflated** into one, creating a false impression of causality: Consumption has declined mainly among more educated, wealthier Americans, while obesity and diabetes disproportionately afflict the poor." (par. 11)

Meaning:

Effect:

4. "'**Disparities** in sugar-sweetened soda consumption mirror obesity **disparities**,' said a study of New York City soda drinkers." (par. 11)

Meaning:

Effect:

5. "Many parents, though not a majority, thought Sunny D and Capri Sun juice drinks were healthy. The words "vitamin" and juice" **connote** health." (par. 17)

Meaning:

Effect:

6. "In general, the industry has been able to make nutritional labels as **feeble** and confusing as possible." (par. 21)

Meaning:

Effect:

7. "'They struggle with calorie numbers, never mind grams of sugar. The easier you make it to comprehend, the more likely that information will be **influential**.'" (par. 25)

Meaning:

Effect:

8. "**Conveying** information is not the only purpose of labels." (par. 29)

Meaning:

Effect:

9. "The other labeled product, of course, is tobacco. In 80 countries — and the number is growing — cigarette packs are covered with gross, full-colored pictures of **gangrenous** toes, cancerous lungs and rotted teeth, along with deathbed photos of cancer victims." (par. 34)

Meaning:

Effect:

10. "Here's a clue: In 2009, Congress **mandated** graphic warning labels covering 50 percent of the pack." (par. 37)

Meaning:

Effect:

September 13, 2001: Hatred Is Unworthy of Us (p. 380)

Leonard Pitts

For each term in bold below, determine the meaning of the word in the context of the sentence, and then describe the effect of the word: how the author's word choice contributes to the meaning and tone of the sentence(s).

1. "This is, after all, a troubling **strain** of our national personality that rises reliably to the surface in moments like this." (par. 5)

Meaning:

Effect:

2. "During the Second World War, Americans of Japanese heritage were rounded up by the government and **interned**." (par. 6)

Meaning:

Effect:

3. "During the Iranian hostage crisis, Americans of Middle Eastern heritage were **reviled** amid loose talk of mass deportation." (par. 6)

Meaning:

Effect:

4. "In the wake of **sentiments** like those and against the backdrop of our history, let me say just one thing to my sister and brother Americans. Don't. Please, don't." (par. 7-8)

Meaning:

Effect:

5. "But in the wake of Tuesday's events, it's **tantamount** to giving aid and comfort to the enemy, a group of petty thugs who tried to bring us down to their level, make us just like them." (par. 9)

Meaning:

Effect:

6. "The work of saving Americans continues **apace**." (par. 12)

Meaning:

Effect:

7. "Meaning, an experiment in individual liberty, a research project in human tolerance, a people bound to one another not by blood but by **fealty** to a extraordinary ideal." (par. 13)

Meaning:

Effect:

8. "In this moment when emotions are high, it seems **prudent** - vital - that we stop and remind ourselves of what is meant by 'all.'" (par. 15)

Meaning:

Effect:

9. "We're a people of rainbow **hues** and multiple faiths." (par. 16)

Meaning:

Effect:

10. "The madmen who **commandeered** those planes don't represent the followers of Islam any more than the madmen who blow up abortion clinics represent the followers of Christ." (par. 18)

Meaning:

Effect:

Hiroshima Speech (p. 383)
Barack Obama

For each term in bold below, determine the meaning of the word in the context of the sentence, and then describe the effect of the word: how the author's word choice contributes to the meaning and tone of the sentence(s).

1. "On every continent, the history of civilization is filled with war, whether driven by scarcity of grain or hunger for gold, compelled by nationalist **fervor** or religious **zeal**." (par. 4)

Meaning (fervor):

Meaning (zeal):

Effect:

2. "Peoples have been **subjugated** and liberated." (par. 4)

Meaning:

Effect:

3. "And yet the war grew out of the same base instinct for domination or conquest that had caused conflicts among the simplest tribes, an old pattern **amplified** by new capabilities and without new constraints." (par. 5)

Meaning:

Effect:

4. "Yet in the image of a mushroom cloud that rose into these skies, we are most **starkly** reminded of humanity's core contradiction." (par. 7)

Meaning:

Effect:

5. "How often does material advancement or social **innovation** blind us to this truth?" (par. 8)

Meaning:

Effect:

6. "But those same stories have so often been used to **oppress** and dehumanize those who are

different." (par. 10)

Meaning:

Effect:

7. "Technological progress without an **equivalent** progress in human institutions can doom us." (par. 12)

Meaning:

Effect:

8. "That memory allows us to fight **complacency**. It fuels our moral imagination. It allows us to change." (par. 15)

Meaning:

Effect:

9. "The United States and Japan have **forged** not only an alliance but a friendship that has won far more for our people than we could ever claim through war." (par. 16)

Meaning:

Effect:

10. "My own nation's story began with simple words: All men are created equal and **endowed** by our creator with certain unalienable rights including life, liberty and the pursuit of happiness." (par. 22)

Meaning:

Effect:

What's Wrong with Cinderella? **(p. 389)**

Peggy Orenstein

For each term in bold below, determine the meaning of the word in the context of the sentence, and then describe the effect of the word: how the author's word choice contributes to the meaning and tone of the sentence(s).

1. "Meanwhile in 2001, Mattel brought out its own "world of girl" line of princess Barbie dolls, DVDs, toys, clothing, home décor and **myriad** other products." (par. 7)

Meaning:

Effect:

2. "Saks bought Club Libby Lu in 2003 for $12 million and has since expanded it to 87 outlets; by 2005, with only **scant** local advertising, revenues hovered around the $46 million mark, a 53 percent jump from the previous year." (par. 7)

Meaning:

Effect:

3. "Even Dora the Explorer, the **intrepid**, dirty-kneed adventurer, has ascended to the throne: in 2004, after a two-part episode in which she turns into a "true princess," the Nickelodeon and Viacom consumer-products division released a satin-gowned "Magic Hair Fairytale Dora," with hair that grows or shortens when her crown is touched." (par. 8)

Meaning:

Effect:

4. "As a feminist mother — not to mention a **nostalgic** product of the Garanimals era — I have been taken by surprise by the princess craze and the girlie-girl culture that has risen around it." (par. 9)

Meaning:

Effect:

5. "I watch my fellow mothers, women who once swore they'd never be dependent on a man, smile **indulgently** at daughters who warble "So This Is Love" or insist on being called Snow White." (par. 9)

Meaning:

Effect:

6. "Maybe princesses are in fact a sign of progress, an indication that girls can embrace their **predilection** for pink without compromising strength or ambition; that, at long last, they can 'have it all.'" (par. 11)

Meaning:

Effect:

7. "'Standing in line in the arena, I was surrounded by little girls dressed head to toe as princesses,' he told me last summer in his **palatial** office, then located in Burbank, and speaking in a rolling Scottish burr." (par. 13)

Meaning:

Effect:

8. "Every reporter Mooney talks to asks some version of my next question: Aren't the Princesses, who are interested only in clothes, jewelry and **cadging** the handsome prince, somewhat retrograde role models?" (par. 15)

Meaning:

Effect:

9. "'Look,' he said, 'I have friends whose son went through the Power Rangers phase who **castigated** themselves over what they must've done wrong.'" (par. 16)

Meaning:

Effect:

10. "Mooney has a point: There are no studies proving that playing princess directly damages girls' self-esteem or dampens other **aspirations**." (par. 17)

Meaning:

Effect:

I'm a Twelve-Year-Old Girl: Why Don't the Characters in My Apps Look Like Me?
(p. 399)
Madeline Messer

For each term in bold below, determine the meaning of the word in the context of the sentence, and then describe the effect of the word: how the author's word choice contributes to the meaning and tone of the sentence(s).

1. "Does this mean that girls aren't **capable** of escaping a bear, but Santa is?" (par. 6)

Meaning:

Effect:

2. "Sometimes there are small differences in being a boy or a girl — at one point in one of the Temple games, a boy receives a shield, whereas a girl gets a burst of speed — but nothing to **warrant** a huge price tag." (par. 7)

Meaning:

Effect:

3. "These **biases** affect young girls like me." (par. 8)

Meaning:

Effect:

4. "The lack of girl characters **implies** that girls are not equal to boys and they don't deserve characters that look like them." (par. 8)

Meaning:

Effect:

5. "If I were an app maker, the **ethical** issue of charging for girl characters and not boy characters would be enough reason to change." (par. 9)

Meaning:

Effect:

When I Saw Prince, I Saw a Vital New Black Masculinity (p. 401)
Terryn Hall

For each term in bold below, determine the meaning of the word in the context of the sentence, and then describe the effect of the word: how the author's word choice contributes to the meaning and tone of the sentence(s).

1. "My youth in the 1990s was **quintessentially** American and black." (par. 1)

Meaning:

Effect:

2. "And what I knew about blackness and how it should be performed, particularly masculinity, was **immensely** shaped by the hip-hop that blasted out of the car radio and the stereo system my mother kept in our living room." (par. 1)

Meaning:

Effect:

3. "These **projected** a very firm definition of manhood." (par. 1)

 Meaning:

Effect:

4. "The only other **consistent** example of black manhood was my daily interaction with the grandfather who helped my single mother raise me." (par. 2)

Meaning:

Effect:

5. "Biggie Smalls, on the other hand, was delightful, **raunchy**…. (Yep, there were plenty of lessons in male desire in hip-hop.)" (par. 4)

Meaning:

Effect:

6. "Prince did none of that. And yet he was just as – if not more – sexual than the hip-hop I enjoyed as a teenager. … his music exposed me to a masculine sensuality that allowed a space for vulnerability, **ambiguity** and fluidity." (par. 5)

Meaning:

Effect:

7. "Never before had I seen such energy, such masculinity, if you like, **emanate** from a stage." (par. 6)

Meaning:

Effect:

8. "For me, Prince's voice, his music, his entire artistic being existed in the **liminal** space between the sexual and spiritual, something that I had, and have, heard all too rarely." (par. 7)

Meaning:

Effect:

9. "Seeing a strong, unapologetically black man direct an audience of thousands and ultimately, my heart, made it clear that being yourself could take you further than being an **approximation** of someone else." (par. 8)

Meaning:

Effect:

10. "Maxwell and André 3000 owe Prince a debt – my subsequent crushes on the both of them are largely due to my initial **infatuation** with Prince." (par. 8)

Meaning:

Effect:

Don't Ban Photos of Skinny Models (p. 404)

Vanessa Friedman

For each term in bold below, determine the meaning of the word in the context of the sentence, and then describe the effect of the word: how the author's word choice contributes to the meaning and tone of the sentence(s).

1. "Just as the White House hosted the first United States of Women summit meeting, which **culminated** in Oprah Winfrey's noting, in conversation1 with Michelle Obama, 'We live in a world where you are constantly being bombarded by images,' across the ocean the new mayor of London was announcing a policy that would ban ads on public transport that might cause women to feel pressured 'into unrealistic expectations surrounding their bodies.'" (par. 2)

Meaning:

Effect:

2. "But it is, rather, an old idea, and one that reinforces stereotypes instead of grappling with the real issue: How do we change the **paradigm** altogether?" (par. 3)

Meaning:

Effect:

3. "The immediate **impetus** for the ban, which will be carried out by the London transit authority via a steering committee that will rule on ads case by case, was a 2015 diet pill ad depicting a very tan, very curvy woman (the kind who is a staple of lad mags) in a bright yellow bikini alongside the words, 'Are you beach body ready?'" (par. 4)

Meaning:

Effect:

4. "While I have no doubt that Mr. Khan had the best intentions (he made a reference to his desire to protect his daughters), and there is no question that studies have shown that depictions of thin women in idealized or overly airbrushed photographs can be an important factor in eating disorders4 and other types of body **dysmorphia**." (par. 6)

Meaning:

Effect:

5. "And I say that as someone with two daughters (and a son) who is **acutely** aware of the distortions of the fashion world and their dangers." (par. 6)

Meaning:

Effect:

6. "Indeed, when the Gucci ad was banned, it immediately resulted in a **torrent** of new articles and social media posts prominently featuring said ad." (par. 7)

Meaning:

Effect:

7. "Just because a judgment is supposedly coming from a good place does not **obviate** the fact that it's a personal judgment, handed down from afar by a third party, bringing another set of prejudices and preconceptions to bear." (par. 9)

Meaning:

Effect:

8. "Yet that power — the ability of each individual to decide on her body for herself — is one we should be cultivating, not **relinquishing**." (par. 10)

Meaning:

Effect:

9. "To ban an ad **depicting** a specific body type is to demonize that type, labeling it publicly as bad." (par. 11)

Meaning:

Effect:

10. "There's a growing movement on social media among a broad range of women to reject the marketing of anxiety and to embrace physical **authenticity**." (par. 13)

Meaning:

Effect:

from *Gender Bias Without Borders* (p. 408)
Geena Davis Institute on Gender in the Media

For each term in bold below, determine the meaning of the word in the context of the sentence, and then describe the effect of the word: how the author's word choice contributes to the meaning and tone of the sentence(s).

1. "At the most micro level, discrimination **impedes** girls and women from achieving their individual hopes and dreams." (par. 1)

Meaning:

Effect:

2. "Despite a push to promote females worldwide, one example of where progress remains **stagnant** is the U.S. film industry." (par. 1)

Meaning:

Effect:

3. "Is this **tendency** to under- and misrepresent woman an American phenomenon, or does gender imbalance occur on a worldwide scale?" (par. 2)

Meaning:

Effect:

4. "Every speaking (i.e., utters one or more words **discernibly** on screen) or named character was evaluated in this investigation for demographics, sexualization, occupation and STEM careers." (par. 4)

Meaning:

Effect:

5. "Six countries did not have any films with gender **parity**." (par. 8)

Meaning:

Effect:

6. "It is interesting to note that the U.K. independent sample is very different than the U.S./U.K. collaboration sample across all three **prevalence** indicators." (par. 9)

Meaning:

Effect:

7. "The explanation reflects the **adage**, 'write what you know.'" (par. 16)

Meaning:

Effect:

8. "Gender inequality is **rampant** in global films." (par. 17)

Meaning:

Effect:

9. "These findings may represent a step in the right direction, but should be interpreted cautiously as only 27 films were **demarcated** for younger audiences." (par. 23)

Meaning:

Effect:

10. "For Obvious reasons, the U.S.'U.K. sample is not compared to any real-world **correlate**." (par. 25)

Meaning:

Effect:

Name_____

Date_____Class_____

Toxic Masculinity Is Killing Men: The Roots of Male Trauma (p. 414)

Kali Holloway

For each term in bold below, determine the meaning of the word in the context of the sentence, and then describe the effect of the word: how the author's word choice contributes to the meaning and tone of the sentence(s).

1. "It is impossible to downplay the concurrent influence of images and messages about masculinity **embedded** in our media." (par. 1)

Meaning:

Effect:

2. "But certainly, we all recognize the traits that are valued among men in film, television, videogames, comic books, and more: strength, **valor**, independence, the ability to provide and protect." (par. 1)

Meaning:

Effect:

3. "While depictions of men have grown more complicated, **nuanced** and human over time (we're long past the days of 'Father Knows Best' and 'Superman' archetypes), certain 'masculine' qualities remain valued over others." (par. 2)

Meaning:

Effect:

4. "As Amanda D. Lotz writes in her 2014 book, Cable Guys: Television and Masculinities in the 21st Century, though depictions of men in media have become more diverse, 'storytelling has nevertheless performed significant ideological work by consistently supporting...male characters it constructs as heroic or admirable, while **denigrating** others.'" (par. 2)

Meaning:

Effect:

5. "So although television series may have displayed a range of men and masculinities, they also **circumscribed** a 'preferred' or 'best' masculinity through attributes that were consistently idealized." (par. 2)

Meaning:

Effect:

6. "They are fearless action heroes;... psychopaths in Grand Theft Auto; shlubby, housework-averse sitcom dads with **inexplicably** beautiful wives; bumbling stoner twentysomethings who still manage to [get] the hot girl in the end; and still, the impenetrable Superman." (par. 3)

Meaning:

Effect:

7. "Couple those numbers with violence in film and other media, and the numbers are likely **astronomical**." (par. 3)

Meaning:

Effect:

8. "It leaves little boys, and later, men, emotionally **disembodied**, afraid to show weakness and often unable to fully access, recognize or cope with their feelings." (par. 4)

Meaning:

Effect:

9. "The cliche about men not being in touch with their emotions says nothing about **inherent** markers of maleness." (par. 5)

Meaning:

Effect:

10. "'It's traumatic. It's traumatic to be forced to **abdicate** half of your own humanity.'" (par. 5)

Meaning:

Effect:

Name_____

Date_____Class_____

How "Master of None" Subverts Stereotypical Masculinity by Totally Ignoring It
(p. 416)
Jack O'Keefe

For each term in bold below, determine the meaning of the word in the context of the sentence, and then describe the effect of the word: how the author's word choice contributes to the meaning and tone of the sentence(s).

1. "But for all these **paragons** of masculinity, flexing their muscles and sacrificing themselves for the ones they love, the most accurate portrayal of masculinity you'll see anytime soon is on Master Of None1, because there isn't much of what is usually defined as traditional, stereotypical "masculinity" in the show." (par. 1)

Meaning:

Effect:

2. "Many sitcoms rely on **archetypes** of masculinity to find humor." (par. 3)

Meaning:

Effect:

3. "More nuanced sitcoms like How I Met Your Mother, the **pinnacle** of 21st-century rom- sitcoms, still played with the drastic ends of masculinity for humor." (par. 3)

Meaning:

Effect:

4. "**Prominent** male characters in television — from Mad Men's Don Draper to Parks and Recreation's Ron Swanson and beyond — are often defined by an inability to truly express themselves, shackled by the notion that men aren't allowed to be emotional." (par. 5)

Meaning:

Effect:

5. "Dev ends up spending a long afternoon with his girlfriend's grandmother, and instead of being embarrassed to be seen alone with an old woman who isn't his own grandmother or being bored by her stories, Dev is **enthralled** with learning about her history." (par. 6)

Meaning:

Effect:

6. "For Derek, masculinity appears to be very cut and dry, and directly linked to **heterosexuality**." (par. 9)

Meaning:

Effect:

7. "Don Draper, Barney Stinson, and New Girl's Schmidt are all primarily defined by their relationships (or lack thereof) with the women they sleep with, and assert their manhood by "collecting" as many intimate partners as possible, objectifying women in their own **pursuit** of male dominance." (par. 9)

Meaning:

Effect:

8. "Dev, Arnold, and the other men of Master of None aren't one-dimensional archetypes fitting into some kind of Alpha-male or Beta-male **dichotomy**." (par. 10)

Meaning:

Effect:

9. "Masculinity defines a series of traits that help enforce culturally enforced gender roles which are growing increasingly **obsolete**." (par. 10)

Meaning:

Effect:

10. "Master of None does more than **subvert** masculinity, it straight up ignores it and by doing so, makes a massive statement about masculinity on TV — that a man doesn't need it to be a man." (par. 10)

Meaning:

Effect:

Name_____
Date_____Class_____

Let's Kill All the Mosquitoes (p. 421)
Daniel Engber

For each term in bold below, determine the meaning of the word in the context of the sentence, and then describe the effect of the word: how the author's word choice contributes to the meaning and tone of the sentence(s).

1. "But New Yorkers, like everyone else in the United States, can take **solace** in two simple facts." (par. 2)

Meaning:

Effect:

2. "Indeed, these sweat-sniffing, bloodsucking parasites might reasonably be counted among the greatest **fiends** in human history." (par. 4)

Meaning:

Effect:

3. "But each of these modes of warfare leaves room for activism and **dissent**." (par. 8)

Meaning:

Effect:

4. "They use what's called 'Integrated Mosquito Management,' a **euphemism** for doing lots of little things at once: keeping track of where mosquitoes breed, spraying them with chemicals, fixing broken drains and picking up discarded tires, eliminating swamps." (par. 10)

Meaning:

Effect:

5. "In 1962, Rachel Carson published SILENT SPRING, her **epochal** broadside against the chemical industry." (par. 13)

Meaning:

Effect:

6. "An **incipient** attempt in the Florida Keys, however, has run afoul of some locals, who worry over being guinea pigs in a Frankenfly experiment." (par. 16)

Meaning:

Effect:

7. "These gene-drive techniques are so **potent**—so vast in their destructive potential— that it has been very hard for scientists to test them, even in large outdoor field enclosures." (par. 20)

Meaning:

Effect:

8. "A poorly run experiment could **decimate** global populations, or even make them disappear." (par. 20)

Meaning:

Effect:

9. "'There's no food chain that we know of where mosquitoes are an **inevitable** link in a crucial process,' one mosquito-control expert told me." (par. 23)

Meaning:

Effect:

10. "We've wiped out lots of species in the past, of course, through our **blithe** indifference to the natural world." (par. 24)

Meaning:

Effect:

from *Why Online Harassment Is Still Ruining Lives—and How We Can Stop It*
(p. 429)
Sarah Kessler

For each term in bold below, determine the meaning of the word in the context of the sentence, and then describe the effect of the word: how the author's word choice contributes to the meaning and tone of the sentence(s).

1. "On June 1, the Supreme Court voided that conviction, explaining that the standard the court had used to judge whether Elonis's threats were 'true threats' was not **sufficient**." (par. 3)

Meaning:

Effect:

2. "When crimes like stalking, threatening someone with violence, calling for others to physically harm someone, and **defamation** take place online, they are often treated less seriously by law enforcement, friends and family, and bystanders than when they are committed in a physical, offline place." (par. 5)

Meaning:

Effect:

3. "High-profile stories over the last couple of years have raised the profile of these crimes–stories like that of Caroline Criado-Perez, a blogger and cofounder of the Women's Room website who led a campaign to put a woman on the back of the British bank note–and consequently received a **deluge** of death and rape threats." (par. 6)

Meaning:

Effect:

4. "You can be sued for defamation, invading privacy in certain ways, and intentionally inflicting emotional **distress**." (par. 9)

Meaning:

Effect:

5. "But those laws aren't being frequently **enforced**." (par. 12)

Meaning:

Effect:

6. "Social media companies do not want to implement technologies that censor their platforms by mistaking healthy debate for **malicious** harassment; for the same reason, companies are reluctant to automatically suspend user accounts." (par. 15)

Meaning:

Effect:

7. "One woman I spoke with about the online harassment she **endured** said she was so stricken with anxiety that her partner had to deliver medication to her in bed." (par. 24)

Meaning:

Effect:

8. "**Anecdotally**, many women admit they don't participate on platforms like Twitter as much as they might otherwise, for fear of harassment." (par. 28)

Meaning:

Effect:

9. "'Because I know if I do comment on it, I'm just going to end up being **inundated** with nutjobs.'" (par. 28)

Meaning:

Effect:

10. "Most of us aren't going to find ourselves in the same situation that Richards was caught up in, but after hearing her story, we might hesitate to participate in public **discourse**, afraid that one day we'll be the ones who find ourselves in a swirling whirlwind of rage." (par. 31)

Meaning:

Effect:

Advice to Youth (p. 437)

Mark Twain

For each term in bold below, determine the meaning of the word in the context of the sentence, and then describe the effect of the word: how the author's word choice contributes to the meaning and tone of the sentence(s).

1. "They said it should be something suitable to youth-something **didactic**, instructive, or something in the nature of good advice." (par. 1)

Meaning:

Effect:

2. "First, then, I will say to you my young friends—and I say it **beseechingly**, urgently— Always obey your parents, when they are present." (par. 1-2)

Meaning:

Effect:

3. "Leave dynamite to the low and **unrefined**." (par. 3)

Meaning:

Effect:

4. "It gives you a **splendid** reputation with everybody to know that you get up with the lark; and if you get the right kind of lark, and work at him right, you can easily train him to get up at half past nine, every time -- it's no trick at all." (par. 4)

Meaning:

Effect:

5. "That of course, is putting it rather stronger than necessary; still while I cannot go quite so far as that, I do maintain, and I believe I am right, that the young ought to be **temperate** in the use of this great art until practice and experience shall give them that confidence, elegance, and precision which alone can make the accomplishment graceful and profitable." (par. 5)

Meaning:

Effect:

6. "Patience, diligence, painstaking attention to detail—these are requirements; these in time, will make the student perfect; upon these only, may he rely as the sure foundation for future **eminence**." (par. 5)

Meaning:

Effect:

7. "Think what **tedious** years of study, thought, practice, experience, went to the equipment of that peerless old master who was able to impose upon the whole world the lofty and sounding maxim that 'Truth is mighty and will prevail'—the most majestic compound fracture of fact which any of woman born has yet achieved." (par. 5)

Meaning:

Effect:

8. "A feeble, stupid, **preposterous** lie will not live two years—except it be a **slander** upon somebody." (par. 5)

Meaning (preposterous):

Meaning (slander):

Effect:

9. "The **sorrow** and suffering that have been caused through the innocent but heedless handling of firearms by the young!" (par. 6)

Meaning:

Effect:

10. "Therefore, just the same, don't you meddle with old unloaded firearms; they are the most deadly and **unerring** things that have ever been created by man." (par. 6)

Meaning:

Effect:

Letter from Delano (p. 443)

Cesar Chavez

For each term in bold below, determine the meaning of the word in the context of the sentence, and then describe the effect of the word: how the author's word choice contributes to the meaning and tone of the sentence(s).

1. "If for any reason you fail to come forth to **substantiate** your charges, then you must be held responsible for committing violence against us, albeit violence of the tongue." (par. 2)

Meaning:

Effect:

2. "I am convinced that you as a human being did not mean what you said but rather acted **hastily** under pressure from the public relations firm that has been hired to try to counteract the tremendous moral force of our movement." (par. 2)

Meaning:

Effect:

3. "How many times we ourselves have felt the need to lash out in anger and **bitterness**." (par. 2)

Meaning:

Effect:

4. "For our part I admit that we have **seized** upon every tactic and strategy consistent with the morality of our cause to expose that injustice and thus to heighten the sensitivity of the American conscience so that farm workers will have without bloodshed their own union and the dignity of bargaining with their agribusiness employers." (par. 3)

Meaning:

Effect:

5. "Unwittingly perhaps, you may unleash that other force which our union by discipline and deed, censure and education has sought to avoid, that **panacea** shortcut, that senseless violence which honors no color, class or neighborhood." (par. 3)

Meaning:

Effect:

6. "You must understand—I must make you understand—that our membership and the hopes and aspirations of the hundreds of thousands of the poor and **dispossessed** that have been raised on our account are, above all, human beings, no better and no worse than any other cross-section of human society; we are not saints because we are poor, but by the same measure neither are we immoral." (par. 4)

Meaning:

Effect:

7. "We are men and women who have suffered and endured much, and not only because of our **abject** poverty but because we have been kept poor." (par. 4)

Meaning:

Effect:

8. "And this struggle itself gives meaning to our life and **ennobles** our dying." (par. 4)

Meaning:

Effect:

9. "To resist not with retaliation in kind but to overcome with love and compassion, with ingenuity and creativity, with hard work and longer hours, with stamina and patient **tenacity**, with truth and public appeal, with friends and allies, with nobility and discipline, with politics and law, and with prayer and fasting." (par. 5)

Meaning:

Effect:

10. "I ask you to recognize and bargain with our union before the economic pressure of the boycott and strike takes an **irrevocable** toll; but if not, I ask you to at least sit down with us to discuss the safeguards necessary to keep our historical struggle free of violence." (par. 7)

Meaning:

Effect:

Home Court (p. 492)

José Olivarez

For each term in bold below, determine the meaning of the word in the context of the sentence, and then describe the effect of the word: how the author's word choice contributes to the meaning and tone of the sentence(s).

1. "We played with shadows
    of death threatening to touch, we were **defiant**, we
    were still alive, we sweat the fever
    of hurt from our bodies, our small hands
    aching to be held."
    (lines 5-9)

Meaning:

Effect:

2. "We played all day

    and it was more prayer than basketball, the
    jumper's follow through:
    a small, noiseless **plea**." (lines 9-12)

Meaning:

Effect:

3. "We put up a thousand shots of **penance**,
    all of us trying to gather all of the magic left in
    our wrists." (lines 14-16)

Meaning:

Effect:

4. "We were striking anything we could touch, our
    eyes dry and **vengeful**." (lines 22-23)

Meaning:

Effect:

5. "That was nothing compared to our hearts
    when we looked at our hands and saw

our whole bodies were made of **Grief**." (lines 30-32)

Meaning:

Effect:

The Raven (p. 494)

Edgar Allan Poe

For each term in bold below, determine the meaning of the word in the context of the sentence, and then describe the effect of the word: how the author's word choice contributes to the meaning and tone of the sentence(s).

1. "Once upon a midnight dreary, while I pondered, weak and **weary**," (line 1)

Meaning:

Effect:

2. "Over many a **quaint** and curious volume of forgotten lore—" (line 2)

Meaning:

Effect:

3. "Not the least **obeisance** made he; not a minute stopped or stayed he;" (line. 39)

Meaning:

Effect:

4. "But, with **mien** of lord or lady, perched above my chamber door—" (line 40)

Meaning:

Effect:

5. "Then this ebony bird **beguiling** my sad fancy into smiling," (line 43)

Meaning:

Effect:

6. "Till the **dirges** of his Hope that **melancholy** burden bore Of 'Never—nevermore'." (lines 65-66)

Meaning:

Effect:

7. "What this grim, ungainly, ghastly, gaunt, and **ominous** bird of yore
    Meant in croaking 'Nevermore.'" (lines 71-72)

Meaning:

Effect:

8. "**Desolate** yet all undaunted, on this desert land enchanted—" (line 87)

Meaning:

Effect:

9. "Tell this soul with sorrow **laden** if, within the distant Aidenn,
    It shall clasp a sainted maiden whom the angels name Lenore—" (lines 93-94)

Meaning:

Effect:

10. "On the **pallid** bust of Pallas just above my chamber door;
    And his eyes have all the seeming of a demon's that is dreaming," (lines 105-106)

Meaning:

Effect:

What I Will (p. 500)
Suheir Hammad

For each term in bold below, determine the meaning of the word in the context of the sentence, and then describe the effect of the word: how the author's word choice contributes to the meaning and tone of the sentence(s).

1. "I know
   intimately that skin
   you are hitting." (lines 9-11)

Meaning:

Effect:

2. "I will not **mourn**
   the dead with murder nor suicide."
   (lines 22-24)

Meaning:

Effect:

3. "Life is a right not
   collateral or casual." (lines 28-29)

Meaning:

Effect:

4. "I
   will **craft** my own drum. Gather my beloved near
   and our chanting
   will be dancing." (lines 31-34)

Meaning:

Effect:

5. "I will dance
   and resist and dance and
   persist and dance." (lines 39-41)

Meaning:

Effect:

Name_____

Date_____Class_____

Transmission (p. 502)

Rachel Richardson

For each term in bold below, determine the meaning of the word in the context of the sentence, and then describe the effect of the word: how the author's word choice contributes to the meaning and tone of the sentence(s).

1. "...she and her navigator
   alternately cursing and defining their position by
   latitude..." (lines 3-5)

Meaning:

Effect:

2. "...as best they could read it
   in the **bellowing** wind..." (lines 5-6)

Meaning:

Effect:

3. "...and by what
   they could **surmise** of their rate per hour, last
   land they'd seen." (lines 6-8)

Meaning:

Effect:

4. "Stay with me, someone,
   and the girl wrote each word
   in her composition book, kept the channel tuned,
   hunched to the receiver
   when static overtook the line." (lines 8-12)

Meaning:

Effect:

5. "The coast guard laughed at her father
   holding out the schoolgirl **scrawl**
   and sent him home ashamed." (lines 14-16)

Meaning:

Effect:

Money (p. 505)

Dana Gioia

For each term in bold below, determine the meaning of the word in the context of the sentence, and then describe the effect of the word: how the author's word choice contributes to the meaning and tone of the sentence(s).

1. "Money, the long green,
   cash, stash, **rhino**, jack
   or just plain dough." (lines 1-3)

Meaning:

Effect:

2. "**Chock** it up, fork it over,
   shell it out." (lines 4-5)

Meaning:

Effect:

3. "Greenbacks, **double eagles**, megabucks and
   Ginnie Maes." (lines 8-9)

Meaning:

Effect:

4. "It greases the palm, **feathers** a nest,
   holds heads above water,
   makes both ends meet." (lines 10-12)

Meaning:

Effect:

5. "Gathering interest, **compounding** daily.
   Always in circulation." (lines 14-15)

Meaning:

Effect:

Flames (p. 506)
Billy Collins

For each term in bold below, determine the meaning of the word in the context of the sentence, and then describe the effect of the word: how the author's word choice contributes to the meaning and tone of the sentence(s).

1. "His ranger's hat is **cocked**
   at a disturbing angle." (lines 5-6)

Meaning:

Effect:

2. "His brown fur **gleams**…" (line 7)

Meaning:

Effect:

3. "…as his paws, the size of
   catcher's mitts,
   crackle into the distance." (lines 9-11)

Meaning:

Effect:

4. "He is sick of **dispensing**
   warnings…" (lines 12-13)

Meaning:

Effect:

5. "…the careless,
   the **half-wit** camper,
   the dumbbell hiker." (lines 13-15)

Meaning:

Effect:

Name_____
Date_____Class_____

Find Your Way and You—American Boy (p. 508)
Jenni B. Baker

For each term in bold below, determine the meaning of the word in the context of the sentence, and then describe the effect of the word: how the author's word choice contributes to the meaning and tone of the sentence(s).

1. "But for real Scouting fun and excitement with the gang, you'll want to travel farther **afield**." (page 509, par. 3)

Meaning:

Effect:

2. "You want to feel yourself **akin** to the scouts of old—the Indian, the pioneer, the guide, the tracker, the explorer, the men who traveled across America." (page 509, par. 3)

Meaning:

Effect:

3. "Do you hear in your imagination the almost soundless dip-dip of Indian canoe paddles or ring of the ax of an early pioneer **hewing** a home out of the American wilderness?" (page 510, par. 1)

Meaning:

Effect:

4. "Have you followed with your mind's eye the covered wagons on the **trek** across our continent?" (page 510, par. 1)

Meaning:

Effect:

5. "Have you thought of the men and women who built our country by their determination and **devotion**?" (page 510, par. 1)

Meaning:

Effect:

Harold's Chicken Shack #86 (p. 512)
Nate Marshall

For each term in bold below, determine the meaning of the word in the context of the sentence, and then describe the effect of the word: how the author's word choice contributes to the meaning and tone of the sentence(s).

1. "when i went to summer camp the white kids had a **tendency**
   to shorten names of important institutions. " (lines 1-2)

Meaning:

Effect:

2. "eventually i started
   unintentionally introducing myself as Nate." (lines 6-7)

Meaning:

Effect:

3. "Mick-daniel, Nick-thaniel, MacDonnel shot across the courts like
   wild **heaves** toward the basket. " (lines 11-12)

Meaning:

Effect:

4. "the **subconscious** visual
   of a chicken shack seems a poor fit for national expansion." (lines 12-13)

Meaning:

Effect:

5. "shack sounds too much like home of
   poor people, like **haven** for weary like
   building our own." (lines 15-17)

Meaning:

Effect:

Kindness (p. 515)
Naomi Shihab Nye

For each term in bold below, determine the meaning of the word in the context of the sentence, and then describe the effect of the word: how the author's word choice contributes to the meaning and tone of the sentence(s).

1. "Before you know what kindness really is you
    must lose things,
    feel the future **dissolve** in a moment
    like salt in a weakened broth." (lines 1-4)

Meaning:

Effect:

2. "What you held in your hand,
    what you counted and carefully saved, all
    this must go so you know
    how **desolate** the landscape can be
    between the regions of kindness." (lines 5-9)

Meaning:

Effect:

3. "How you ride and ride thinking the
    bus will never stop,
    the passengers eating **maize** and chicken
    will stare out the window forever." (lines 10-13)

Meaning:

Effect:

4. "Before you learn the **tender** gravity of kindness you
    must travel where the Indian in a white poncho lies dead
    by the side of the road." (lines 14-16)

Meaning:

Effect:

5. "Before you know kindness as the deepest thing inside,

you must know **sorrow** as the other deepest thing." (lines 21-22)

Meaning:

Effect:

Sweet Like A Crow (p. 517)

Michael Ondaatje

For each term in bold below, determine the meaning of the word in the context of the sentence, and then describe the effect of the word: how the author's word choice contributes to the meaning and tone of the sentence(s).

1. "Your voice sounds like a **scorpion** being pushed
   through a glass tube…" (lines 1-2)

Meaning:

Effect:

2. "…like someone has just **trod** on a peacock…" (line 3)

Meaning:

Effect:

3. "…a **pariah** dog
   with a magpie in its mouth…" (lines 13-14)

Meaning:

Effect:

4. "…a dolphin **reciting** epic poetry to a sleepy audience…" (line 22)

Meaning:

Effect:

5. "…like 3 old ladies locked in the **lavatory**…" (line 30)

Meaning:

Effect:

Sonnet 18: Shall I compare thee to a summer's day? (p. 520)
William Shakespeare

For each term in bold below, determine the meaning of the word in the context of the sentence, and then describe the effect of the word: how the author's word choice contributes to the meaning and tone of the sentence(s).

1. "Thou art more lovely and more **temperate**:" (line 2)

Meaning:

Effect:

2. "Rough winds do shake the **darling** buds of May..." (line 3)

Meaning:

Effect:

3. "And summer's **lease** hath all too short a date:" (line 4)

Meaning:

Effect:

4. "By chance or nature's changing course **untrimm'd**;" (line 8)

Meaning:

Effect:

5. "But thy **eternal** summer shall not fade..." (line 9)

Meaning:

Effect:

We Real Cool (p. 522)
Gwendolyn Brooks

For each term in bold below, determine the meaning of the word in the context of the sentence, and then describe the effect of the word: how the author's word choice contributes to the meaning and tone of the sentence(s).

1. "We

    Lurk late." (lines 2-3)

Meaning:

Effect:

2. "We
    Strike straight." (lines 5-6)

Meaning:

Effect:

3. "We

    Sing **sin**." (lines 6-7)

Meaning:

Effect:

4. "We
    Thin **gin**." (lines 7-8)

Meaning:

Effect:

5. "We

    Jazz June." (lines 8-9)

Meaning:

Effect:

In Chicano Park (p. 524)

David Tomas Martinez

For each term in bold below, determine the meaning of the word in the context of the sentence, and then describe the effect of the word: how the author's word choice contributes to the meaning and tone of the sentence(s).

1. "No matter if half the park is concrete
    and **stanchions** supporting a bridge..." (lines 1-2)

Meaning:

Effect:

2. "...near industrial buildings yellow in the sun, their
    stalks of smoke soaring awake..." (lines 3-4)

Meaning:

Effect:

3. "No matter if all the murals **decay**..." (line 11)

Meaning:

Effect:

4. "And between rolls,
    wipe the dust off the dice, as bills **coil** a foot..." (lines 17-18)

Meaning:

Effect:

5. "Not even bags of chips, cheetahs with wind,
    avoid being tackled, **gouged**, and ripped apart." (lines 21-22)

Meaning:

Effect:

Because I Could Not Stop for Death (p. 526)
Emily Dickinson

For each term in bold below, determine the meaning of the word in the context of the sentence, and then describe the effect of the word: how the author's word choice contributes to the meaning and tone of the sentence(s).

1. "We slowly drove – He knew no **haste**" (line 5)

Meaning:

Effect:

2. "And I had put away
   My labor and my **leisure** too, For His
   Civility—" (lines 6-8)

Meaning (leisure):

Meaning (civility):

Effect:

3. "We passed the School, where Children **strove**…" (line 9)

Meaning:

Effect:

4. "The Dews drew **quivering** and chill—" (line 14)

Meaning:

Effect:

5. "We paused before a House that seemed A
   Swelling of the Ground—
   The Roof was **scarcely** visible—
   The Cornice—in the Ground—" (lines 17-20)

Meaning:

Effect:

T.S.A. (p. 528)
Amit Majmudar

For each term in bold below, determine the meaning of the word in the context of the sentence, and then describe the effect of the word: how the author's word choice contributes to the meaning and tone of the sentence(s).

1. At O'Hare, at Atlanta, at Dallas/Fort Worth, it
      happens every trip,
at LaGuardia, Logan, and Washington Dulles, the
      customary strip..." (lines 5-8)

Meaning:

Effect:

2. "Lest the randomness of it be doubted, observe how
      Myrtle's searched in **tandem**..." (lines 11-12)

Meaning:

Effect:

3. "How polite of the screeners to sham **paranoia**..." (line 15)

Meaning:

Effect:

4. "   ...when what they really want
  is to pick out the **swarthiest**, scruffiest of us and
      pat us top to toe..." (lines 16-18)

Meaning:

Effect:

5. "   ...my dark unshaven brothers
  whose names overlap with the crazies and God **fiends**..." (lines 22-23)

Meaning:

Effect:

Ways of Talking (p. 530)

Ha Jin

For each term in bold below, determine the meaning of the word in the context of the sentence, and then describe the effect of the word: how the author's word choice contributes to the meaning and tone of the sentence(s).

1. "Even if there was no grief
    we wouldn't stop **lamenting**..." (lines 4-5)

Meaning:

Effect:

2. "...as though longing for the charm of a
    distressed face." (lines 6-7)

Meaning:

Effect:

3. "So many things **descended** without warning..." (line

Meaning:

Effect:

4. "...labor wasted, loves lost, houses gone,
    marriages broken, friends **estranged**,
    ambitions worn away by immediate needs." (lines 10-12)

Meaning:

Effect:

5. "**Grief** seemed like an endless river—
    The only immortal flow of life." (lines 15-16)

Meaning:

Effect:

Let America Be America Again (p. 532)
Langston Hughes

For each term in bold below, determine the meaning of the word in the context of the sentence, and then describe the effect of the word: how the author's word choice contributes to the meaning and tone of the sentence(s).

1. "Let it be the **pioneer** on the plain
   Seeking a home where he himself is free." (lines 3-4)

Meaning:

Effect:

2. "Let it be that great strong land of love
   Where never kings **connive** nor tyrants scheme..." (lines 7-8)

Meaning:

Effect:

3. "I am the people, **humble**, hungry, mean—" (line 34)

Meaning:

Effect:

4. "I am the man who never got ahead,
   The poorest worker **bartered** through the years." (lines 38-39)

Meaning:

Effect:

5. "Whose sweat and blood, whose faith and pain,
   Whose hand at the **foundry**, whose plow in the rain,
   Must bring back our mighty dream again." (lines 67-69)

Meaning:

Effect:

6. "We, the people, must **redeem**
   The land, the mines, the plants, the rivers." (lines 82-83)

Meaning:

Effect:

The New Colossus **(p. 538)**
Emma Lazarus

For each term in bold below, determine the meaning of the word in the context of the sentence, and then describe the effect of the word: how the author's word choice contributes to the meaning and tone of the sentence(s).

1. "Not like the **brazen** giant of Greek fame…" (line 1)

Meaning:

Effect:

2. "With conquering limbs **astride** from land to land…" (line 2)

Meaning:

Effect:

3. "Is the imprisoned lightning, and her name
   Mother of Exiles. From her **beacon**-hand
   Glows world-wide welcome…" (lines 5-7)

Meaning:

Effect:

4. "'Keep, ancient lands, your storied **pomp**!'" (line 9)

Meaning:

Effect:

5. "'Give me your tired, your poor,
   Your huddled masses yearning to breathe free,
   The wretched refuse of your **teeming** shore.'" (lines 10-12)

Meaning:

Effect:

Remembrances for the 100ᵗʰ Anniversary of the Statue of Liberty (p. 540)

Concord Oral History Program

For each term in bold below, determine the meaning of the word in the context of the sentence, and then describe the effect of the word: how the author's word choice contributes to the meaning and tone of the sentence(s).

1. "My family and I followed my grand uncle into **exile** in England." (par. 3)

Meaning:

Effect:

2. "We were part of a **convoy** of about 50 ships that included cargo vessels and oil tankers along with the troop transports." (par. 4)

Meaning:

Effect:

3. "And because it was wartime the route taken was a **circuitous** one. " (par. 4)

Meaning:

Effect:

4. "At the end of the **harrowing** voyage, there was the Statue of Liberty." (par. 5)

Meaning:

Effect:

5. "The boat that I left on from Bremerhaven was filled with **refugees** from Eastern bloc countries entering as part of a special refugee quota passed during the Eisenhower Administration." (par. 7)

Meaning:

Effect:

6. "Living conditions were **primitive** compared to the U.S." (par. 16)

Meaning:

Effect:

lady liberty (p. 543)

Tato Laviera

For each term in bold below, determine the meaning of the word in the context of the sentence, and then describe the effect of the word: how the author's word choice contributes to the meaning and tone of the sentence(s).

1. "for liberty, your day filled in **splendor**..." (line 1)

Meaning:

Effect:

2. "wall street a backdrop of centennial **adulation**..." (line 6)

Meaning:

Effect:

3. "...palms blistered and calloused, feet
    embroidered in rust, centennial
    decay..." (lines 25-27)

Meaning:

Effect:

4. "...**incarcerating** the body as
    she prepared to receive
    her twentieth-century transplant..." (lines 37-39)

Meaning:

Effect:

5. "...and lady liberty decided to reflect
    on lincoln's emancipatory **resoluteness**
    on washington's patriotism..." (lines 47-49)

Meaning:

Effect:

6. "...on jefferson's **lucidity**..." (line 50)

Meaning:

Effect:

7. "...she spoke for the principles, for
    the **preamble**,
    for the bill of rights,
    and thirty-nine peaceful
    presidential transitions..." (lines 65-69)

Meaning:

Effect:

8. "hunger **abounds**, our soil is plentiful, our
    technology advanced enough
    to feed the world,
    to feed humanity's hunger . . ." (lines 86-89)

Meaning:

Effect:

9. "...for we will never be free
    if indeed freedom is **subjugated**
    to trampling upon people's needs." (lines 96-98)

Meaning:

Effect:

10. "...celebrating in the name of equality,
     in the **pursuit** of happiness..." (lines 117-118)

Meaning:

Effect:

Slant (p. 546)

Suji Kwock Kim

For each term in bold below, determine the meaning of the word in the context of the sentence, and then describe the effect of the word: how the author's word choice contributes to the meaning and tone of the sentence(s).

1. "If the angle of an eye is all,
    the **slant** of hope, the **slant** of dreaming, according to each life…" (lines 1-2)

Meaning:

Effect:

2. "…light of Lady Liberty, **possessor** of the most famous armpit in the world…" (line 4)

Meaning:

Effect:

3. "…the **oglers** wearing fern-wilting quantities of cologne, strutting, trash-talking,
    glorious…" (line 14)

Meaning:

Effect:

4. "the immigrants, the refugees, the peddlars, stockbrokers and janitors, **stenographers**
        and cooks,
    all of us making and unmaking ourselves…" (lines 15-16)

Meaning:

Effect:

5. "Quick, quick, ask heaven of it, of every mortal relation,
    feeling that is **fleeing**…" (lines 20-21)

Meaning:

Effect:

The Statue of Liberty Was Born a Muslim (p. 494)

Michael Daly

For each term in bold below, determine the meaning of the word in the context of the sentence, and then describe the effect of the word: how the author's word choice contributes to the meaning and tone of the sentence(s).

1. "Bartholdi remained determined to **erect** a colossus on the scale of the one in ancient Rhodes." (par. 2)

Meaning:

Effect:

2. "Too many of us have joined Christie in allowing the photos of the **carnage** in Paris to make us forget those images of little Aylan." (par. 14)

Meaning:

Effect:

3. "But in our **subsequent** grief and anger we ended up becoming so unlike ourselves that we engaged in torture." (par. 20)

Meaning:

Effect:

4. "That only made sense, as the French largely paid for the statue; not the central government, but some 180 **municipalities**, including Paris." (par. 24)

Meaning:

Effect:

5. "The Twin Towers were still gone, yet the very fact that you could again peer out Lady Liberty's crown **imparted** a sense that America was recovering itself." (par. 28)

Meaning:

Effect:

6. "Yes, we need to be **vigilant**." (par. 32)

Meaning:

Effect:

7. "But whatever damage an agent might be able to **inflict** would be nothing compared to what we would do to ourselves by going against what makes us great." (par. 35)

Meaning:

Effect:

8. "Anyway, the latest **jihadi** in the U.S. known to be taking direct instructions from ISIS was a 20-year-old raised on Staten Island, an American citizen the same way all except possibly one of the Paris attackers were French or Belgian citizens." (par. 36)

Meaning:

Effect:

9. "A few yards away by the South Memorial Pool were inscribed the names of the firefighters and cops who had **perished** in the 9/11 attacks while showing us that the way to beat terrorists is to refuse to be terrorized." (par. 39)

Meaning:

Effect:

10. "And those words in the inscription must apply to everyone, most particularly youngsters who are in a **plight** such as Aylan's, but are not yet beyond saving, who might still reach the golden door. (par. 42)

Meaning:

Effect:

Black Statue of Liberty (p. 551)
jessica Care moore

For each term in bold below, determine the meaning of the word in the context of the sentence, and then describe the effect of the word: how the author's word choice contributes to the meaning and tone of the sentence(s).

1. "I'm a symbol of freedom, but I'm still not free
   I suffer from class, race, and gender **inequality**." (lines 9-10)

Meaning:

Effect:

2. "I wear a crown of knowledge, 'cause I'm a **conscious** queen…" (line 11)

Meaning:

Effect:

3. "My mask is one of happiness, though my history here is full of misery.
   Done **deliberately**." (lines 12-13)

Meaning:

Effect:

4. "You placed a bible under my arm, after you ripped me of my faith And
   made me pray to a fictional **imposter**…" (lines 15-16)

Meaning:

Effect:

5. "In the slums and the ghettos that you find so **uncouth**." (line 20)

Meaning:

Effect:

6. "Looking into her wise eyes will make a blind man see
   How can you dare name a **eurocentric** girl after me?" (lines 28-29)

Meaning:

Effect:

7. "What's the **liberated** woman gotta do?" (line 42)

Meaning:

Effect:

8. "Every month I pay the rent. Put
    my **silhouette** on a stamp
    I'm not a ho, slut or tramp." (lines 44-46)

Meaning:

Effect:

9. "I can bake cookies, bear babies, **preside** over revolutions..." (line 50)

Meaning:

Effect:

10. "My **aura** is unafraid.
     So, no statue in the big apple can mess with me." (lines 53-54)

Meaning:

Effect:

Ego-Tripping *(there may be a reason why)* (p. 555)
Nikki Giovanni

For each term in bold below, determine the meaning of the word in the context of the sentence, and then describe the effect of the word: how the author's word choice contributes to the meaning and tone of the sentence(s).

1. "I was born in the **congo**" (line 1)

Meaning:

Effect:

2. "I designed a pyramid so tough that a star that only
   glows every one hundred years falls
   into the center giving **divine** perfect light" (lines 3-5)

Meaning:

Effect:

3. "I sat on the throne
   drinking **nectar** with allah" (lines 7-8)

Meaning:

Effect:

4. "My son noah built new/ark and I
   stood proudly at the **helm**
   as we sailed on a soft summer day" (lines 26-28)

Meaning:

Effect:

5. "men **intone** my loving name" (line 31)

Meaning:

Effect:

6. "I am so perfect so divine so **ethereal** so surreal I
    cannot be comprehended
    except by my permission" (lines 46-48)

Meaning:

Effect:

Somewhere There Is a Simple Life (p. 557)
Anna Akhmatova

For each term in bold below, determine the meaning of the word in the context of the sentence, and then describe the effect of the word: how the author's word choice contributes to the meaning and tone of the sentence(s).

1. "Somewhere there is a simple life and a world,
    Transparent, warm and joyful. . ." (lines 1-2)

Meaning:

Effect:

2. "But we live ceremoniously and with difficulty
    And we observe the **rites** of our bitter meetings..." (lines 6-7)

Meaning:

Effect:

3. "But not for anything would we exchange this splendid
    Granite city of fame and **calamity**..." (lines 10-11)

Meaning:

Effect:

4. "The sunless, **gloomy** gardens..." (line 13)

Meaning:

Effect:

5. "And, barely audible, the **Muse's** voice." (line 14)

Meaning:

Effect:

Four Elements of Ghost-dance (p. 559)
Reed Bobroff

For each term in bold below, determine the meaning of the word in the context of the sentence, and then describe the effect of the word: how the author's word choice contributes to the meaning and tone of the sentence(s).

1. "I want to go back

          back to when

          drum circle **cipher** sessions

spun the world." (lines 3-6)

Meaning:

Effect:

2. "listen to the way hide grinds

   like pine nuts in **gourd**" (lines 13-14)

Meaning:

Effect:

3. "**Quests** no longer find thin sacks of bones on

   the plains." (lines 17-18)

Meaning:

Effect:

4. "*MY MOCCASINS!*

   need to be tied with a deer hide / fat lace. Spit shined, / sterling silver

      stamp—gotta look **vamp**..." (lines 36-38)

Meaning:

Effect:

5. "Dressed in ghost jerseys,

   we dance on aerosol **petroglyphs**." (lines 65-66)

Meaning:

Effect:

6. "We mix these Gathering Nations in
   until we all **permeate**
   sage." (lines 73-75)

Meaning:

Effect:

Things Chinese (p. 564)

Adrienne Su

For each term in bold below, determine the meaning of the word in the context of the sentence, and then describe the effect of the word: how the author's word choice contributes to the meaning and tone of the sentence(s).

1. "My policy, born of exhaustion with talk about race
   And the quintessentially American wish for **antecedents**..." (lines 7-8)

Meaning:

Effect:

2. "Two of whom stayed Chinese to their final days, Two of
   whom were all but defined by their expertise
   On the food of the country I was trying to **excise**." (lines 10-12)

Meaning:

Effect:

3. "It wiped out my parents' earliest years And
   converted them to 1950s Georgians
   Who'd always attended church and school, like anyone." (lines 16-18)

Meaning:

Effect:

4. "Why **distinctness** and mystery were not advantages..." (line 28)

Meaning:

Effect:

5. "For months I couldn't write anything decent Because
   banned information kept trying to enter
   Like bungled **idioms** in the speech of a foreigner." (lines 31-33)

Meaning:

Effect:

6. "I was my own totalitarian government, An
    HMO that wouldn't pay for a specialist,
    And I was the **dissident** or patient who perished." (lines 34-36)

Meaning:

Effect:

7. "The hope was to **transcend** the profanity of being..." (line 37)

Meaning:

Effect:

Eddie Priest's Barbershop & Notary (p. 567)
Kevin Young

For each term in bold below, determine the meaning of the word in the context of the sentence, and then describe the effect of the word: how the author's word choice contributes to the meaning and tone of the sentence(s).

1. "is having nothing
    better to do   than guess at the years
    of hair **matted** beneath the soiled caps of
    drunks" (lines 9-11)

Meaning:

Effect:

2. "the **tender** heads
    of sons fresh from cornrows" (lines 15-16)

Meaning:

Effect:

3. "grandfathers
    stopping their games of **ivory**
    dominoes   just before they reach the bone yard"
    (lines 27-30)

Meaning:

Effect:

4. "is winking **widowers** announcing
    cut it clean off   I'm through courting
    and hair only gets in the way" (lines 30-32)

Meaning:

Effect:

5. "that sting of wintergreen
    tonic on the neck of a sleeping snow haired
    man" (lines 34-36)

Meaning:

Effect:

Ode on a Grecian Urn (p. 569)

John Keats

For each term in bold below, determine the meaning of the word in the context of the sentence, and then describe the effect of the word: how the author's word choice contributes to the meaning and tone of the sentence(s).

1. "Thou still **unravish'd** bride of quietness," (line 1)

Meaning:

Effect:

2. "What leaf-fring'd legend haunts about thy shape Of

   deities or mortals, or of both," (lines 5-6)

Meaning:

Effect:

3. "Pipe to the spirit **ditties** of no tone:" (line 14)

Meaning:

Effect:

4. "And, happy melodist, **unwearied**,
      For ever piping songs for ever new;" (lines 23-24)

Meaning:

Effect:

5. "What little town by river or sea shore,
      Or mountain-built with peaceful citadel,
      Is emptied of this folk, this **pious** morn?" (lines 35-37)

Meaning:

Effect:

6. "With forest branches and the **trodden** weed;" (line 43)

Meaning:

Effect:

7. "Thou shalt remain, in midst of other **woe**" (line 47)

Meaning:

Effect:

from *Song of Myself* (p. 572)
Walt Whitman

For each term in bold below, determine the meaning of the word in the context of the sentence, and then describe the effect of the word: how the author's word choice contributes to the meaning and tone of the sentence(s).

1. "And what I **assume** you shall **assume**,

    For every atom belonging to me as good belongs to you." (lines 2-3)

Meaning:

Effect:

2. "Creeds and schools in **abeyance**,
    Retiring back a while sufficed at what they are, but never forgotten," (lines 10-11)

Meaning:

Effect:

3. "The **distillation** would intoxicate me also, but I shall not let it." (line 16)

Meaning:

Effect:

4. "The sound of the belch'd words of my voice loos'd to the **eddies** of the wind," (line 25)

Meaning:

Effect:

5. "You shall no longer take things at second or third hand, nor look through the eyes of the dead,
    nor feed on the **spectres** in books," (lines 35-36)

Meaning:

Effect:

6. "There was never any more **inception** than there is now," (line 41)

Meaning:

Effect:

7. "To elaborate is no **avail**, learn'd and unlearn'd feel that it is so." (line 49)

Meaning:

Effect:

8. "Stout as a horse, affectionate, **haughty**, electrical, I
   and this mystery here we stand." (lines 51-52)

Meaning:

Effect:

9. "Showing the best and dividing it from the worst age **vexes** age," (line 56)

Meaning:

Effect:

10. "It **coaxes** me to the vapor and the dusk." (line 74)

Meaning:

Effect:

Stephen King's Guide to Movie Snacks (p. 620)
Stephen King

For each term in bold below, determine the meaning of the word in the context of the sentence, and then describe the effect of the word: how the author's word choice contributes to the meaning and tone of the sentence(s).

1. "The **Bard** of Horror takes a **gastronomical** tour of the movie-theater concession stand— all hail the cholesterol-lowering properties of diet soda" (opening)

Meaning (Bard):

Meaning (gastronomical):

Effect:

2. "Oh, an occasional piece about how much they cost, but few words on their **culinary** wonderfulness." (par. 1)

Meaning:

Effect:

3. "So let me **impart** a few lessons years of snacking have taught me." (par. 1)

Meaning:

Effect:

4. "And I find there's something **giddy** about tossing down $4.50 for a box of Gummi Bears or a bag of chocolate raisins." (par. 3)

Meaning:

Effect:

5. "It makes me feel like a high roller, especially when the **matinee** ticket itself only costs 50 cents more."(par. 3)

Meaning:

Effect:

6. "A big diet cola sops up the calories and **cholesterol** contained in movie snack food just like a big old sponge soaks up water." (par. 4)

Meaning:

Effect:

7. "You know you have a heavy bag when the bottom starts to sag and ooze large drops of a yellow **puslike** substance before you even get into the theater." (par. 6)

Meaning:

Effect:

8. "And while I don't bring **bootleg** food into the movies, I do bring bootleg toothpicks." (par. 8)

Meaning:

Effect:

9. "And although it's a matter of personal choice, I myself don't eat movie meat (go on, **snicker**, I can take it)." (par. 9)

Meaning:

Effect:

Trashed (p. 623)
Derf Backderf

For each term in bold below, determine the meaning of the word in the context of the sentence, and then describe the effect of the word: how the author's word choice contributes to the meaning and tone of the sentence(s).

1. "His comic strip, *The City*, appeared in over 140 publications in its twenty-plus years in **syndication**." (opening)

Meaning:

Effect:

2. "That's when our **forefathers** invented…the dump!" (p. 624)

Meaning:

Effect:

3. "The favorite method of disposal was to simply toss it out the window onto the street, where it would rot and **reek**." (p. 624)

Meaning:

Effect:

4. "In the 1400s, the piles of stinking garbage outside the walls of Paris were so high, city defenses were **compromised**." (p. 625)

Meaning:

Effect:

5. "New York City had so many free-roaming hogs that Charles Dickens in "American Notes" begged city fathers to rid the **metropolis** of the "ugly brutes"." (p. 626)

Meaning:

Effect:

6. "Often communities would "reclaim" **wetlands**." (p. 626)

Meaning:

Effect:

7. "Not until 1979 did the **E.P.A.** issue rules on how landfills were built and operated." (p. 626)

Meaning:

Effect:

8. "From 1960 on, household waste in the U.S. increased drastically, as **conspicuous** consumption and built-in **obsolescence** became the norm." (p. 626)

Meaning (conspicuous):

Meaning (obsolescence):

Effect:

9. "Europeans aren't much better, and Canadians generate more garbage **per capita** than anyone on Earth!" (p. 626)

Meaning:

Effect:

10. "An independent **biannual** study by Columbia University finds our annual garbage total isn't 254 million tons...it's 389 million tons!" (p. 627)

Meaning:

Effect:

Why Teenage Girls Roll Their Eyes (p. 630)
Lisa Damour

For each term in bold below, determine the meaning of the word in the context of the sentence, and then describe the effect of the word: how the author's word choice contributes to the meaning and tone of the sentence(s).

1. "Many people can roll their eyes, but adolescent girls have practically **monopolized** the **ocular** gesture as a form of communication." (par. 1)

Meaning (monopolized):

Meaning (ocular):

Effect:

2. "Given that the drive for **autonomy** is a central force during adolescence, taking orders can be especially annoying for teenagers." (par. 3)

Meaning:

Effect:

3. "Again, **ophthalmic calisthenics** offer a useful solution." (par. 3)

Meaning (ophthalmic):

Meaning (calisthenics):

Effect:

4. "Teens can be easily overwhelmed by their own feelings, and they're often **ambivalent** about leaning on parents for support." (par. 4)

Meaning:

Effect:

5. "If parents hold irrational expectations, make **arbitrary** rules, or recruit shame when ordinary anger would do, girls sometimes stick up for themselves by rolling their eyes." (par. 5)

Meaning:

Effect:

6. "They attack one another and adults with the dismissive, **demeaning** gesture and can provoke reasonable people into **retaliatory** responses." (par. 6)

Meaning (demeaning):

Meaning (retaliatory):

Effect:

7. "When eye-rolling is clearly meant as an insult, parents can try to raise the **relational** bar by saying, "That's rude. I'm trusting you'll soon find a more mature way to let me know what you're thinking," or something along those lines." (par. 6)

Meaning:

Effect:

from *A Theory of Fun for Game Design* (p. 633)
Raph Koster

For each term in bold below, determine the meaning of the word in the context of the sentence, and then describe the effect of the word: how the author's word choice contributes to the meaning and tone of the sentence(s).

1. "Games aren't just a **diversion**; they're something valuable and important." (par. 2)

Meaning:

Effect:

2. "This can happen via physical **stimuli**, **aesthetic** appreciation, or direct chemical manipulation." (par. 6)

Meaning (stimuli):

Meaning (aesthetic):

Effect:

3. "Fun is all about our brains feeling good—the release of **endorphins** into our system...." (par. 7)

Meaning:

Effect:

4. "Endorphins are an **opiate**." (par. 11)

Meaning:

Effect:

5. "Pleasure is not the only thing that gives us this effect, of course—**adrenaline** rushes caused by fear provide a similar sensation." (par. 11)

Meaning:

Effect:

6. "When you feel a piece of music is repetitive or **derivative**, it grows boring because it presents no **cognitive** challenge." (par. 12)

Meaning (cognitive):

Meaning (derivative):

Effect:

7. "If you put a person in a sensory **deprivation** chamber, he or she will get unhappy very quickly." (par. 13)

Meaning:

Effect:

8. "At all times, the brain is casting about trying to learn something, trying to **integrate** information into its worldview." (par. 13)

Meaning:

Effect:

9. "It is **insatiable** in that way." (par. 13)

Meaning:

Effect:

10. "The player might grok that there's a ton of depth to the possible **permutations** in a game, but conclude that these permutations are below their level of interest—sort of like saying, "Yeah, there's a ton of depth in baseball, but memorizing the RBI stats[9] for the past 20 years is not all that useful to me."" (par. 17)

Meaning:

Effect:

Earth without People (p. 640)

Alan Weisman

For each term in bold below, determine the meaning of the word in the context of the sentence, and then describe the effect of the word: how the author's word choice contributes to the meaning and tone of the sentence(s).

1. "A good place to start searching for answers is in Korea, in the 155-mile-long, 2.5-mile- wide mountainous Demilitarized Zone, or DMZ, set up by the **armistice** ending the Korean War." (par. 2)

Meaning:

Effect:

2. "Today those paddies have become barely **discernible**, transformed into pockets of marsh, and the new occupants of these lands arrive as dazzling white squadrons of red- crowned cranes that glide over the bulrushes in perfect formation, touching down so lightly that they detonate no land mines." (par. 2)

Meaning:

Effect:

3. "They winter in the DMZ alongside the endangered white-naped cranes, revered in Asia as sacred **portents** of peace." (par. 2)

Meaning:

Effect:

4. "This has spurred an international coalition of scientists called the DMZ Forum to try to **consecrate** the area for a peace park and nature preserve." (par. 3)

Meaning:

Effect:

5. "The habitat would not revert to a truly natural state until the dams that now divert rivers to **slake** the needs of Seoul's more than 20 million inhabitants failed—a century or two after the humans had gone." (par. 5)

Meaning:

Effect:

6. "Dogs would go **feral**, but they wouldn't last long: They'd never be able to compete." (par. 5)

Meaning:

Effect:

7. "From A.D. 800 to 900, a combination of drought and **internecine** warfare over dwindling farmland brought 2,000 years of civilization crashing down." (par. 6)

Meaning:

Effect:

8. "With nobody to trample seedlings, New York's **prolific** exotic, the Chinese ailanthus tree, would take over." (par. 7)

Meaning:

Effect:

9. "That would **exacerbate** a problem that already plagues New York—rising groundwater." (par. 8)

Meaning:

Effect:

10. "There a chemical weapons plant produced mustard and nerve gas, **incendiary** bombs, napalm, and after World War II, pesticides." (par. 13)

Meaning:

Effect:

11. "Still, at some point thousands of years hence, the last stone walls—perhaps chunks of St. Paul's Chapel on Wall Street, built in 1766 from Manhattan's own hard **schist**—would fall." (par. 16)

Meaning:

Effect:

12. "What **Pleistocene** humans did in 1,500 years to terrestrial life, modern man has done in mere decades to the oceans—"almost," Jackson says." (par. 13)

Meaning:

Effect:

My Daughter's Homework Is Killing Me (p. 649)

Karl Taro Greenfeld

For each term in bold below, determine the meaning of the word in the context of the sentence, and then describe the effect of the word: how the author's word choice contributes to the meaning and tone of the sentence(s).

1. "That's how the notes start, and they only get **murkier** after that." (par. 1)

Meaning:

Effect:

2. "When I ask Esmee what this actually means, she gives me her homework **credo**." (par. 1)

Meaning:

Effect:

3. "(Esmee's algebra class is doing a section on **polynomials**, a word I haven't heard in decades.)" (par. 7)

Meaning:

Effect:

4. ""The term *synergistic* applies to the combined efforts of Tarbuck and Lutgens," says the biographical note at the beginning." (par. 11)

Meaning:

Effect:

5. "In Southern California in the late '70s, it was totally **plausible** that an eighth grader would have no homework at all." (par. 15)

Meaning:

Effect:

6. "These **lamentations** are a ritual whenever we are gathered around kitchen islands talking about our kids' schools." (par. 18)

Meaning:

Effect:

7. "My daughter has done a **commendable** job memorizing the conjugations." (par. 5)

Meaning:

Effect:

8. "That night, in an e-mail chain started by the class parent to seek chaperones for a field trip, I removed the teacher's name, changed the subject line, and then asked the other parents in the class whether their children found the homework load **onerous**." (par. 38)

Meaning:

Effect:

9. "Freedom, in the form of **unfettered** capitalism, also has its downside." (par. 48)   Meaning:

Effect:

10. "It turns out that there is no **correlation** between homework and achievement." (par. 52)

Meaning:

Effect:

from *Quiet: The Power of Introverts in a World that Can't Stop Talking* (p. 661)
Susan Cain

For each term in bold below, determine the meaning of the word in the context of the sentence, and then describe the effect of the word: how the author's word choice contributes to the meaning and tone of the sentence(s).

1. "She stands silently, her mere presence enough to **galvanize** the crowd." (par. 10)

Meaning:

Effect:

2. "They were full of phrases like "radical humility" and "quiet **fortitude**."" (par. 11)

Meaning:

Effect:

3. "Parks herself seemed aware of this **paradox**, calling her autobiography *Quiet Strength*— a title that challenges us to question our assumptions." (par. 12)

Meaning:

Effect:

4. "Take the partnership of Rosa Parks and Martin Luther King Jr.: a formidable orator refusing to give up his seat on a segregated bus wouldn't have had the same effect as a modest woman who'd clearly prefer to keep silent but for the **exigencies** of the situation." (par. 15)

Meaning:

Effect:

5. "We live with a value system that I call the Extrovert Ideal—the omnipresent belief that the ideal self is **gregarious**, alpha, and comfortable in the spotlight." (par. 18)

Meaning:

Effect:

6. "Introversion-along with its cousins sensitivity, seriousness, and shyness-is now a second-class personality trait, somewhere between a disappointment and a **pathology**." (par. 19)

Meaning:

Effect:

7. "The same dynamics apply in groups, where research shows that the **voluble** are considered smarter than the **reticent**-even though there's zero correlation between the gift of gab and good ideas." (par. 20)

Meaning (voluble):

Meaning (reticent):

Effect:

8. "I soon discovered that there is no all-purpose definition of introversion or extroversion; these are not **unitary** categories, like "curly-haired" or "sixteen-year-old," in which everyone can agree on who qualifies for inclusion." (par. 23)

Meaning:

Effect:

9. "A few things introverts are not: The word *introvert* is not a synonym for hermit or **misanthrope**." (par. 29)

Meaning:

Effect:

10. "As Jung **felicitously** put it, "There is no such thing as a pure extrovert or a pure introvert." (par. 35)

Meaning:

Effect:

What Is Your Life's Blueprint? (p. 670)
Martin Luther King Jr.

For each term in bold below, determine the meaning of the word in the context of the sentence, and then describe the effect of the word: how the author's word choice contributes to the meaning and tone of the sentence(s).

1. "You know, it's very unfortunate that in so many instances, our society has placed a **stigma** on the Negroes' color." (par. 3)

Meaning:

Effect:

2. "And I understand all of the **sociological** reasons why we often drop out of school." (par. 5)

Meaning:

Effect:

3. "For if you set out to do that, you have already flunked your **matriculation** exam for entrance into the University of Integration." (par. 6)

Meaning:

Effect:

4. "They and their own lives have walked through long and desolate nights of oppression, and yet they've risen up and plunged against cloud-filled nights of **affliction**." (par. 9)

Meaning:

Effect:

5. "From a poverty-stricken area of Philadelphia, Pennsylvania, Marian Anderson[5] rose up to be the world's greatest **contralto**, so that Toscanini[6] could say that a voice like this comes only once in a century, and Sibelius[7] of Finland could say, "My roof is too low for such a voice."" (par. 11)

Meaning:

Effect:

6. "From crippling circumstances there came a George Washington Carver to carve for himself an imperishable **niche** in the **annals** of science." (par. 13)

Meaning (niche):

Meaning (annals):

Effect:

7. "And then came Ralph Bunche, the grandson of a slave preacher, and he reached up and grabbed it and allowed it to shine in his life with all of its **scintillating** beauty." (par. 14)

Meaning:

Effect:

8. "I close by quoting once more the man that the young lady quoted, that magnificent black **bard** who has now passed on, Langston Hughes." (par. 18)

Meaning:

Effect:

9. "The mother didn't always have her grammar right, but she uttered words of great symbolic **profundity**:" (par. 18)

Meaning:

Effect:

The Politics of the Hoodie (p. 677)

Troy Patterson

For each term in bold below, determine the meaning of the word in the context of the sentence, and then describe the effect of the word: how the author's word choice contributes to the meaning and tone of the sentence(s).

1. ""The Politics of the Hoodie", published in 2016, was part of that series, and is an example of his **astute** observations about the intermingling of politics, culture, and fashion." (opening)

Meaning:

Effect:

2. "Here, projecting catalog-model **cordiality** in the sterile space of an off-white backdrop, was a young black man in a hoodie." (par. 1)

Meaning:

Effect:

3. "Watching Beyoncé's recent video for "Formation," with its set piece showing a black child in a hooded sweatshirt disarming a rank of riot police with his dance moves, most Americans grasped the outfit as a **rhetorical** device serving a dreamlike declaration about protest and civil rights." (par. 3)

Meaning:

Effect:

4. "During the N.F.L. playoffs, football fans saw the quarterback Cam Newton, the **locus** of a running dialogue about blackness, wear hoodies to interviews, and they read tweets that called him a "thug" for it." (par. 3)

Meaning:

Effect:

5. "The hooded sweatshirt emerged as a pop political object after decades of **mundane** hard work." (par. 5)

Meaning:

Effect:

6. "But the hoodie did not warrant enough consideration to earn its **diminutive** nickname until after it was processed by B-boys, graffiti artists and break dancers in the '80s." (par. 6)

Meaning:

Effect:

7. "The hood frames a dirty look, obscures acne and anxiety, masks headphones in study hall, makes a cone of solitude that will suffice for an **autonomous** realm." (par. 7)

Meaning:

Effect:

8. "A glance at almost any police blotter, or a recollection of the forensic sketch of the Unabomber[2], will confirm the hoodie as a wardrobe staple of the criminal class, and this makes it uniquely convenient as a **proxy** for racial profiling or any other exercise of **enmity**." (par. 8)

Meaning (proxy):

Meaning (enmity):

Effect:

9. "All that potential subtext is attached to a generally **evocative** item of clothing." (par. 10)

Meaning:

Effect:

10. "Its visual strength **abets** its powers as a cultural marker, needing just a nudge to create its own contexts." (par. 11)

Meaning:

Effect:

Name_____
Date_____Class_____

Labels, Clothing and Identity: Are You What You Wear? (p. 684)
Michelle Parrinello-Cason

For each term in bold below, determine the meaning of the word in the context of the sentence, and then describe the effect of the word: how the author's word choice contributes to the meaning and tone of the sentence(s).

1. "I am a wife, but that doesn't mean I **ascribe** to all of the traditional **connotations** of 'wife.'"(par. 1)

Meaning (ascribe):

Meaning (connotations):

Effect:

2. "With Geraldo Rivera[1] blaming (and then **recanting**) Martin's death on his hoodie and everyone from entire basketball teams, to college students across the country, to Congressmen **donning** the garment in solidarity with Martin, the hoodie is in the spotlight." (par. 2)

Meaning (recanting):

Meaning (donning):

Effect:

3. "The clothing becomes a **scapegoat** for our own prejudices. [...] " (par. 6)

Meaning:

Effect:

4. "A **hijab** does not make someone a terrorist." (par. 7)

Meaning:

Effect:

5. "While I **unequivocally** agree that we should not use clothing as a scapegoat for our prejudices, I cannot deny that clothing does carry meaning." (par. 8)

Meaning:

Effect:

6. "That message only had meaning as a **rebuttal**." (par. 13)

Meaning:

Effect:

7. "This woman spread vicious (false) rumors about my drug use and **promiscuity** to people all over town." (par. 14)

Meaning:

Effect:

8. "Yes, we choose clothes to send a message about who we are, but the moment that the message is taken out of our control, it becomes a projection of **stereotype** and unwarranted judgment." (par. 15)

Meaning:

Effect:

Women Who Wear Pants: Still Somehow Controversial (p. 688)

Nora Caplan-Bricker

For each term in bold below, determine the meaning of the word in the context of the sentence, and then describe the effect of the word: how the author's word choice contributes to the meaning and tone of the sentence(s).

1. "Like many of women's battles, pants-related activism stretches back centuries and continues with no sign of **abating** in the present day." (par. 2)

Meaning:

Effect:

2. "In addition to **suffrage**, 19th-century feminists such as Elizabeth Cady Stanton advocated what they called "rational dress," a costume with a short skirt over loose trousers that was pioneered by the activist Elizabeth Smith Miller." (par. 3)

Meaning:

Effect:

3. "Even as East Coast suffragettes began to worry about spending their political capital on pants, other women across the country continued to **don** them." (par. 4)

Meaning:

Effect:

4. "Cooper found records of "a 'Marie Susie'" who "**lobbied** the Board of Aldermen for the right to wear pants in Gold Rush–era San Francisco, saying that she had worn 'masculine habiliments' for twenty years and wished to be protected against arrest for doing so."" (par. 4)

Meaning:

Effect:

5. "In the early 20th century, the **subversive** quality of women's pants became a source of chic appeal; fashion designers, starting with Paul Poiret, began to design collections around them." (par. 5)

Meaning:

Effect:

6. "The *Washington Post* reported at the time that Reid's colleagues were "**incredulous**"; one congressman gushed, "I was told there was a lady here in trousers, so I had to come over and see for myself."" (par. 7)

Meaning:

Effect:

7. ""I am really quite serious about my service in the Congress and I wouldn't want to do anything that seemed **facetious**."" (par. 7)

Meaning:

Effect:

8. "Until 1993, a rule in the upper chamber barred women from wearing pants on the floor, but when a small **cadre** of Democrats, including Barbara Mikulski of Maryland, started wearing trousers in protest, female Senate staff joined them, and the **prohibition** was **abolished**." (par. 8)

Meaning (cadre):

Meaning (prohibition):

Meaning (abolished):

Effect:

In Fashion, Cultural Appropriation Is Either Very Wrong or Very Right (p. 695)
Jenni Avins

For each term in bold below, determine the meaning of the word in the context of the sentence, and then describe the effect of the word: how the author's word choice contributes to the meaning and tone of the sentence(s).

1. "This was before the term "cultural **appropriation**" jumped from academia[1] into the realm of Internet outrage and oversensitivity." (par. 2)

Meaning:

Effect:

2. "Such borrowing is how we got treasures such as New York pizza[5] and Japanese denim[6]— not to mention how the West got democratic **discourse**[7], mathematics, and the calendar." (par. 6)

Meaning:

Effect:

3. "Yet as wave upon wave of shrill accusations of cultural appropriation make their way through the Internet outrage cycle, the **rhetoric** ranges from earnest **indignation** to **patronizing** disrespect." (par. 6)

Meaning (rhetoric):

Meaning (indignation):

Meaning (patronizing):

Effect:

4. "And as we watch artists and celebrities being **pilloried** and called racist, it's hard not to fear the reach of the cultural-appropriation police, who jealously track who "owns" what and instantly jump on **transgressors**." (par. 7)

Meaning (pilloried):

Meaning (transgressors):

Effect:

5. "The exchange of ideas, styles, and traditions is one of the **tenets** and joys of a modern, multicultural society." (par. 8)

Meaning:

Effect:

6. "You probably don't need an example, but U.S. fraternity parties[8] are **rife** with them." (par. 11)

Meaning:

Effect:

7. "Sports teams such as the Washington Redskins[9], and their fanbases[10], continue to fight to keep bigoted names and images as mascots—**perpetuating** negative stereotypes and pouring salt into old wounds[11]." (par. 11)

Meaning:

Effect:

8. "Among the evening's best-dressed was Rihanna, who navigated the theme with **aplomb** in a fur-trimmed robe by Guo Pei, a Beijing-based Chinese couturier whose work was also part of the Met's exhibition." (par. 13)

Meaning:

Effect:

9. ""This is **analogous** to casually wearing a Purple Heart or Medal of Honor that was not earned," Simon Moya-Smith, a journalist of the Oglala Lakota Nation, told MTV." (par. 17)

Meaning:

Effect:

From Converse to Kanye: The Rise of Sneaker Culture (p. 699)
Hugh Hart

For each term in bold below, determine the meaning of the word in the context of the sentence, and then describe the effect of the word: how the author's word choice contributes to the meaning and tone of the sentence(s).

1. ""The sneaker is the most **baroque** item of dress in a man's attire," says shoe expert Elizabeth Semmelhack, and she should know." (par. 1)

Meaning:

Effect:

2. "She says, "High heels and sneakers are both **ubiquitous**, yet we don't often ask ourselves 'How is it that we have such emotional reactions to this kind of footwear?'" (par. 3)

Meaning:

Effect:

3. ""The original Chuck Taylor All-Stars shoe from Converse is associated with ideas of anti-fashion, alternative culture, authenticity and **nostalgia**, so those ideas are related to that brand."" (par. 4)

Meaning:

Effect:

4. "By mid-century, the shoe company itself emerges as a self-designated **commodifier** of cool." (par. 6)

Meaning:

Effect:

5. ""Then of course, Nike's swoosh become absolutely integral to the **aesthetic** of the shoes they created." (par. 6)

Meaning:

Effect:

6. ""This **sartorial** expression of high tech cowboy challenges the **brogue** shoes and herd mentality of masculine dress that had formerly been demanded in the work place."" (par. 7)

Meaning (sartorial):

Meaning (brogue):

Effect:

7. "But sneaker **adulation** hit a whole new level in the '80s and '90s after black athletes and musicians embraced the shoes." (par. 8)

Meaning:

Effect:

8. ""When rap stars and high-achieving athletes wear sneakers, they set the tone for why certain sneakers are more desirable than others and find their way into the male wardrobe in a more meaningful way than some pair of **generic** kicks you wear to wash the car on Sunday." (par. 8)

Meaning:

Effect:

9. "After cycling through a succession of materials and technologies geared toward enabling users to jump higher (Reebok Pumps) and run faster (Nike's Foamposite), 21st-century shoe design has now expanded to market style over athletic **prowess**." (par. 10)

Meaning:

Effect:

The Battle over Dress Codes (p. 702)
Peggy Orenstein

For each term in bold below, determine the meaning of the word in the context of the sentence, and then describe the effect of the word: how the author's word choice contributes to the meaning and tone of the sentence(s).

1. "Next they'll be endorsing **Darwinism** in Kansas." (par. 2)

Meaning:

Effect:

2. "Girls, particularly those with **ample** hips or breasts, are almost exclusively singled out, typically told their outfits will "distract boys."" (par. 4)

Meaning:

Effect:

3. "The last time classroom attire was this **contentious** was the late 1960s and early 1970s, when the most high-profile cases centered on boys." (par. 5)

Meaning:

Effect:

4. "According to Jo Paoletti, author of the forthcoming book "Sex and **Unisex**: Fashion, Feminism and the Sexual Revolution," young men with long hair were sometimes attacked by their peers." (par. 5)

Meaning:

Effect:

5. "Boys run afoul of dress codes when they **flout** authority: "hippies" defying the establishment, "thugs" in saggy pants." (par. 6)

Meaning:

Effect:

6. "They are correct: Addressing **leering** or harassment will challenge young men's

assumptions." (par. 7)

Meaning:

Effect:

7. "Even so, while women are not responsible for male misbehavior, and while no amount of dress (or undress) will avert catcalls, cultural change can be glacial, and I have a child trying to **wend** her way safely through our city streets right now." (par. 8)

Meaning:

Effect:

8. "So even as I object to the policing of girls' sexuality, I'm concerned about the **incessant** drumbeat of self-objectification: the pressure young women face to view their bodies as the objects of others' desires." (par. 9)

Meaning:

Effect:

9. "In its landmark 2007 report on the sexualization of girlhood, the American Psychological Association linked self-objectification to poor self-esteem, depression, body dissatisfaction and compromised **cognitive** function." (par. 10)

Meaning:

Effect:

10. "Yet, for today's girls, sexy appearance has been firmly **conflated** with strong womanhood, and at ever younger (not to mention ever older) ages." (par. 11)

Meaning:

Effect:

How One Stupid Tweet Blew Up Justine Sacco's Life (p. 707)

Jon Ronson

For each term in bold below, determine the meaning of the word in the context of the sentence, and then describe the effect of the word: how the author's word choice contributes to the meaning and tone of the sentence(s).

1. "As she made the long journey from New York to South Africa, to visit family during the holidays in 2013, Justine Sacco, 30 years old and the senior director of corporate communications at IAC, began tweeting **acerbic** little jokes about the indignities of travel." (par. 1)

Meaning:

Effect:

2. "She chuckled to herself as she pressed send on this last one, then wandered around Heathrow's international terminal for half an hour, **sporadically** checking her phone." (par. 6)

Meaning:

Effect:

3. "The furor over Sacco's tweet had become not just an **ideological** crusade against her perceived bigotry but also a form of idle entertainment." (par. 11)

Meaning:

Effect:

4. "Her complete ignorance of her predicament for those 11 hours lent the episode both dramatic irony and a pleasing narrative **arc**." (par. 11)

Meaning:

Effect:

5. "It felt as if **hierarchies** were being dismantled, as if justice were being democratized." (par. 16)

Meaning:

Effect:

6. "So for the past two years, I've been interviewing individuals like Justine Sacco: everyday

people **pilloried** brutally, most often for posting some poorly considered joke on social media." (par. 17)

Meaning:

Effect:

7. "But **shorn** of this context, her picture appeared to be a joke not about a sign but about the war dead." (par. 18)

Meaning:

Effect:

8. "In a sermon, the Rev. Nathan Strong, of Hartford, Conn., entreated his flock to be less **exuberant** at executions." (par. 41)

Meaning:

Effect:

9. ""**Ignominy** is universally acknowledged to be a worse punishment than death," he wrote." (par. 42)

Meaning:

Effect:

10. "An 1867 editorial in The Times **excoriated** the state for its **obstinacy**." (par. 43)

Meaning (excoriated):

Meaning (obstinacy):

Effect:

11. "But I did find plenty of people from centuries past **bemoaning** the outsize cruelty of the practice, warning that well-meaning people, in a crowd, often take punishment too far." (par. 44)

Meaning:

Effect:

from *Men Explain Things to Me* (p. 716)
Rebecca Solnit

For each term in bold below, determine the meaning of the word in the context of the sentence, and then describe the effect of the word: how the author's word choice contributes to the meaning and tone of the sentence(s).

1. "The house was great–if you like Ralph Lauren-style chalets–a rugged luxury cabin at 9,000 feet complete with elk antlers, lots of **kilims**, and a wood-burning stove." (par. 1)

Meaning:

Effect:

2. "So caught up was I in my assigned role as **ingénue** that I was perfectly willing to entertain the possibility that another book on the same subject had come out simultaneously and I'd somehow missed it." (par. 7)

Meaning:

Effect:

3. "When *River of Shadows* came out, some **pedant** wrote a snarky letter to the *New York Times* explaining that, though Muybridge had made improvements in camera technology, he had not made any breakthroughs in photographic chemistry." (par. 11)

Meaning:

Effect:

4. "And perhaps because the book was about the **virile** subjects of cinema and technology, the Men Who Knew came out of the woodwork." (par. 11)

Meaning:

Effect:

5. "He carped, for example, that to **aggrandize** Muybridge's standing I left out technological predecessors like Henry R. Heyl." (par. 12)

Meaning:

Effect:

6. "I wouldn't be surprised if part of the **trajectory** of American politics since 2001 was shaped

by, say, the inability to hear Coleen Rowley, the FBI woman who issued those early warnings about al-Qaeda, and it was certainly shaped by a Bush administration to which you couldn't tell anything, including that Iraq had no links to al-Qaeda and no WMDs, or that the war was not going to be a "cakewalk."" (par. 15)

Meaning:

Effect:

7. "Arrogance might have had something to do with the war, but this syndrome is a war that nearly every woman faces every day, a war within herself too, a belief in her **superfluity**, an invitation to silence, one from which a fairly nice career as a writer (with a lot of research and facts correctly deployed) has not entirely freed me." (par. 16)

Meaning:

Effect:

8. "After all, there was a moment there when I was willing to let Mr. Important and his **overweening** confidence bowl over my more shaky certainty." (par. 16)

Meaning:

Effect:

9. "There's a happy medium between these poles to which the genders have been pushed, a warm **equatorial** belt of give and take where we should all meet." (par. 17)

Meaning:

Effect:

10. "Not yet, but according to the **actuarial** tables, I may have another forty-something years to live, more or less, so it could happen." (par. 24)

Meaning:

Effect:

Name_____

Date_____Class_____

On Chicken Tenders **(p. 721)**

Helen Rosner

For each term in bold below, determine the meaning of the word in the context of the sentence, and then describe the effect of the word: how the author's word choice contributes to the meaning and tone of the sentence(s).

1. "You might not ever eat them—you might be a vegetarian or a vegan, or not consume birds for whatever reason, or not want to deal with the carbs, or not think it's okay for adult humans with serious opinions about **fracking** to dip a toe into the children's menu—but that's a choice about ingesting them." (par. 1)

Meaning:

Effect:

2. "Their **ubiquity** on kids' menus isn't a mark against their perfection, but rather proof of it: the kids' menu is where all perfect foods live." (par. 2)

Meaning:

Effect:

3. "Perfection is a **precarious** state." (par. 3)

Meaning:

Effect:

4. "A miraculous adaptation, the **inverse** of the receptive adjustments we perform when faced with unpleasantness: just as we naturally tune out familiar noises or lingering foul smells, we can also become **inured** to delight." (par. 6)

Meaning (inverse):

Meaning (inured):

Effect:

5. "You hear a hundred explanations of how to order, smile your thanks at a thousand *amuse bouches*, read a million back-of-the-menu culinary **manifestos**." (par. 6)

Meaning:

Effect:

6. "A true connoisseur of the chicken tender knows that there are three **immutable** rules." (par. 8)

Meaning:

Effect:

7. "The crispness of the exterior is what creates the tenderness of the interior, its structural **cohesion** when submerged in hot oil helps the chicken inside stay juicy and good." (par. 10)

Meaning:

Effect:

8. "If you want a vehicle for ranch dressing, order the **crudités**." (par. 11)

Meaning:

Effect:

9. "Even the other kids' menu **stalwarts** have more history to them than the chicken tender, a relatively new addition to the gastronomic landscape that only reached deep-fryer ubiquity in the 1990s." (par. 15)

Meaning:

Effect:

10. "(This itself is a fascinatingly rare phenomenon: when was the last time something truly novel hit the culinary **zeitgeist** that didn't have a trademark appended to it?)" (par. 15)

Meaning:

Effect:

11. "It takes more than one generation to develop the intricate root system of nostalgia that anchors the ballpark pastoral of hot dogs or nachos, the picket-fence **vignette** of fried bologna sandwiches, or the dusty-road Americana of a burger and an ice-cold Coke." (par. 15)

Meaning:

Effect:

Black Bodies in Motion and Pain (p. 726)

Edwidge Danticat

For each term in bold below, determine the meaning of the word in the context of the sentence, and then describe the effect of the word: how the author's word choice contributes to the meaning and tone of the sentence(s).

1. "I'd somehow expected them to be as **colossal** as their subject, the fifty-five-year-plus mass migration of more than six million African-Americans from the rural south to urban centers in the northern United States." (par. 1)

Meaning:

Effect:

2. "The sixty spare and, at times, appropriately **stark** tempera paintings in the series each measure twelve-by-eighteen inches and are underscored by descriptive captions written by the artist, whose parents moved from Virginia and South Carolina to New Jersey, where he was born." (par. 1)

Meaning:

Effect:

3. "The bowed heads of the hungry and the curved backs of mourners helped the Great Migration to gain and keep its **momentum**, along with the promise of less **abject** poverty in the North, better educational opportunities, and the right to vote." (par. 2)

Meaning (momentum):

Meaning (abject):

Effect:

4. "And yet before they were massacred they were subjected to a variation of the same **detestable vitriol** that unwanted immigrants everywhere face: "You're taking over our country, and you have to go."" (par. 4)

Meaning (detestable):

Meaning (vitriol):

Effect:

5. "This bigoted young man charged himself with deciding who can stay and who can go, and

the only uncontestable way he knew to carry out his **venomous** decree was to kill." (par. 5)

Meaning:

Effect:

6. "**Xenophobes** often speak of migrants and immigrants as though they are an invasion force or something **akin** to biological warfare." (par. 9)

Meaning (Xenophobes):

Meaning (akin):

Effect:

7. "Even children are migrating by the thousands in our **hemisphere**, crossing several borders to flee gang violence in Central America, while hoping to be reunited with their U.S.- based parents." (par. 10)

Meaning:

Effect:

Name_____
Date_____Class_____

On the Decay of Friendship (p. 730)
Samuel Johnson

For each term in bold below, determine the meaning of the word in the context of the sentence, and then describe the effect of the word: how the author's word choice contributes to the meaning and tone of the sentence(s).

1. "Many have talked in very exalted language, of the **perpetuity** of friendship, of invincible constancy, and unalienable kindness; and some examples have been seen of men who have continued faithful to their earliest choice, and whose affection has predominated over changes of fortune, and **contrariety** of opinion." (par. 2)

Meaning (perpetuity):

Meaning (contrariety):

Effect:

2. "A man deprived of the companion to whom he used to open his bosom, and with whom he shared the hours of leisure and merriment, feels the day at first hanging heavy on him; his difficulties oppress, and his doubts distract him; he sees time come and go without his **wonted** gratification, and all is sadness within, and solitude about him." (par. 6)

Meaning:

Effect:

3. "But this uneasiness never lasts long; necessity produces **expedients**, new amusements are discovered, and new conversation is admitted." (par. 6)

Meaning:

Effect:

4. "The first hour convinces them that the pleasure which they have formerly enjoyed, is forever at an end; different scenes have made different impressions; the opinions of both are changed; and that **similitude** of manners and sentiment is lost which confirmed them both in the **approbation** of themselves." (par. 7)

Meaning (similitude):

Meaning (approbation):

Effect:

5. "This minute ambition is sometimes crossed before it is known, and sometimes defeated by **wanton petulance**; but such attacks are seldom made without the loss of friendship; for whoever has once found the vulnerable part will always be feared, and the resentment will burn on in secret, of which shame hinders the discovery." (par. 8)

Meaning (wanton):

Meaning (petulance):

Effect:

6. "This, however, is a slow **malignity**, which a wise man will **obviate** as inconsistent with quiet, and a good man will repress as contrary to virtue; but human happiness is sometimes violated by some more sudden strokes." (par. 9)

Meaning (malignity):

Meaning (obviate):

Effect:

7. "A dispute begun in jest upon a subject which a moment before was on both parts regarded with careless indifference, is continued by the desire of conquest, till vanity kindles into rage, and opposition **rankles** into enmity." (par. 10)

Meaning:

Effect:

8. "Those who are angry may be reconciled; those who have been injured may receive a recompense: but when the desire of pleasing and willingness to be pleased is silently diminished, the renovation of friendship is hopeless; as, when the vital powers sink into **languor**, there is no longer any use of the physician." (par. 12)

Meaning:

Effect:

By Any Other Name (p. 770)

Santha Rama Rau

For each term in bold below, determine the meaning of the word in the context of the sentence, and then describe the effect of the word: how the author's word choice contributes to the meaning and tone of the sentence(s).

1. "At the **Anglo-Indian** day school in Zorinabad to which my sister and I were sent when she was eight and I was five and a half, they changed our names." (par. 1)

Meaning:

Effect:

2. "We had been sent to that school because my father, among his responsibilities as an officer of the civil service, had a tour of duty to perform in the villages around that steamy little **provincial** town, where he had his headquarters at that time." (par. 5)

Meaning:

Effect:

3. "Up to then, my mother had refused to send Premila to school in the British-run establishments of that time, because, she used to say, "you can bury a dog's tail for seven years and it still comes out curly, and you can take a Britisher away from his home for a lifetime and he still remains **insular**."" (par. 6)

Meaning:

Effect:

4. "I was very sleepy after lunch, because at home we always took a **siesta**." (par. 18) Meaning:

Effect:

5. "It was usually a pleasant time of day, with the bedroom darkened against the harsh afternoon sun, the drifting off into sleep with the sound of Mother's voice reading a story in one's mind, and, finally, the shrill, fussy voice of the **ayah** waking one for tea." (par. 18)

Meaning:

Effect:

6. "It seemed like an eternity since I had seen her that morning—a **wizened**, affectionate figure

in her white cotton sari, giving me dozens of urgent and useless instructions on how to be a good girl at school." (par. 22)

Meaning:

Effect:

7. "Premila followed more **sedately**, and she told me on the way home never to do that again in front of the other children." (par. 22)

Meaning:

Effect:

8. "We quarreled in our usual way, waded in the **tepid** water under the lime trees, and waited for the night to bring out the smell of the jasmine." (par. 26)

Meaning:

Effect:

9. "Occasionally a horse-drawn **tonga** passed us, and the women, in their pink or green silks, stared at Premila and me trudging along on the side of the road." (par. 34)

Meaning:

Effect:

10. "I walked more and more slowly, and shouted to Premila, from time to time, "Wait for me!" with increasing **peevishness**." (par. 34)

Meaning:

Effect:

from *Is Everyone Hanging Out without Me?* (p. 776)

Mindy Kaling

For each term in bold below, determine the meaning of the word in the context of the sentence, and then describe the effect of the word: how the author's word choice contributes to the meaning and tone of the sentence(s).

1. "It **behooves** anyone who lives in a Tudor house to make it look like a witch cottage once in a while." (par. 1)

Meaning:

Effect:

2. "The Church Lady's catchphrases were our catchphrases, and we repeated them until my mother said, **exasperated**: "Please stop saying 'Isn't that special?' in that strange voice." (par. 2)

Meaning:

Effect:

3. "Nothing says impenetrability and closeness like a silk-screened T-shirt with an **acronym** most people don't understand." (par. 5)

Meaning:

Effect:

4. "It's as if their parents had hoped that by naming them these manly, **ornate** names, they might have a fighting chance of being the leading men of our school." (par. 8)

Meaning:

Effect:

5. "But our school was behind the times, and the **aesthetic** that ruled was the curvy, petite, all-American Tiffani Amber Thiessen look, which Polly and Lauren had to some degree." (par. 9)

Meaning:

Effect:

6. "If it sounds weird and **compartmentalized**, that's because it was." (par. 10)

Meaning:

Effect:

7. "The very same sketch that had made Mavis and me clutch our chests in **diaphragm**-hurting laughter had **rendered** my best friends bored and silent." (par. 12)

Meaning (diaphragm):

Meaning (rendered):

Effect:

8. "I made the classic mistake of trying to explain why it was so funny, as though a great explanation would be the key to **eliciting** a huge laugh from them." (par. 12)

Meaning:

Effect:

9. "Presenting a homemade knitted object to my parents was actually like handing them a detailed backlog of my **idleness**." (par. 15)

Meaning:

Effect:

from *Yes, Chef* (p. 783)

Marcus Samuelsson

For each term in bold below, determine the meaning of the word in the context of the sentence, and then describe the effect of the word: how the author's word choice contributes to the meaning and tone of the sentence(s).

1. "That my mother was intelligent rings true because I know she had to be **shrewd** to save the lives of myself and my sister, which is what she did, in the most mysterious and miraculous of ways." (par. 2)

Meaning:

Effect:

2. "Right now, if I could, I would lead you to the red tin in my kitchen, one of the dozens I keep by the stove in my apartment in Harlem, filled with my own blend and marked with blue electrical tape and my own **illegible scrawl**." (par. 4)

Meaning (illegible):

Meaning (scrawl):

Effect:

3. "The woman has her food and **wares** in her bag, which is slung across her chest and rests on her hip." (par. 6)

Meaning:

Effect:

4. "My mother, sister and I would walk the Sidama **savannah** for four hours a day, to and from her job selling crafts in the market." (par. 7)

Meaning:

Effect:

5. "It was a **henna** tattoo of a cross, henna taking the place of the jewelry she could not afford or even dream of having." (par. 8)

Meaning:

Effect:

6. "I was two when a **tuberculosis** epidemic hit Ethiopia." (par. 10)

Meaning:

Effect:

7. "We were all coughing up blood and my mother had seen enough in her young life to measure the **ravages** of that disease." (par. 10)

Meaning:

Effect:

8. "It was all coming at her now: the fatigue and the fever; pieces of her lung splintering and mixing with her throw-up; the **calcifications** on her bones, where the disease had already spread." (par. 10)

Meaning:

Effect:

9. "Her identity remains stubbornly **shrouded** in the past, so I feed myself and the people I love the food that she made." (par. 11)

Meaning:

Effect:

My Father's Previous Life (p. 788)
Monique Truong

For each term in bold below, determine the meaning of the word in the context of the sentence, and then describe the effect of the word: how the author's word choice contributes to the meaning and tone of the sentence(s).

1. "My father's desk in 1979 sat **imposingly** in a corner of our living room in Centerville, Ohio." (par. 1)

Meaning:

Effect:

2. "In our house, the permanence of ink and the clumsy, **wayward** hands of a child were reasons enough to keep such instruments hidden." (par. 1)

Meaning:

Effect:

3. "I don't remember her smiling, but rather looking **inquisitively** into the lens." (par. 2)
Meaning:

Effect:

4. "I loved my father dearly, but his **demeanor** was even more **august** than his desk." (par. 4)

Meaning (demeanor):

Meaning (august):

Effect:

5. "Curiosity and instinct must have made me brave, because I did ask him, and the story he told forever disrupted the **static**, simple definition of family for me." (par. 4)

Meaning:

Effect:

6. "Our age difference was **insurmountable** then." (par. 7)

Meaning:

Effect:

7. "The real-life girl was a typical older sister, uninterested in me and even a bit **scornful** of my existence." (par. 7)

Meaning:

 Effect:

8. "We managed to communicate, via her competent English and my **remedial** French, that we were linked not by a father, but by a man who was a mystery to us both." (par. 8)

Meaning:

Effect:

9. "Our father's **legacy** to us wasn't really a void, but an understanding that families are created with care and effort." (par. 9)

Meaning:

Effect:

You, Me, and the Sea (p. 791)

Steven Hall

For each term in bold below, determine the meaning of the word in the context of the sentence, and then describe the effect of the word: how the author's word choice contributes to the meaning and tone of the sentence(s).

1. "The tide is almost all the way out, exposing the rock pools beyond the **breakwater**." (par. 2)

Meaning:

Effect:

2. "A **sinuous**, solid black something." (par. 7)

Meaning:

Effect:

3. "It flips or flaps like a muscle **spasm**—up off the sand, then it falls back, lying flat." (par. 7)

Meaning:

Effect:

4. "It has the full **complement** of stiff, triangular fins, a long, curved tail, a big round shark- eye looking up at me from the sand, and a C-shaped mouth full of teeth." (par. 19)

Meaning:

Effect:

5. "Not just because I hate to see any animal suffer, but because there is a task to be performed here, and the task is so stripped down and obvious, and the situation so very **surreal**, that it takes on the unnatural, stylised air of myth or **parable**, despite the fact that it is also entirely real and happening in the here-and-now." (par. 24)

Meaning (surreal):

Meaning (parable):

Effect:

6. "How **robust**?" (par. 34)

Meaning:

Effect:

7. "The moment I have hold of it, the shark arches itself into a tense C-shape, like a **taut** bow, trying to get its mouth around to bite me." (par. 36)

Meaning:

Effect:

8. "The shark darts away amongst the **submerged** rock pools." (par. 38)

Meaning:

Effect:

9. "Understanding that I have no control whatsoever over what happens the moment I let go, I throw the shark forward, and it slides into the sea a few feet away with an **aerodynamic** plop." (par. 52)

Meaning:

Effect:

Music Lessons (p. 796)
Sarah Vowell

For each term in bold below, determine the meaning of the word in the context of the sentence, and then describe the effect of the word: how the author's word choice contributes to the meaning and tone of the sentence(s).

1. "I was standing in line in my silver **spats** down past the end zone waiting to go on." (par. 2)

Meaning:

Effect:

2. "The shako's purpose is to make a scrubby assortment of adolescents look **magisterial**." (par. 2)

Meaning:

Effect:

3. "But it not only prevented me from breathing, it rendered me and my **comrades** in the horn section unstable, so that even though my job was to march around as some kind of sick metaphor for teenage military precision, I moved through time and space with the grace and confidence of a puppy walking on a beach ball." (par. 2)

Meaning:

Effect:

4. "But that didn't stop the choir girls from making everyone temporarily forget their locker combinations thanks to an **impromptu**, uncalled-for burst from *Brigadoon*.[3]" (par. 10)

Meaning:

Effect:

5. "I especially loved the **illicitly** named spit valve." (par. 18)

Meaning:

Effect:

6. "I found out that the reason I had **shoddy** tone and trouble hitting the high notes was because of the shape of my jaw." (par. 20)

Meaning:

Effect:

7. "I was outraged that a person's fate could depend on something as **arbitrary** as the angles of her teeth." (par. 20)

Meaning:

Effect:

8. "They were difficult, unlistenable, and wildly **pretentious**, though, thankfully, I didn't learn the word "pretentious" until I was eighteen, thereby freeing me up to be unbearably guilt-free for most of my adolescence." (par. 22)

Meaning:

Effect:

9. "Why waste all that time developing an idea over an extended period of time when you could **encapsulate** the entire concept in one big, loud twelve-second piece!" (par. 22)

Meaning:

Effect:

10. "I was also acceptable at the baritone, shaky on the xylophone, and **putrid** on the piano." (par. 27)

Meaning:

Effect:

from *Hunger Makes Me a Modern Girl* (p. 803)

Carrie Brownstein

For each term in bold below, determine the meaning of the word in the context of the sentence, and then describe the effect of the word: how the author's word choice contributes to the meaning and tone of the sentence(s).

1. "From the burgundy insides of a Chevy Blazer, we all turned to look at a jogger, a woman, a **sinewy** form **devoid** of curves, angles only, rib cage and clavicles protruding, like some sort of moving body diagram, inside out." (par. 1)

Meaning (sinewy):

Meaning (devoid):

Effect:

2. "After all, who else among their kids' friends was mature enough to understand the **nuanced** joys of a recently **procured** coffee-table book on the Kennedys or the acquisition of a delicious chocolate fondue recipe?" (par. 9)

Meaning (nuanced):

Meaning (procured):

Effect:

3. "Later, in the school bathroom during lunch, I delivered the story to our other friends with the gravity and **stoicism** of a nightly-news anchor." (par. 10)

Meaning:

Effect:

4. "These **convivial** but otherwise **circuitous** talks are likely why my dad's brother, Uncle Mike, often stepped up as the family storyteller and entertainer." (par. 14)

Meaning (convivial):

Meaning (circuitous):

Effect:

5. "We **vacillated** between shouting and silence, the megaphone and the mute." (par. 19)

Meaning:

Effect:

6. "Her upwardly mobile sense of middle-class **decorum** was still intact, despite the fact that *her* clothing drooped, almost slithered, off her body as if it were seeking elsewhere to perch, looking hardly different on her than it would on a wire hanger." (par. 20)

Meaning:

Effect:

7. "I felt sophomoric and **callow**, but I was only fourteen." (par. 21)

Meaning:

Effect:

8. "Or that the vulnerability, heartache and fear will leave you open to illness—you'll enter healthy and leave **enervated**, or not leave at all." (par. 25)

Meaning:

Effect:

9. "It was glaring **blitheness** on my father's part." (par. 29)

Meaning:

Effect:

La Gringuita (p. 811)
Julia Alvarez

For each term in bold below, determine the meaning of the word in the context of the sentence, and then describe the effect of the word: how the author's word choice contributes to the meaning and tone of the sentence(s).

1. "Decades later, hearing the story, my father, ever vigilant and jealous of his wife and daughters, was convinced—no matter what my mother said about **idiomatic** expressions— that the sailor had made an advance." (par. 4)

Meaning:

Effect:

2. "As rebellious adolescents, we soon figured out that conducting our **filial** business in English gave us an edge over our strict, Spanish-speaking parents." (par. 7)

Meaning:

Effect:

3. "My father was a pushover for **pithy** quotes from Shakespeare, and a recitation of "The quality of mercy is not strained" could usually get me what I wanted." (par. 7)

Meaning:

Effect:

4. "We couldn't just skirt **culpability** by using the reflexive: the bag of cookies did not finish itself, nor did the money disappear itself from Mami's purse." (par. 8)

Meaning:

Effect:

5. "The **litmus** test was dancing merengue, our national, fast-moving, lots-of-hip-action dance." (par. 20)

Meaning:

Effect:

6. "Or actually, in English, I could have said half a dozen **ambivalent**, soothing things." (par. 28)

Meaning:

Effect:

7. "But not having a complicated vocabulary in Spanish, I didn't know the fancy, smooth-talking ways of delaying and **deterring**." (par. 28)

Meaning:

Effect:

8. "The comment came out sounding **inane**." (par. 28)

Meaning:

Effect:

9. "But I wonder if after the Latina **protagonist** makes love with her novio, she doesn't sit up in bed and tell him the story of her life in English with a few palabritas thrown in to capture the rhythm of her Latin heartbeat?" (par. 33)

Meaning:

Effect:

10. "A woman who has joined her life with the life of a man who grew up on a farm in Nebraska, whose great-grandparents came over from Germany and discouraged their own children from speaking German because of the **antipathy** that erupted in their new country towards anything German with the outbreak of World War I." (par. 42)

Meaning:

Effect:

from *Coming into Language* (p. 820)
Jimmy Santiago Baca ,

For each term in bold below, determine the meaning of the word in the context of the sentence, and then describe the effect of the word: how the author's word choice contributes to the meaning and tone of the sentence(s).

1. "On the cover were black-and-white photos: Padre Hidalgo **exhorting** Mexican peasants to revolt against the Spanish dictators; Anglo vigilantes hanging two Mexicans from a tree; a young Mexican woman with rifle and ammunition belts crisscrossing her breast; Cesar Chavez and field workers marching for fair wages; Chicano railroad workers laying **creosote** ties; Chicanas laboring at machines in textile factories; Chicanas picketing and hoisting boycott signs." (par. 2)

Meaning (exhorting):

Meaning (creosote):

Effect:

2. "There was nothing so humiliating as being unable to express myself, and my **inarticulateness** increased my sense of jeopardy." (par. 4)

Meaning:

Effect:

3. "Listening to the words of these writers, I felt that invisible threat from without lessen- my sense of teetering on a rotting plank over swamp water where **famished** alligators clapped their horny snouts for my blood." (par. 5)

Meaning:

Effect:

4. "And when they closed the books, these Chicanos, and went into their own Chicano language, they made **barrio** life come alive for me in the fullness of its vitality." (par. 6)

Meaning:

Effect:

5. "Words now pleaded back with the bleak **lucidity** of hurt." (par. 10)

Meaning:

Effect:

6. "Each word steamed with the hot lava juices of my **primordial** making, and I crawled out of **stanzas** dripping with birth-blood, reborn and freed from the chaos of my life." (par. 11)

Meaning (primordial):

Meaning (stanzas):

Effect:

7. "I wrote to **sublimate** my rage, from a place where all hope is gone, from a madness of having been damaged too much, from a silence of killing rage." (par. 15)

Meaning:

Effect:

8. "I wrote with a deep groan of doom in my blood, bewildered and dumbstruck; from an indestructible love of life, to affirm breath and laughter and the **abiding** innocence of things." (par. 15)

Meaning:

Effect:

from *Black Boy* (p. 823)

Richard Wright

For each term in bold below, determine the meaning of the word in the context of the sentence, and then describe the effect of the word: how the author's word choice contributes to the meaning and tone of the sentence(s).

1. "That night in my rented room, while letting the hot water run over my can of pork and beans in the sink, I opened *A Book of **Prefaces*** and began to read." (par. 1)

Meaning:

Effect:

2. "I was **jarred** and shocked by the style, the clear, clean, sweeping sentences." (par. 1)

Meaning:

Effect:

3. "I pictured the man as a raging demon, slashing with his pen, consumed with hate, **denouncing** everything American, **extolling** everything European or German, laughing at the weaknesses of people, mocking God, authority." (par. 1)

Meaning (denouncing):

Meaning (extolling):

Effect:

4. "I had once tried to write, had once **reveled** in feeling, had let my crude imagination roam, but the impulse to dream had been slowly beaten out of me by experience." (par. 3)

Meaning:

Effect:

5. ""You'll **addle** your brains if you don't watch out."" (par. 12)

Meaning:

Effect:

6. "I read Dreiser's *Jennie Gerhardt* and *Sister Carrie* and they revived in me a **vivid** sense of my mother's suffering; I was overwhelmed." (par. 13)

Meaning:

Effect:

7. "All my life had shaped me for the realism, the **naturalism** of the modern novel, and I could not read enough of them." (par. 13)

Meaning:

Effect:

8. "Steeped in new moods and ideas, I bought a **ream** of paper and tried to write; but nothing would come, or what did come was flat beyond telling." (par. 14)

Meaning:

Effect:

9. "In **buoying** me up, reading also cast me down, made me see what was possible, what I had missed." (par. 15)

Meaning:

Effect:

Confessions of a Code Switcher (p. 826)

Joshua Adams

For each term in bold below, determine the meaning of the word in the context of the sentence, and then describe the effect of the word: how the author's word choice contributes to the meaning and tone of the sentence(s).

1. "For those who don't know, there's a common idea amongst many black people that forces in society compel us to be **adept** at adapting." (par. 1)

Meaning:

Effect:

2. "The Mississippi Delta **drawl** I and many black people from the south and west sides of Chicago speak with is why many characterize us as being "the South of the North"." (par. 2)

Meaning:

Effect:

3. "When I've said another Black person talks white, I never once meant to imply that I was equating being **articulate** to "whiteness" (or isolating it from blackness), though that is the conclusion most people reach." (par. 4)

Meaning:

Effect:

4. "It was also an ignorant assumption about engaging in Black cultural **solidarity**." (par. 5)

Meaning:

Effect:

5. "This may be **semantics**, but I didn't assume all Black people talk the same, I just assumed all Black people don't talk like White people." (par. 5)

Meaning:

Effect:

6. "I mistook their "why can't I be a Black person who talks educated?" as re- **propagating** the idea that talking "black" means talking dumb, not rebelling against it (since the **antithesis** is usually a condemnation of someone who talks "ghetto")." (par. 5)

Meaning (propagating):

Meaning (antithesis):

Effect:

7. "Blackness is not a **monolithic** structure, and these aren't the sole reasons why any one Black person would loathe being accused of "talking white"." (par. 7)

Meaning:

Effect:

8. "I was born in Chicago, arguably the **quintessence** of American multiculturalism in the midst of segregation." (par. 9)

Meaning:

Effect:

9. "It has always been the latent means to a very real and **tangible** end, whether I choose to do it or not." (par. 11)

Meaning:

Effect:

They're, Like, Way Ahead of the Linguistic Currrrve (p. 830)
Douglas Quenqua

For each term in bold below, determine the meaning of the word in the context of the sentence, and then describe the effect of the word: how the author's word choice contributes to the meaning and tone of the sentence(s).

1. "Whether it be uptalk (pronouncing statements as if they were questions? Like this?), creating slang words like "bitchin'" and "ridic," or the **incessant** use of "like" as a conversation filler, vocal trends associated with young women are often seen as markers of immaturity or even stupidity." (par. 2)

Meaning:

Effect:

2. "But **linguists** — many of whom once promoted theories consistent with that attitude — now say such thinking is outmoded." (par. 4)

Meaning:

Effect:

3. "Girls and women in their teens and 20s deserve credit for pioneering vocal trends and popular slang, they say, adding that young women use these **embellishments** in much more sophisticated ways than people tend to realize." (par. 4)

Meaning:

Effect:

4. "Working with what they acknowledged was a very small sample — recorded speech from 34 women ages 18 to 25 — the professors said they had found evidence of a new trend among female college students: a **guttural** fluttering of the vocal cords they called "vocal fry."" (par. 6)

Meaning:

Effect:

5. ""They use this as a tool to **convey** something," she said." (par. 9)

Meaning:

Effect:

6. "The idea that young women serve as **incubators** of vocal trends for the culture at large has longstanding roots in linguistics." (par. 12)

Meaning:

Effect:

7. "As Paris is to fashion, the thinking goes, so are young women to linguistic **innovation**." (par. 12)

Meaning:

Effect:

8. "Others say women use language to assert their power in a culture that, at least in days gone by, asked them to be **sedate** and **decorous**." (par. 14)

Meaning (sedate):

Meaning (decorous):

Effect:

The Seven Words I Cannot Say (Around My Children) **(p. 833)**
Jessica Wolf

For each term in bold below, determine the meaning of the word in the context of the sentence, and then describe the effect of the word: how the author's word choice contributes to the meaning and tone of the sentence(s).

1. "I already knew he was planning to **allot** me only one slice, adding the rest to his heaping plate of eggs." (par. 2)

Meaning:

Effect:

2. "I've done my due **diligence**, and in my view, that's my initiation fee." (par. 6)

Meaning:

Effect:

3. "But to my boys, I'm barging up the ladder to the tree house, **blatantly** ignoring the sign that says Keep Out." (par. 6)

Meaning:

Effect:

4. "When my older son and his friends are together, listening to them talk is like trying to **decipher** the clicking of the Bantu." (par. 7)

Meaning:

Effect:

5. "It's all delivered so fast – recognizable words **cavorting** with the unfamiliar – and there's not even a moment to ground myself in context clues." (par. 7)

Meaning:

Effect:

6. "I think of it as a unique **dialect**, perhaps specific to our town – possibly even to our high school." (par. 7)

Meaning:

Effect:

7. "My parents liked words too, and when you grow up in a home rich with vocabulary, it feels good and right to be curious and expand your personal **lexicon**." (par. 8)

Meaning:

Effect:

8. "I'm not allowed to call my beloved new boots "dope," but if I refer to "weed" as "pot," they correct me, making sure I'm using the more current **vernacular**." (par. 13)

Meaning:

Effect:

9. "Obviously, some of my **verboten** words are fine to use in a middle-aged context." (par. 14)

Meaning:

Effect:

10. "What's the big deal if I find a poppin' new word to break up the **monotony**?" (par. 14)

Meaning:

Effect:

from *The Art of Asking* (p. 837)
Amanda Palmer

For each term in bold below, determine the meaning of the word in the context of the sentence, and then describe the effect of the word: how the author's word choice contributes to the meaning and tone of the sentence(s).

1. "I also learned over those four years that a diet of hummus, cookies, and cereal makes you fat, that it's impossible to tap a keg unless it's been properly chilled, and that DJ-ing a college radio show from three to five in the morning doesn't expand your social circle one **iota**." (par. 9)

Meaning:

Effect:

2. "I took a barista job, rented a room in a **dilapidated** share house in Somerville, Massachusetts, and decided I'd be a statue." (par. 16)

Meaning:

Effect:

3. "Toscanini's Ice Cream, where I worked as a sorbet-scooping espresso puller along with a **motley** bunch of twentysomethings, was a local operation with three Cambridge locations owned and lovingly managed by an incredible guy named Gus Rancatore." (par. 17)

Meaning:

Effect:

4. "So I took an hour-long **amble** along the banks of the river that flowed gracefully alongside the Harvard dorms, feeling very entrepreneurial, resourceful, *and* bohemian, picking any flower with an actual blossom that looked presentable until I had about fifty." (par. 25)

Meaning:

Effect:

5. "My **mantra** of **masochism** broke the minute the first few people curiously wandered up to me." (par. 37)

Meaning (mantra):

Meaning (masochism):

Effect:

6. "I'd then mechanically **proffer** up a small gift (an exotic coin, a candy, an antique key), unless, of course, I'd landed in one of the "suicide" spots, in which case I mimed a clownish mini-tragedy, killing myself with a variety of prop weapons." (par. 59)

Meaning:

Effect:

7. "It was whimsical but **grisly**, sort of *Harold and Maude* meets Marcel Marceau." (par. 60)

Meaning:

Effect:

8. "I'd been viewing my role on the street as a performance artist who would share the gift of her weird, arty impulses with the **amenable** public." (par. 76)

Meaning:

Effect:

9. "In my mute, frozen state, time and space took on a fascinating new quality, measured from one **liberated** movement to another, and I created an internal spoken dialogue with the world around me." (par. 85)

Meaning:

Effect:

from *What I Talk About When I Talk About Running* (p. 872)
Haruki Murakami

For each term in bold below, determine the meaning of the word in the context of the sentence, and then describe the effect of the word: how the author's word choice contributes to the meaning and tone of the sentence(s).

1. "The trees that line the walking path along the river provide plenty of cool shade, and Harvard and Boston University students are always out on the glittering river practicing for a **regatta**." (par. 1)

Meaning:

Effect:

2. "Industrious squirrels are running around like crazy trying to gather up enough **provisions** to last them through the winter." (par. 2)

Meaning:

Effect:

3. "Once Halloween is over, winter, like some capable tax collector, sets in, **concisely** and silently." (par. 3)

Meaning:

Effect:

4. "The wind blowing across the river is as cold and sharp as a newly **honed** hatchet." (par. 3)

Meaning:

Effect:

5. "Clouds of all sizes show up and move on, and the surface of the river, lit by the sun, reflects these white shapes as they come and go, sometimes faithfully, sometimes **distortedly**." (par. 7)

Meaning:

Effect:

6. "Whenever the seasons change, the direction of the wind **fluctuates** like someone threw a switch." (par. 7)

Meaning:

Effect:

7. "You can definitely feel a sort of aggressive challenge **emanating** from them." (par. 18)

Meaning:

Effect:

8. "She's in her sixties, I imagine, has elegant features, and is always **impeccably** dressed." (par. 22)

Meaning:

Effect:

9. "One time she had on an elegant **sari**, another time an oversize sweatshirt with a university's name on it." (par. 22)

Meaning:

Effect:

10. "It's not too brash or **contrived**." (par. 24)

Meaning:

Effect:

from *Boxcar—El Vagon* (p. 918)

Silvia Gonzalez S.

For each term in bold below, determine the meaning of the word in the context of the sentence, and then describe the effect of the word: how the author's word choice contributes to the meaning and tone of the sentence(s).

1. "Gonzalez's inspiration for writing "Boxcar" (1997) came after hearing about the tragic deaths of **undocumented** workers in a railroad boxcar." (opening)

Meaning:

Effect:

2. "(**Amiable**) How many times do we have to go through this?" (Scene 1, line 6)

Meaning:

Effect:

3. "There was betrayal, lies, cover-ups, **deceptive** acts, and marrying the wealthy Mexican rancher's daughters." (Scene 1, line 30)

Meaning:

Effect:

4. "I can tell by the features of a face where someone is **descended** from." (Scene 1, line 69)

Meaning:

Effect:

5. "An **anthropological** lesson with a touch of history." (Scene 1, line 90)

Meaning:

Effect:

6. "*Huero approaches, **ecstatic** he found the boxcar.*" (Scene 3, line 12)

Meaning:

Effect:

7. "With **enticements**!" (Scene 4, line 63)

Meaning:

Effect:

8. "They're **exploited**, and that's not the American way." (Scene 4, line 103)

Meaning:

Effect:

9. "Most us were **delirious**." (Scene 8, line 34)

Meaning:

Effect:

10. "They marveled at his **tenacity** and will to make it here all alone, and for walking from so far." (Scene 9, line 40)

Meaning:

Effect:

from *The Social Conquest of Earth* (p. 1012)
E. O. Wilson

For each term in bold below, determine the meaning of the word in the context of the sentence, and then describe the effect of the word: how the author's word choice contributes to the meaning and tone of the sentence(s).

1. "To form groups, drawing **visceral** comfort and pride from familiar fellowship, and to defend the group enthusiastically against rival groups—these are among the absolute universals of human nature and hence of culture." (par. 1)

Meaning:

Effect:

2. "Once a group has been established with a defined purpose, however, its boundaries are **malleable**." (par. 1)

Meaning:

Effect:

3. "Some of the fans wear bizarre costumes and face makeup in **homage** to their team." (par. 4)

Meaning:

Effect:

4. "Brown then added an important point: "Identification with a sports team has in it something of the **arbitrariness** of the minimal groups." (par. 5)

Meaning:

Effect:

5. "In its power and universality, the tendency to form groups and then favor in-group members has the **earmarks** of instinct." (par. 7)

Meaning:

Effect:

6. "But even if such experience does play a role, it would be an example of what psychologists call prepared learning, the inborn **propensity** to learn something swiftly and decisively." (par. 7)

Meaning:

Effect:

7. "Other **cogent** examples of prepared learning in the human **repertoire** include language, incest avoidance, and the acquisition of phobias." (par. 7)

Meaning (cogent):

Meaning (repertoire):

Effect:

8. "And exactly this **phenomenon** has been discovered by cognitive psychologists." (par. 8)

Meaning:

Effect:

9. "People are prone to **ethnocentrism**." (par. 9)

Meaning:

Effect:

Why We're Patriotic (p. 1016)
Adam Piore

For each term in bold below, determine the meaning of the word in the context of the sentence, and then describe the effect of the word: how the author's word choice contributes to the meaning and tone of the sentence(s).

1. "It was 1940 and such **spontaneous** outpourings, this one described in a letter to the song's creator Irving Berlin, were not unusual." (par. 4)

Meaning:

Effect:

2. "His family fled Russia to escape a wave of murderous **pogroms** directed at Jews." (par. 5)

Meaning:

Effect:

3. ""And not casually, but with emotion which was almost **exaltation**," Berlin later recalled." (par. 5)

Meaning:

Effect:

4. "Patriotism is an **innate** human sentiment." (par. 8)

Meaning:

Effect:

5. "It's a **partisan** strategy, as predictable every election year as campaign buttons and patriotic bunting." (par. 10)

Meaning:

Effect:

6. "Some groups were **delineated** by a preference for abstract art, others by their ability to estimate the number of dots in a picture." (par. 11)

Meaning:

Effect:

7. "Whereas patriotism is something everyone should possess as a **virtue**."" (par. 18)

Meaning:

Effect:

8. "You are under the shelter of a more powerful **transcendental entity** and you do not have to worry about your own personal individual failures and anxieties."" (par. 22)

Meaning (transcendental):

Meaning (entity):

Effect:

9. "Tolerance, openness, and **empathy** arise from deep in human nature." (par. 25)

Meaning:

Effect:

from *People Like Us* **(p. 1020)**
David Brooks

For each term in bold below, determine the meaning of the word in the context of the sentence, and then describe the effect of the word: how the author's word choice contributes to the meaning and tone of the sentence(s).

1. "We don't really care about **diversity** all that much in America, even though we talk about it a great deal." (par. 1)

Meaning:

Effect:

2. "Instead, what I have seen all around the country is people making **strenuous** efforts to group themselves with people who are basically like themselves." (par. 1)

Meaning:

Effect:

3. "People are less often tied down to factories and mills, and they can search for places to live on the basis of cultural **affinity**." (par. 3)

Meaning:

Effect:

4. "Once Boulder, Colorado, became known as **congenial** to politically progressive mountain bikers, half the politically progressive mountain bikers in the country (it seems) moved there; they made the place so culturally pure that it has become practically a **parody** of itself." (par. 3)

Meaning (congenial):

Meaning (parody):

Effect:

5. "Make no mistake—we are increasing our happiness by segmenting off so **rigorously**." (par. 4)

Meaning:

Effect:

6. "The United States might be a diverse nation when considered as a whole, but block by block and institution by institution it is a relatively **homogeneous** nation." (par. 5)

Meaning:

Effect:

7. "Some go to **charismatic** churches; some go to mainstream churches." (par. 8)

Meaning:

Effect:

8. "These **distortions** are believed because it feels good to believe them." (par. 9)

Meaning:

Effect:

9. "Sure, it would be **superficial** familiarity, but it beats the iron curtains that now separate the nation's various cultural zones." (par. 11)

Meaning:

Effect:

from *Why Are All the Black Kids Sitting Together in the Cafeteria?* (p. 1024)
Beverly Daniel Tatum

For each term in bold below, determine the meaning of the word in the context of the sentence, and then describe the effect of the word: how the author's word choice contributes to the meaning and tone of the sentence(s).

1. "If you walk into racially mixed elementary schools, you will often see young children of **diverse** racial backgrounds playing with one another, sitting at the snack table together, crossing racial boundaries with an ease uncommon in adolescence." (par. 2)

Meaning:

Effect:

2. "As he stops in town with his new bicycle, does a police officer hassle him, asking where he got it, **implying** that it might be stolen?" (par. 5)

Meaning:

Effect:

3. "Each of these experiences **conveys** a racial message." (par. 5)

Meaning:

Effect:

4. "Malcolm's emotional response was typical-anger, confusion, and **alienation**." (par. 6)

Meaning:

Effect:

5. "He withdrew from his White classmates, stopped participating in class, and eventually left his **predominately** white Michigan home to live with his sister in Roxbury, a Black community in Boston." (par. 6)

Meaning:

Effect:

6. "In another example, a young Black woman attending a **desegregated** school to which she was bussed was encouraged by a teacher to attend the upcoming school dance." (par. 8)

Meaning:

Effect:

7. "Imagine the young eighth-grade girl who experienced the teacher's use of "you people" and the dancing stereotype as a racial **affront**." (par. 9)

Meaning:

Effect:

8. "When feelings, rational or irrational, are **invalidated**, most people disengage." (par. 9)

Meaning:

Effect:

9. "Not only are Black adolescents encountering racism and reflecting on their identity, but their White peers, even when they are not the **perpetrators** (and sometimes they are), are unprepared to respond in supportive ways." (par. 10)

Meaning:

Effect:

10. "They have absorbed the **stereotypical** images of Black youth in the popular culture and are reflecting those images in their self-presentation." (par. 11)

Meaning:

Effect:

Bringing Home the Wrong Race (p. 1028)
Diane Farr

For each term in bold below, determine the meaning of the word in the context of the sentence, and then describe the effect of the word: how the author's word choice contributes to the meaning and tone of the sentence(s).

1. "When she then looked up at Seung and **scowled**, I gave her a big bright smile as a gentle warning to **refrain** from girl-on-girl hating." (par. 2)

Meaning (scowled):

Meaning (refrain):

Effect:

2. "Once seated, I began to dissect my burrito, looking to expel anything that might **singe** my half-Irish, half-Italian and wholly American palate." (par. 3)

Meaning:

Effect:

3. "As my smile began to **wane**, he finally replied, "I'm supposed to marry a Korean girl."" (par. 5)

Meaning:

Effect:

4. "Maybe Seung could tell I was on the verge of **rescinding** my earlier "I love you," so he jumped to the bottom line: "My parents are not going to easily accept this relationship." (par. 9)

Meaning:

Effect:

5. "Finally the **catastrophizing** in my head stopped." (par. 10)

Meaning:

Effect:

6. "He explained that, weeks before, he had begun a campaign to make his parents like, accept or at least not hate me, and to not **disown** him." (par. 13)

Meaning:

Effect:

7. "This campaign included **systematic** leaks of information to his parents by family members who were sympathetic to his affection for someone outside of their race." (par. 13)

Meaning:

Effect:

8. "What shocked me was less my peers' admissions of their parents' restrictions than their willingness to **abide** by them." (par. 26)

Meaning:

Effect:

9. "At least in our case, I'm thankful to say, it turns out that people are easier to accept than an **abstraction**." (par. 29)

Meaning:

Effect:

Sports, Politics, Tribe, Violence, and the Social Human Animal's Drive to Survive (p. 1031)
David Ropeik

For each term in bold below, determine the meaning of the word in the context of the sentence, and then describe the effect of the word: how the author's word choice contributes to the meaning and tone of the sentence(s).

1. "In this piece, Ropeik introduces the **tongue-in-cheek acronyms** BIRG and CORF." (opening)

Meaning (tongue-in-cheek):

Meaning (acronyms):

Effect:

2. "This **phenomenon** is evidence that rooting for the home team is about something WAY deeper than sports." (par. 1)

Meaning:

Effect:

3. "And from Maine to Cape Cod, and from Athens to Atlanta down to Albany Georgia, the **lament** is "THEY lost."" (par. 2)

Meaning:

Effect:

4. "This behavior, and language, comes from someplace deeper, more instinctive, more ancient, more tribal...someplace that I would suggest is tied to nothing less than the deepest instinctive **imperative** of all, to survive." (par. 4)

Meaning:

Effect:

5. "We subconsciously choose our views on many issues so they match the views in the groups we most strongly identify with, a theory called Cultural **Cognition**." (par. 5)

Meaning:

Effect:

6. "Sports are only less violent **surrogates** of precisely the same human need, to belong to a tribe that's doing well because as the tribe's chances go, so go yours." (par. 6)

Meaning:

Effect:

7. "And if everything goes as hoped, the season ends with a championship capped by huge **civic** rallies in which everyone chants and screams "WE won!"" (par. 7)

Meaning:

Effect:

8. "But BIRGing and CORFing is not much different from the **polarized** closed-minded **antipathy** people on the right and left feel toward each other, the **virulent** and often violent hatred people in the orthodox branches of various faiths feel toward people outside their sect, not much different from the antipathy Kikuyus in Kenya feel toward the Luo tribe or the violence between Pashtuns and other tribes in Afghanistan or the angry feelings people in so many nations have toward the people in other countries." (par. 76)

Meaning (polarized):

Meaning (antipathy):

Meaning (virulent):

Effect:

9. "They represent the social human animal's *need* for tribal affiliation and **cohesion**, a belonging which is vital to nothing less motivating than survival itself." (par. 85)

Meaning:

Effect:

A Roz by Any Other Name (p. 1036)
B. T. Ryback

For each term in bold below, determine the meaning of the word in the context of the sentence, and then describe the effect of the word: how the author's word choice contributes to the meaning and tone of the sentence(s).

1. "I'll report Romeo to his parents and suggest that Lord Montague demand a pound of Juliet's flesh in **restitution** for this embarrassment." (line 42)

Meaning:

Effect:

2. "What **allegiance** do you owe that Mule?" (line 59)

Meaning:

Effect:

3. "Why do you think there has been a **resurrection** in the fights between the two houses?" (line 105)

Meaning:

Effect:

4. "The minute people find out that Rosalind Constantini has been **trumped** by a Capulet, I'm ruined." (line 174)

Meaning:

Effect:

5. "Perhaps I will dress as a boy, befriend Romeo, and then convince him to take back his true love, the **lustrous** Rosalind!" (line 186)

Meaning:

Effect:

6. "I come of my own **accord**, I swear!" (line 230)

Meaning:

Effect:

7. "When I saw you run into the house, I thought for sure I had lost you, until the light from yonder window broke upon the dew-kissed grass, betraying your secret **counsel**, leading me to the fair maiden of the house!" (line 252)

Meaning:

Effect:

8. "Very small, very brief, but I saw it in the heaviness of her breath; and all my disappointment, all the night's boredom and embarrassment felt so **inconsequential** in the face of such pure...sadness." (line 441)

Meaning:

Effect:

9. "Surely, you caught me in some **ponderous** moment, wherein I remembered some tragic detail of my vast responsibilities as a princess." (line 452)

Meaning:

Effect:

10. "It's much like being **canonized** if I remember correctly." (line 525)

Meaning:

Effect:

Name_____

Date_____Class_____

The Treasures of the Gods (p. 1089)

Neil Gaiman

For each term in bold below, determine the meaning of the word in the context of the sentence, and then describe the effect of the word: how the author's word choice contributes to the meaning and tone of the sentence(s).

1. "A hundred expressions chased each other across Loki's face: **cunning** and shiftiness, **truculence** and confusion." (par. 13)

Meaning (cunning):

Meaning (truculence):

Effect:

2. "The most **ingenious** craftsmen of them all, he decided, were the three dwarfs known as the sons of Ivaldi." (par. 26)

Meaning:

Effect:

3. "Loki looked as **guileless** as he could, which was amazingly guileless." (par. 37)

Meaning:

Effect:

4. ""You work the **bellows**, Brokk." (par. 48)

Meaning:

Effect:

5. "It flew in and circled the room in a **malicious** way." (par. 50)

Meaning:

Effect:

6. "The black fly, up on the corner of the ceiling **seethed** with resentment and irritation." (par. 58)

Meaning:

Effect:

7. "Eitri picked up an **ingot** of pig iron, bigger than any ingot that the black fly (who was Loki) had ever seen before, and he hefted it into the forge." (par. 69)

Meaning:

Effect:

8. "It was a beautiful spear, carved with intricate **runes**." (par. 86)

Meaning:

Effect:

9. "Loki was glaring with **impotent** fury." (par. 131)

Meaning:

Effect:

from *The Odyssey* (p. 1099)

Homer

For each term in bold below, determine the meaning of the word in the context of the sentence, and then describe the effect of the word: how the author's word choice contributes to the meaning and tone of the sentence(s).

1. "And when long years and seasons wheeling
brought around that point of time
ordained for him to make his passage homeward, trials
and dangers, even so, attended him
even in Ithaka, near those he loved." (Book 1, lines 24-28)

Meaning:

Effect:

2. "Now he has paid the **reckoning** in full." (Book 1, line 53)

Meaning:

Effect:

3. "But my own heart is broken for Odysseus, the
master mind of war, so long a castaway upon an
island in the running sea;
a wooded island, in the sea's middle,
and there's a goddess in the place, the daughter of
one whose **baleful** mind knows all the deepsof the
blue sea—Atlas, who holds the columns
that bear from land the great thrust of the sky." (Book 1, lines 58-65)

Meaning:

Effect:

4. "Naturally, the god, after the blinding—
mind you, he does not kill the man;
he only **buffets** him away from home." (Book 1, lines 88-90)

Meaning:

Effect:

5. "Poseidon must relent
for being quarrelsome will get him nowhere,

one god, **flouting** the will of all the gods." (Book 1, lines 93-95)

Meaning:

Effect:

6. "He found the criers with **clarion** voices and told them
to muster the unshorn Akhaians in full assembly." (Book 2, lines 7-8)

Meaning:

Effect:

7. "They **squander** everything." (Book 2, line 28)

Meaning:

Effect:

8. "My house is being **plundered**: is this courtesy?" (Book 2, line 34)

Meaning:

Effect:

9. "It is a shroud I weave for Lord Laërtês,
when cold death comes to lay him on his **bier**." (Book 2, lines 70-71)

Meaning:

Effect:

10. "O goddess,
what **guile** is hidden here?" (Book 5, lines 25-26)

Meaning:

Effect:

from *The Odyssey* (p. 1109)
Homer

For each term in bold below, determine the meaning of the word in the context of the sentence, and then describe the effect of the word: how the author's word choice contributes to the meaning and tone of the sentence(s).

1. "Nine days I drifted on the **teeming** sea
before dangerous high winds." (Book 9, lines 1-2)

Meaning:

Effect:

2. "All ships' companies
mustered alongside for the mid-day meal." (Book 9, lines 5-6)

Meaning:

Effect:

3. "In the next land we found were Kyklopês,
giants, **louts**, without a law to bless them." (Book 9, lines 24-25)

Meaning:

Effect:

4. "This isle—seagoing folk would have annexed it and
built their homesteads on it: all good land, fertile for
every crop in season: lush
well-watered meads along the shore, vines in **profusion**, prairie,
clear for the plow, where grain would grow
chin high by harvest time, and rich sub-soil." (Book 9, lines 51-56)

Meaning:

Effect:

5. "A **prodigious** man
slept in this cave alone, and took his flocks
to graze afield—remote from all companions,
knowing none but savage ways, a brute
so huge, he seemed no man at all of those
who eat good wheaten bread; but he seemed rather
a shaggy mountain reared in solitude." (Book 9, lines 108-114)

Meaning:

Effect:

6. "A wineskin full
I brought along, and **victuals** in a bag,
for in my bones I knew some towering brute would be
upon us soon—all outward power,
a wild man, ignorant of civility." (Book 9, lines 133-137)

Meaning:

Effect:

7. "Or are you wandering **rogues**, who cast your lives
like dice, and ravage other folk by sea?" (Book 9, lines 180-181)

Meaning:

Effect:

8. "That **carrion** rogue
and his accurst companions burnt it out
when he had conquered all my wits with wine." (Book 9, lines 387-389)

Meaning:

Effect:

9. "So we moved out, sad in the vast **offing**,
having our precious lives, but not our friends." (Book 9, lines 463-464)

Meaning:

Effect:

10. "The lovely voices in **ardor** appealing over the water
made me crave to listen, and I tried to say
'Untie me!' to the crew, jerking my brows;
but they bent steady to the oars." (Book 12, lines 35-38)

Meaning:

Effect:

11. "But scarcely had that island faded
in blue air than I saw smoke
and white water, with sound of waves in **tumult**—
a sound the men heard, and it terrified them." (Book 12, lines 47-50)

Meaning:

Effect:

12. "But when she swallowed the sea water down we
saw the funnel of the **maelstrom**, heard
the rock bellowing all around, and dark
sand raged on the bottom far below." (Book 12, lines 93-96)

Meaning:

Effect:

from *The Odyssey* (p. 1122)
Homer

For each term in bold below, determine the meaning of the word in the context of the sentence, and then describe the effect of the word: how the author's word choice contributes to the meaning and tone of the sentence(s).

1. "When Telémakhos came,
the wolvish troop of watchdogs only **fawned** on him as he
advanced." (Book 16, lines 5-7)

Meaning:

Effect:

2. "They are drunk, drunk on **impudence**, they might
injure my guest—and how could I bear that?" (Book 16, lines 48-49)

Meaning:

Effect:

3. "I mean this **wanton** game they play, these fellows,
riding roughshod over you in your own house, admirable
as you are." (Book 16, lines 56-58)

Meaning:

Effect:

4. "Be kind to us, we'll make you fair **oblation**
and gifts of hammered gold." (Book 16, lines 92-93)

Meaning:

Effect:

5. "And one **disdainful** suitor added this:
"May his fortune grow an inch for every inch he bends it!"" (Book 21, lines 56-57)

Meaning:

Effect:

6. "In the hushed hall it **smote** the suitors
and all their faces changed." (Book 21, lines 67-68)

Meaning:

Effect:

7. "To glory over slain men is no **piety**." (Book 22, line 57)

Meaning:

Effect:

8. "But in reply the great **tactician** said:
"Not yet." (Book 22, lines 76-77)

Meaning:

Effect:

9. "So now in turn each woman thrust her head into
a noose and swung, yanked high in air,
to perish there most **piteously**." (Book 22, lines 118-120)

Meaning:

Effect:

10. "Their secret! as she heard it told, her knees
grew **tremulous** and weak, her heart failed her." (Book 23, lines 73-74)

Meaning:

Effect:

Heroic Acts to Protect the Word Hero (p. 1137)
Linton Weeks

For each term in bold below, determine the meaning of the word in the context of the sentence, and then describe the effect of the word: how the author's word choice contributes to the meaning and tone of the sentence(s).

1. "According to CNN, Philadelphia Eagles quarterback Michael Vick, who spent time in prison for animal abuse, "is being honored as a hero next month at a black-tie event in Norfolk, Va., for his **'resilience** in overcoming obstacles' and becoming 'a true example of life success for all to **emulate**,' according to event organizers."" (par. 4)

Meaning (resilience):

Meaning (emulate):

Effect:

2. "Other people who use the word "hero" may do so in different **contexts**, Rutkowski says, "but since we do not have exclusive rights to the word, it is **counterproductive** to cringe on hearing same." (par. 6)

Meaning (contexts):

Meaning (counterproductive):

Effect:

3. ""I suspect that if the American public's nerves weren't quite so badly frayed by all the over-attention to bad behavior, if we weren't all addicted to a culture of celebrity and extreme amplification of every news story, in other words, if the whole country were only a little bit more sane," Webber writes on *The Washington Post* website, "then we'd have a more **modulated** reaction to most events, the good, the bad and the ugly." (par. 10)

Meaning:

Effect:

4. "And we'd reserve the word 'hero' ... for actions and circumstances that actually **merit** their application."" (par. 10)

Meaning:

Effect:

5. "The dictionary traces the word's meaning from "a being of godlike **prowess** and **beneficence**" to "a warrior-chieftain of special strength, courage or ability" during the Homeric period of ancient Greece." (par. 14)

Meaning (prowess):

Meaning (beneficence):

Effect:

6. "About a fifth of the awards have been granted **posthumously**." (par. 17)

Meaning:

Effect:

7. "In the midst of continuing, well-earned acclaim for his cool competency, he took the measure of his act and **demurred** from the title 'hero.'" (par. 24)

Meaning:

Effect:

Is Anybody Watching My Do-Gooding? (p. 1141)
Katy Waldman

For each term in bold below, determine the meaning of the word in the context of the sentence, and then describe the effect of the word: how the author's word choice contributes to the meaning and tone of the sentence(s).

1. "We still want him around (DC Comics recently announced 10 new superhero films to unspool over the next six years, including one about a *her*: Wonder Woman), but his **omnipresence** makes him easy to mock." (par. 1)

Meaning:

Effect:

2. "Part of our **ambivalence** may also stem from the suspicion that his noble deeds are not as selfless as they seem, motivated instead by a thirst for attention, rational egotism, or even masochism." (par. 1)

Meaning:

Effect:

3. "Is extreme self-sacrifice the result of a pained **calculus**, a weighing of desire and obligation, or an instinct?" (par. 2)

Meaning:

Effect:

4. "Study author David Rand noted that people playing economic games are similarly less likely to share resources when they **ruminate** about their moves, but more generous when they don't take time to consider strategy." (par. 3)

Meaning:

Effect:

5. "The Yale study adds to a rich tradition of scientific inquiry into **altruism**, generosity, and the better angels/cannily perceptive salespeople of our nature." (par. 4)

Meaning:

Effect:

6. "One-year-olds will comfort an experimenter in **feigned** distress." (par. 5)

Meaning:

Effect:

7. "In fact, suddenly introducing an **extrinsic** motivation can undermine the internal glow of doing good—and drive subsequent helping rates down." (par. 6)

Meaning:

Effect:

8. "This overjustification effect is the **bane** of helicopter parents everywhere." (par. 6)

Meaning:

Effect:

9. "(Related but more **prosaic**: Studies suggest that "sensation-seeking" is positively correlated with the willingness to give blood.)" (par. 13)

Meaning:

Effect:

10. "Meanwhile, for show-offy altruists, there are **philanthropic** golden boys Bruce Wayne and Tony Stark, or that one male ally in your Twitter feed who always blurs the line between feminist support and benevolent sexism." (par. 14)

Meaning:

Effect:

Seeing through the Illusions of the Sports Hero **(p. 1146)**

William Rhoden

For each term in bold below, determine the meaning of the word in the context of the sentence, and then describe the effect of the word: how the author's word choice contributes to the meaning and tone of the sentence(s).

1. "A star with the Phoenix Suns at the time, Barkley was **lambasted** by a large portion of the news media who insisted that high-profile athletes, by virtue of their celebrity, should act like **paragons** of virtue, even if they weren't." (par. 2)

Meaning (lambasted):

Meaning (paragons):

Effect:

2. "In light of the dramatic falls of Michael Vick, Marion Jones, Barry Bonds, Roger Clemens, Tiger Woods and now Lance Armstrong, we need to either **recalibrate** our definition of the sports hero or scrap it altogether." (par. 3)

Meaning:

Effect:

3. "Owens is being hailed as the greatest track and field athlete of all time, same thing goes for 'Dead Pan' Joe Louis, whose decisive defeat of Carnera has sent the scribes scurrying to the dictionaries seeking **superlatives** of greater scope than any they've used before.'"" (par. 6)

Meaning:

Effect:

4. "There is the **propaganda** of heroism." (par. 7)

Meaning:

Effect:

5. "Louis battled drug addiction for years, was forced to fight past his prime and wound up **destitute**." (par. 10)

Meaning:

Effect:

6. "As Owens headed to the ballpark one afternoon to participate in yet another cheesy moneymaking exhibition, he came across an article in that day's New York Post that **poignantly** described his condition." (par. 12)

Meaning:

Effect:

7. "There is the **hypocrisy** of heroism." (par. 14)

Meaning:

Effect:

8. "Nike said it was betrayed and misled, though certainly no more than the world was deceived by Woods, who **implied** — or allowed marketers to **infer** — that his great character was at the root of his athletic success." (par. 17)

Meaning (implied):

Meaning (infer):

Effect:

Joining the Military Doesn't Make You a Hero (p. 1149)
Stephen Kinzer

For each term in bold below, determine the meaning of the word in the context of the sentence, and then describe the effect of the word: how the author's word choice contributes to the meaning and tone of the sentence(s).

1. "Now we pretend they are **demi-gods**." (par. 1)

Meaning:

Effect:

2. "Yet we also felt this way at the height of the Cold War, and we did not **fetishize** soldiers then the way we do now." (par. 2)

Meaning:

Effect:

3. "We are mature enough to know that a banker's suit does not always reflect honesty and that a **cleric**'s robe may not cloak a pure soul." (par. 3)

Meaning:

Effect:

4. "That honor is reserved for those whose individual **merit** may be limited to their choice — perhaps motivated by a variety of factors — to put on a uniform." (par. 6)

Meaning:

Effect:

5. "Now, with the emergence of the all-volunteer army, society has transferred the burden of war to a small, self-contained **caste** cut off from the American mainstream." (par. 7)

Meaning:

Effect:

6. "This distance allows civilians to develop **extravagant** fantasies about soldiers that feed the militarist impulse." (par. 7)

Meaning:

Effect:

7. "This serves the **cynical** interests of those who, for political or business reasons, want to encourage American involvement in foreign wars." (par. 8)

Meaning:

Effect:

8. "Even worse, it distracts attention away from the **scandalous** way we treat our veterans." (par. 8)

Meaning:

Effect:

9. "Cheering for them in public and saluting them in **cliché**-ridden speeches is a way to disguise the fact that our society **callously** discards many of them." (par. 8)

Meaning (cliché):

Meaning (callously):

Effect:

Why Wonder Woman Is the Hero We Need Today (p. 1152)
Emily Wanamaker

For each term in bold below, determine the meaning of the word in the context of the sentence, and then describe the effect of the word: how the author's word choice contributes to the meaning and tone of the sentence(s).

1. "Just her name alone **conjures** up the image of a towering Amazon, clad in red, white, and blue, ready to save the world with her golden lasso and silver bracelets." (par. 2)

Meaning:

Effect:

2. "She is, in her own words, "a **disciple** of peace and love."" (par. 2)

Meaning:

Effect:

3. "In the 1940s, she fought constantly for equality between men and women, fighting against Nazis and **misogynistic** criminals who posed a threat to those she chose to defend." (par. 3)

Meaning:

Effect:

4. "As Brooke stated, Wonder Woman has become **entrenched** in the feminist movements of the past decades." (par. 7)

Meaning:

Effect:

5. "One of the most **iconic** Wonder Woman quotes is as follows: "We have a saying, my people, 'Don't kill if you can wound, don't wound if you can subdue, don't subdue if you can **pacify**, and don't raise your hand at all until you've first extended it.'"" (par. 8)

Meaning (iconic):

Meaning (pacify):

Effect:

6. "The country has descended into another chaos, a chaos in which people on both sides of an argument spend so much time pointing fingers and **fearmongering** in order to turn the other

side into the villain, resulting in a world where the people choose to live in blind hatred of others rather than taking the time to stop and listen to their complaints and analyze what has caused them to be raised in order to reach a better understanding." (par. 10)

Meaning:

Effect:

7. "A world in which members of each side of the argument have painted the other in such a negative light that to engage with the opposing side in a positive manner is to **ostracize** oneself from one's original allies." (par. 10)

Meaning:

Effect:

8. ""If the prospect of living in a world where trying to respect the basic rights of those around you and valuing each other simply because we exist are such **daunting**, impossible tasks then what sort of world are we left with?" (par. 15)

Meaning:

Effect:

9. "With this statement, Wonder Woman **encapsulates** the central issue of this constant fight occurring at this moment in the United States – if all we are capable of doing is to argue, then how are we ever going to make the world a better place?" (par. 15)

Meaning:

Effect:

from *Gilgamesh: A Verse Play* (p. 1158)
Yusef Komunyakaa and Chad Gracia

For each term in bold below, determine the meaning of the word in the context of the sentence, and then describe the effect of the word: how the author's word choice contributes to the meaning and tone of the sentence(s).

1. "We are here to see into the past and the future, and not to run **amuck** with the dumb brutes of the forest and rejoice in their darkness." (Act 1, Scene 1, line 33)

Meaning:

Effect:

2. "Son, in your sleep last night you were restless as a fretted **lyre**, like a feverish child wrestling a demon." (Act 1, Scene 2, line 4)

Meaning:

Effect:

3. "I always hear the wildest **litanies** on the day of credits and debits." (Act 1, Scene 2, line 62)

Meaning:

Effect:

4. "This tale is conjured to **swindle** me of my rightful gifts of fur and meat." (Act 1, Scene 2, line 67)

Meaning:

Effect:

5. "If he **succumbs** to her, he is a man, and you may live." (Act 1, Scene 2, line 94)

Meaning:

Effect:

6. "Then you are a **godsend**, if ever a godsend was goodness." (Act 1, Scene 5, line 47)

Meaning:

Effect:

7. "I ache from **pate** to toes, as if I have wrestled with myself in the dirt the whole night." (Act 1, Scene 6, line 12)

Meaning:

Effect:

8. "I am afraid I have fed you too much food of the gods—words, myths, and **delicacies** bitter and sweet." (Act 1, Scene 6, line 37)

Meaning:

Effect:

9. "I am here to honor my god-given **birthright**." (Act 1, Scene 7, line 27)

Meaning:

Effect:

10. "You are **foolhardy**." (Act 1, Scene 7, line 102)

Meaning:

Effect:

from *Gilgamesh: A Verse Play* (p. 1158)
Yusef Komunyakaa and Chad Gracia

For each term in bold below, determine the meaning of the word in the context of the sentence, and then describe the effect of the word: how the author's word choice contributes to the meaning and tone of the sentence(s).

1. Humbaba can **wheel**
   and turn like a fire-chariot. (Act 1, Scene 10, lines 39-40)

Meaning:

Effect:

2. For ten days
   I counted your footsteps, and
   now here you stand
   at the forbidden **threshold.** (Act 1, Scene 10, lines 96-99)

Meaning:

Effect:

3. **Brandish** him till he calls
   my name,
   but please do not kill him. (Act 1, Scene 10, lines 123-25)

Meaning:

Effect:

4. *Gilgamesh swings his sword again and again,* ***hewing*** *Humbaba to pieces.* (Act 1, Scene 10, stage directions following line 159)

Meaning:

Effect:

5. My mother has taught me well
   the **genus** and **hex** of my name. (Act 1, Scene 11, lines 13-14)

Meaning:

Effect:

6. I shall speak for you.
   I shall **fend** for you. (Act 1, Scene 11, lines 44-45)

Meaning:

Effect:

7. I curse your heart
   for bringing me to this
   juncture, to this crook
   In the long road home. (Act 1, Scene 11, lines 84-87)

Meaning:

Effect:

8. And I sit here —
   in my **immense** aloneness. (Act 1, Scene 11, lines 109-10)

Meaning:

Effect:

9. we will give Enkidu
   a hero's ceremony of crossed swords
   and a **volley** of drums. (Act 2, Scene 10, lines 14-16)

Meaning:

Effect:

10. I could not **acquiesce** to the worms,
    to the quiet tyranny of springtime. (Act 2, Scene 10, lines 18-19)

Meaning:

Effect:

11. When I saw you carrying your burden as
    carrion birds circled overhead patrolling
    the dusky sky,
    I thought I was in **purgatory**. (Act 2, Scene 10, lines 20-23)

Meaning:

Effect:

from *The Veldt* (p. 165)
Ray Bradbury

Read and analyze the following passage from "The Veldt," using annotation to investigate how Bradbury uses language and style to convey his meaning effectively.

"And lock the nursery for a few days until I get my nerves settled."

"You know how difficult Peter is about that. When I punished him a month

ago by locking the nursery for even a few hours - the tantrum he threw! And

Wendy too.

They live for the nursery."

"It's got to be locked, that's all there is to it."

"All right." Reluctantly he locked the huge door. "You've been working too
hard.

You need a rest."

"I don't know - I don't know," she said, blowing her nose, sitting down in a

chair that immediately began to rock and comfort her. "Maybe I don't have

enough to do.

Maybe I have time to think too much. Why don't we shut the whole house off for a

few days and take a vacation?"

"You mean you want to fry my eggs for me?" "Yes." She nodded.

"And dam my socks?"

"Yes." A frantic, watery-eyed nodding. "And sweep the house?"

"Yes, yes - oh, yes!''

"But I thought that's why we bought this house, so we wouldn't have to do anything?"

"That's just it. I feel like I don't belong here. The house is wife and mother now, and nursemaid. Can I compete with an African veldt? Can I give a bath and scrub the children as efficiently or quickly as the automatic scrub bath can? I cannot. And it isn't just me. It's you. You've been awfully nervous lately."

from *Reindeer Games* (p. 176)

Sherman Alexie

Read and analyze the following passage from "Reindeer Games," using annotation to investigate how Alexie uses language and style to convey his meaning effectively.

So we walked through the front and into the loud gym. Which

immediately went silent.

Absolutely quiet.

My fellow tribal members saw me and they all stopped cheering,

talking, and moving.

I think they stopped breathing.

And, then, as one, they all turned their backs on me. It was a fricking

awesome display of contempt.

I was impressed. So were my teammates. Especially Roger.

He just looked at me and whistled.

I was mad. If these dang Indians had been this organized when I went

to school here, maybe I would have had more reasons to stay.

That thought made me laugh.

So I laughed.

And my laughter was the only sound in the gym.

And then I noticed that the only Indian who hadn't turned his back on me was Rowdy. He was standing on the other end of the court. He passed a basketball around his back, around his back, around his back, like a clock. And he glared at me.

He wanted to play.

He didn't want to turn his back on me. He wanted to kill me, face-to-face.

That made me laugh some more.

from *Mirror Image* (p. 184)
Lena Coakley

Read and analyze the following passage from "Mirror Image," using annotation to investigate how Coakley uses language and style to convey her meaning effectively.

Alice had to re-learn how to move in the hospital, and to speak. At first the world was nothing but a mush of dark images, disconnected voices and prickly feelings all over her skin. If someone touched her arm she wasn't sure from which part of her body the sensation came. Colors seemed different. People's voices were pitched a tone higher. When she tried to speak she bit her tongue, which seemed enormous in her mouth and tasted funny. When she finally learned, the tone was different, but the inflections and the slight Maritime accent were the same. She'd had an accident, they said. But long before the psychiatrist told her, she knew. These weren't her hands. This wasn't her breath.

from *What, of This Goldfish, Would You Wish?* (p. 192)
Etgar Keret

Read and analyze the following passage from "What, of This Goldfish, Would You Wish?" using annotation to investigate how Keret uses language and style to convey his meaning effectively.

"I can restore him," says the goldfish. "I can bring him back to life." "No one's asking," Sergei says.

"I can bring him back to the moment before," the goldfish says. "To before he knocks on your door. I can put him back to right there. I can do it. All you need to do is ask."

"To wish my wish," Sergei says. "My last."

The fish swishes his fish tail back and forth in the water, the way he does, Sergei knows, when he's truly excited. The goldfish can already taste freedom. Sergei can see it on him.

After the last wish, Sergei won't have a choice. He'll have to let the goldfish go. His magic goldfish. His friend.

"Fixable," Sergei says. "I'll just mop up the blood. A good sponge and it'll be like it never was."

That tail just goes back and forth, the fish's head steady.

Sergei takes a deep breath. He steps out into the middle of the kitchen, out into the puddle. "When I'm fishing, while it's dark and the world's asleep," he says, half to himself and half to the fish, "I'll tie the kid to a rock and dump him in the sea. Not a chance, not in a million years, will anyone ever find *him*."

"You killed him, Sergei," the goldfish says. "You murdered someone—but you're not a murderer." The goldfish stops swishing his tail. "If, on this, you won't waste a wish, then tell me, Sergei, what is it good for?"

from *The Cask of Amontillado* (p. 198)
Edgar Allan Poe

Read and analyze the following passage from "The Cask of Amontillado," using annotation to investigate how Poe uses language and style to convey his meaning effectively.

At the most remote end of the crypt there appeared another less spacious. Its walls had been lined with human remains, piled to the vault overhead, in the fashion of the great catacombs of Paris. Three sides of this interior crypt were still ornamented in this manner. From the fourth side the bones had been thrown down, and lay promiscuously upon the earth, forming at one point a mound of some size. Within the wall thus exposed by the displacing of the bones, we perceived a still interior crypt or recess, in depth about four feet, in width three, in height six or seven. It seemed to have been constructed for no especial use within itself, but formed merely the interval between two of the colossal supports of the roof of the catacombs, and was backed by one of their circumscribing walls of solid granite.

It was in vain that Fortunato, uplifting his dull torch, endeavoured to pry into the depth of the recess. Its termination the feeble light did not enable us to see.

"Proceed," I said; "herein is the Amontillado. As for Luchresi—"

"He is an ignoramus," interrupted my friend, as he stepped unsteadily forward, while I followed immediately at his heels. In niche, and finding an instant he had reached the extremity of the niche, and finding his progress arrested by the rock, stood stupidly bewildered. A moment more and I had fettered him to the granite. In its surface were two iron staples, distant from each other about two feet, horizontally. From one of these depended a short chain, from the other a padlock. Throwing the links about his waist, it was but the work of a few seconds to secure it. He was too much astounded to resist. Withdrawing the key I stepped back from the recess.

from *The Most Dangerous Game* (p. 212)

Richard Connell

Read and analyze the following passage from "The Most Dangerous Game," using annotation to investigate how Connell uses language and style to convey his meaning effectively.

Following the trail with the sureness of a bloodhound came General Zaroff. Nothing escaped those searching black eyes, no crushed blade of grass, no bent twig, no mark, no matter how faint, in the moss. So intent was the Cossack on his stalking that he was upon the thing Rainsford had made before he saw it. His foot touched the protruding bough that was the trigger. Even as he touched it, the general sensed his danger and leaped back with the agility of an ape. But he was not quite quick enough; the dead tree, delicately adjusted to rest on the cut living one, crashed down and struck the general a glancing blow on the shoulder as it fell; but for his alertness, he must have been smashed beneath it. He staggered, but he did not fall; nor did he drop his revolver. He stood there, rubbing his injured shoulder, and Rainsford, with fear again gripping his heart, heard the general's mocking laugh ring through the jungle.

"Rainsford," called the general, "if you are within sound of my voice, as I suppose you are, let me congratulate you. Not many men know how to make a Malay mancatcher. Luckily for me I, too, have hunted in Malacca. You are proving interesting, Mr. Rainsford. I am going now to have my wound dressed; it's only a slight one. But I shall be back. I shall be back."

When the general, nursing his bruised shoulder, had gone, Rainsford took up his flight again. It was flight now, a desperate, hopeless flight, that carried him on for some hours. Dusk came, then darkness, and still he pressed on. The ground grew softer under his moccasins; the vegetation grew ranker, denser; insects bit him savagely.

from *Lelah* (p. 228)
Angela Flournoy

Read and analyze the following passage from "Lelah," using annotation to investigate how Flournoy uses language and style to convey her meaning effectively.

This happened to Lelah sometimes in the casino, a stranger high off a big win gave her money just for bearing witness, and each time she felt like crying. Because a stranger could be so generous, when she'd never once thought to do that after a win. Because she wanted the money so much. Because, truthfully, it didn't take much to make Lelah feel like crying. But feeling like crying was not the same as actually crying, and Lelah was up twenty dollars.

She'd been down to less than twenty bucks and pulled ahead before. There was a red convertible sitting on top of the Wheel of Fortune slots, and though she despised slots as an amateur, vulgar game, she imagined winning so much at a table that they gave the damn thing to her; just put a ramp over the front slots so she could climb up, drive her new Corvette down, and pick up the rest of her winnings at the cashier. Or maybe she'd only get a few hundred, but it would be enough to buy her some time, so she'd resist the urge to try to flip the money. No, she'd run out of there, hundreds in her pocket, and check into a nice hotel. Yes, a nice hotel would be a good start, and then she'd take a day or two to figure out what to do next. This was a lot more plausible than the car scenario, she knew; she just had to strategize.

from *Two Kinds* (p. 237)

Amy Tan

Read and analyze the following passage from "Two Kinds," using annotation to investigate how Tan uses language and style to convey her meaning effectively.

The instructor of the beauty training school had to lop off these soggy clumps to make my hair even again. "Peter Pan is very popular these days" the instructor assured my mother. I now had bad hair the length of a boy's; with curly bangs that hung at a slant two inches above my eyebrows. I liked the haircut, and it made me actually look forward to my future fame.

In fact, in the beginning I was just as excited as my mother, maybe even more so. I pictured this prodigy part of me as many different images, and I tried each one on for size. I was a dainty ballerina girl standing by the curtain, waiting to hear the music that would send me floating on my tiptoes. I was like the Christ child lifted out of the straw manger, crying with holy indignity. I was Cinderella stepping from her pumpkin carriage with sparkly cartoon music filling the air. In all of my imaginings I was filled with a sense that I would soon become perfect: My mother and father would adore me. I would be beyond reproach. I would never feel the need to sulk, or to clamor for anything. But sometimes the prodigy in me became impatient. "If you don't hurry up and get me out of here, I'm disappearing for good," it warned. "And then you'll always be nothing."

from *Outliers* (p. 250)
Malcolm Gladwell

Read and analyze the following passage from "Outliers," using annotation to investigate how Gladwell uses language and style to convey his meaning effectively.

Everyone from all three groups started playing at roughly the same age, around five years old. In those first few years, everyone practiced roughly the same amount, about two or three hours a week. But when the students were around the age of eight, real differences started to emerge. The students who would end up the best in their class began to practice more than everyone else: six hours a week by age nine, eight hours a week by age twelve, sixteen hours a week by age fourteen, and up and up, until by the age of twenty they were practicing-that is, purposefully and single-mindedly playing their instruments with the intent to get better-well over thirty hours a week. In fact, by the age of twenty, the elite performers had each totaled ten thousand hours of practice. By contrast, the merely good students had totaled eight thousand hours, and the future music teachers had totaled just over four thousand hours.

Ericsson and his colleagues then compared amateur pianists with professional pianists. The same pattern emerged. The amateurs never practiced more than about three hours a week over the course of their childhood, and by the age of twenty they had totaled two thousand hours of practice. The professionals, on the other hand, steadily increased their practice time every year, until by the age of twenty they, like the violinists, had reached ten thousand hours.

from *Battle Hymn of the Tiger Mother* (p. 253)
Amy Chua

Read and analyze the following passage from "Battle Hymn of the Tiger Mother," using annotation to investigate how Chua uses language and style to convey her meaning effectively.

As an adult, I once did the same thing to Sophia, calling her garbage in English when she acted extremely disrespectfully toward me. When I mentioned that I had done this at a dinner party, I was immediately ostracized. One guest named Marcy got so upset she broke down in tears and had to leave early. My friend Susan, the host, tried to rehabilitate me with the remaining guests.

"Oh dear, it's just a misunderstanding. Amy was speaking metaphorically—right, Amy? You didn't actually call Sophia 'garbage.'"

"Um, yes, I did; But it's all in the context," I tried to explain. "It's a Chinese immigrant thing."

"But you're not a Chinese immigrant," somebody pointed out.

"Good point," I conceded. "No wonder it didn't work."

I was just trying to be conciliatory. In fact, it had worked great with Sophia.

The fact is that Chinese parents can do things that would seem unimaginable—even legally actionable—to Westerners. Chinese mothers can say to their daughters, "Hey fatty— lose some weight." By contrast, Western parents have to tiptoe around the issue, talking in terms of "health" and never ever mentioning the f-word, and their kids still end up in therapy for eating disorders and negative self-image. (I also once heard a Western father toast his adult daughter by calling her "beautiful and incredibly competent." She later told me that made her feel like garbage.) Chinese parents can order their kids to get straight As. Western parents can only ask their kids to try their best. Chinese parents can say, "You're lazy. All your classmates getting ahead of you." By contrast, Western parents have to struggle with their own conflicted feelings about achievement, and try to persuade themselves that they're not disappointed about how their kids turned out.

from *How to Raise a Creative Child. Step One: Back Off* (p. 259)
Adam Grant

Read and analyze the following passage from "How to Raise a Creative Child. Step One: Back Off," using annotation to investigate how Grant uses language and style to convey his meaning effectively.

Even then, though, parents didn't shove their values down their children's throats. When psychologists compared America's most creative architects with a group of highly skilled but unoriginal peers, there was something unique about the parents of the creative architects: "Emphasis was placed on the development of one's own ethical code."

Yes, parents encouraged their children to pursue excellence and success — but they also encouraged them to find "joy in work." Their children had freedom to sort out their own values and discover their own interests. And that set them up to flourish as creative adults.

When the psychologist Benjamin Bloom led a study of the early roots of world-class musicians, artists, athletes and scientists, he learned that their parents didn't dream of raising superstar kids. They weren't drill sergeants or slave drivers. They responded to the intrinsic motivation of their children. When their children showed interest and enthusiasm in a skill, the parents supported them.

Top concert pianists didn't have elite teachers from the time they could walk; their first lessons came from instructors who happened to live nearby and made learning fun. Mozart showed interest in music before taking lessons, not the other way around. Mary Lou Williams learned to play the piano on her own; Itzhak Perlman began teaching himself the violin after being rejected from music school.

from *Drive* (p. 262)
Daniel Pink

Read and analyze the following passage from "Drive," using annotation to investigate how Pink uses language and style to convey his meaning effectively.

To be clear, it wasn't necessarily the rewards themselves that dampened the children's interest. Remember: When children didn't expect a reward, receiving one had little impact on their intrinsic motivation. Only contingent rewards-if you do this, then you'll get that-had the negative effect. Why? "If-then" rewards require people to forfeit some of their autonomy. Like the gentlemen driving carriages for money instead of fun, they're no longer fully controlling their lives. And that can spring a hole in the bottom of their motivational bucket, draining an activity of its enjoyment.

Lepper and Greene replicated these results in several subsequent experiments with children. As time went on, other researchers found similar results with adults. Over and over again, they discovered that extrinsic rewards-in particular, contingent, expected, "if- then" rewards-snuffed out the third drive.

These insights proved so controversial-after all, they called into question a standard practice of most companies and schools-that in 1999 Deci and two colleagues reanalyzed nearly three decades of studies on the subject to confirm the findings. "Careful consideration of reward effects reported in 128 experiments lead to the conclusion that tangible rewards tend to have a substantially negative effect on intrinsic motivation," they determined. "When institutions--families, schools, businesses, and athletic teams, for example—focus on the short-term and opt for controlling people's behavior," they do considerable long-term damage.

from *Open* (p. 266)
Andre Agassi

Read and analyze the following passage from "Open," using annotation to investigate how Agassi uses language and style to convey his meaning effectively.

Wouldn't that feel like heaven, Andre? To just quit? To never play tennis again? But I can't. Not only would my father chase me around the house with my racket, but something in my gut, some deep unseen muscle, won't let me. I hate tennis, hate it with all my heart, and still I keep playing, keep hitting all morning, and all afternoon, because I have no choice. No matter how much I want to stop, I don't. I keep begging myself to stop, and I keep playing, and this gap, this contradiction between what I want to do and what I actually do, feels like the core of my life. At the moment my hatred for tennis is focused on the dragon, a ball machine modified by my fire-belching father. Midnight black, set on big rubber wheels, the word PRINCE painted in white block letters along its base, the dragon looks at first glance like the ball machine at every country club in America, but it's actually a living, breathing creature straight out of my comic books. The dragon has a brain, a will, a black heart—and a horrifying voice. Sucking another ball into its belly, the dragon makes a series of sickening sounds. As pressure builds inside its throat, it groans. As the ball rises slowly to its mouth, it shrieks. For a moment the dragon sounds almost silly, like the fudge machine swallowing Augustus Gloop in Willy Wonka & the Chocolate Factory. But when the dragon takes dead aim at me and fires a ball 110 miles an hour, the sound it makes is a bloodcurdling roar. I flinch every time. My father has deliberately made the dragon fearsome.

from *Once Upon a Time* (p. 271)
Nadine Gordimer

Read and analyze the following passage from "Once Upon a Time," using annotation to investigate how Gordimer uses language and style to convey her meaning effectively.

When the man and wife and little boy took the pet dog for its walk round the neighborhood streets they no longer paused to admire this show of roses or that perfect lawn; these were hidden behind an array of different varieties of security fences, walls and devices. The man, wife, little boy and dog passed a remarkable choice: there was the low-cost option of pieces of broken glass embedded in cement along the top of walls, there were iron grilles ending in lance-points, there were attempts at reconciling the aesthetics of prison architecture with the Spanish Villa style (spikes painted pink) and with the plaster urns of neoclassical facades (twelve-inch pikes finned like zigzags of lightning and painted pure white). Some walls had a small board affixed, giving the name and telephone number of the firm responsible for the installation of the devices. While the little boy and the pet dog raced ahead, the husband and wife found themselves comparing the possible effectiveness of each style against its appearance; and after several weeks when they paused before this barricade or that without needing to speak, both came out with the conclusion that only one was worth considering. It was the ugliest but the most honest in its suggestion of the pure concentration-camp style, no frills, all evident efficacy. Placed the length of walls, it consisted of a continuous coil of stiff and shining metal serrated into jagged blades, so that there would be no way of climbing over it and no way through its tunnel without getting entangled in its fangs. There would be no way out, only a struggle getting bloodier and bloodier, a deeper and sharper hooking and tearing of flesh.

from *Nemecia* (p. 278)
Kirstin Valdez Quade

Read and analyze the following passage from "Nemecia," using annotation to investigate how Valdez Quade uses language and style to convey her meaning effectively.

After her fourteenth birthday, Nemecia's skin turned red and oily and swollen with pustules. It looked tender. She began to laugh at me for my thick eyebrows and crooked teeth, things I hadn't noticed about myself until then.

One night she came into our bedroom and looked at herself in the mirror for a long time. When she moved away, she crossed to where I sat on the bed and dug her nail into my right cheek. I yelped, jerked my head. "Shh," she said kindly. With one hand she smoothed my hair, and I felt myself soften under her hands as she worked her nail through my skin. It hurt only a little bit, and what did I, at seven years old, care about beauty? As I sat snug between Nemecia's knees, my face in her hands, her attention swept over me the way I imagined a wave would, warm and slow and salty.

Night after night I sat between her knees while she opened and reopened the wound. One day she'd make a game of it, tell me that I looked like a pirate; another day she'd say it was her duty to mark me because I had sinned. Daily she and my mother worked against each other, my mother spreading salve on the scab each morning, Nemecia easing it open each night with her nails. "Why don't you heal, hijita?" my mother wondered as she fed me cloves of raw garlic. Why didn't I tell her? I don't know exactly, but I suppose I needed to be drawn into Nemecia's story.

By the time Nemecia finally lost interest and let my cheek heal, the scar reached from the side of my nose to my lip. It made me look dissatisfied, and it turned purple in the winter.

Name_____

Date_____Class_____

from *Story of an Hour* **(p. 292)**

Kate Chopin

Read and analyze the following passage from "Story of an Hour," using annotation to investigate how Chopin uses language and style to convey her meaning effectively.

She was young, with a fair, calm face, whose lines bespoke repression and even a certain strength. But now there was a dull stare in her eyes, whose gaze was fixed away off yonder on one of those patches of blue sky. It was not a glance of reflection, but rather indicated a suspension of intelligent thought.

There was something coming to her and she was waiting for it, fearfully. What was it? She did not know; it was too subtle and elusive to name. But she felt it, creeping out of the sky, reaching toward her through the sounds, the scents, the color that filled the air.

Now her bosom rose and fell tumultuously. She was beginning to recognize this thing that was approaching to possess her, and she was striving to beat it back with her will--as powerless as her two white slender hands would have been. When she abandoned herself a little whispered word escaped her slightly parted lips. She said it over and over under her breath: "free, free, free!" The vacant stare and the look of terror that had followed it went from her eyes. They stayed keen and bright. Her pulses beat fast, and the coursing blood warmed and relaxed every inch of her body.

from *Why School Should Start Later in the Day* (p. 349)

Lisa Lewis

Read and analyze the following passage from "Why School Should Start Later in the Day," using annotation to investigate how Lewis uses language and style to convey her meaning effectively.

Many districts are reluctant to change their schedules because they see the shift as too expensive and disruptive. But that's short-sighted. In the long run, a later start could actually save schools money — and benefit society at large.

Later start times can mean less missed school — absences dropped 15% in Bonneville County, Idaho, after it instituted such a change, according to a 2014 Children's National Medical Center report. In states such as California where state funding for schools is tied to attendance, it follows that later start times could translate into extra dollars. Megan Reilly, chief financial officer for the Los Angeles Unified School District, has estimated that boosting attendance by just 1% districtwide would bring in an additional $40 million per year.

Repeated studies also show that when the school day starts later and teens get more sleep, both grades and standardized test scores go up. A Colby College economist, Finley Edwards, found that a one-hour delay in start time increased math test and reading test scores by three percentile points. Even more striking, the lowest-scoring students showed the biggest jumps.

Compared to other strategies for boosting performance, delaying the start of the school day is easy and efficient. Teny M. Shapiro, an economist at Santa Clara University, estimates that a one-hour change produces the same benefit as shrinking class size by one-third or replacing a teacher in the 50th percentile of effectiveness with one in the 84th percentile.

from *End the Gun Epidemic in America* (p. 352)
New York Times Editorial Board

Read and analyze the following passage from "End the Gun Epidemic in America," using annotation to investigate how the New York Times Editorial Board uses language and style to convey their meaning effectively.

It is a moral outrage and a national disgrace that civilians can legally purchase weapons designed specifically to kill people with brutal speed and efficiency. These are weapons of war, barely modified and deliberately marketed as tools of macho vigilantism and even insurrection. America's elected leaders offer prayers for gun victims and then, callously and without fear of consequence, reject the most basic restrictions on weapons of mass killing, as they did on Thursday. They distract us with arguments about the word terrorism. Let's be clear: These spree killings are all, in their own ways, acts of terrorism.

from *History Shows the Folly of Disarming Lawful People* (p. 354)
Thomas Sowell

Read and analyze the following passage from "History Shows the Folly of Disarming Lawful People," using annotation to investigate how Sowell uses language and style to convey his meaning effectively.

The fatal fallacy of gun control laws in general is the assumption that such laws actually control guns. Criminals who disobey other laws are not likely to be stopped by gun control laws. What such laws actually do is increase the number of disarmed and defenseless victims.

Mass shootings are often used as examples of a need for gun control. But what puts a stop to mass shootings? Usually the arrival on the scene of somebody else with a gun. Mass shooters are often portrayed as "irrational" people engaged in "senseless" acts. But mass shooters are usually rational enough to attack schools, churches and other places where there is far less likelihood of someone being on the scene who is armed.

Seldom do we hear about these "irrational" shooters engaging in "senseless" attacks on meetings of the National Rifle Association or a local gun show or a National Guard armory.

The fallacy of believing that the way to reduce shootings is to disarm peaceful people extends from domestic gun control laws to international disarmament agreements. If disarmament agreements reduced the dangers of war, there would never have been a World War II.

from *Why Was Harambe the Gorilla in a Zoo in the First Place?* (p. 357)
Marc Bekoff

Read and analyze the following passage from "Why Was Harambe the Gorilla in a Zoo in the First Place?" using annotation to investigate how Bekoff uses language and style to convey his meaning effectively.

An analysis of Harambe's behavior published in another essay I wrote indicates that he was doing what one would expect a western lowland gorilla to do with a youngster. Harambe's hold on the child and his sheltering of the youngster are indicators of protection. He didn't seem to be afraid. He examined the boy but also was attentive to the reaction of the crowd who saw what happened and the communication between the child's mother and her son.

Along these lines, it's essential that the people who work with zoo-ed animals know their behavior in detail, and those people who know individuals the best—the caretakers who interact with certain individuals daily—be called in in emergency situations. Each animal has a unique personality and this knowledge could be put to use to avoid what happened to Harambe.

For people who want to know more about what was going on in Harambe's head and heart, think about your companion dog, for example. How do they respond when someone trespasses into where they feel safe? I like to ask people to use their companion animals to close the empathy gap because people get incredibly upset when a dog is harmed because they see dogs as sentient, feeling beings. So too, was Harambe.

So, would you allow your dog to be put in a zoo? If not, then why Harambe and millions of other individuals who languish behind bars?

from *Is It Immoral to Watch the Super Bowl?* (p. 362)
Steve Almond

Read and analyze the following passage from "Is It Immoral to Watch the Super Bowl," using annotation to investigate how Almond uses language and style to convey his meaning effectively.

Just so we're clear on this: I still love football. I love the grace and the poise of the athletes. I love the tension between the ornate structure of the game and its improvisatory chaos, and I love the way great players find opportunity, even a mystical kind of order, in the midst of that chaos.

The problem is that I can no longer indulge these pleasures without feeling complicit. It was easier years ago, when injuries like Stingley's could be filed away as freakish accidents. TV coverage was relatively primitive, the players hidden under helmets and pads, obscured by fuzzy reception, more superheroes than men. Today we see the cruelty of the game in high definition. Slow-motion replays show us the precise angle of a grotesquely twisted ankle and a quarterback's contorted face at the exact moment he is concussed.

The sport's incredible popularity has turned players into national celebrities and has made their mental and physical deterioration front-page news. In 2012, the former All-Pro linebacker Junior Seau killed himself. The autopsy confirmed that he had chronic traumatic encephalopathy, or C.T.E., the cause of the dementia that is increasingly prevalent among former players. A whole new crop of retired stars, including Tony Dorsett and Brett Favre, are just beginning to report symptoms like memory loss and depression.

Name_____

Date_____Class_____

from *The Paranoid Style of American Policing* (p. 370)
Ta-Nehisi Coates

Read and analyze the following passage from "The Paranoid Style of American Policing," using annotation to investigate how Coates uses language and style to convey his meaning effectively.

When policing is delegitimized, when it becomes an occupying force, the community suffers. The neighbor-on-neighbor violence in Chicago, and in black communities around the country, is not an optical illusion. Policing is (one) part of the solution to that violence. But if citizens don't trust officers, then policing can't actually work. And in Chicago, it is very hard to muster reasons for trust.

When Bettie Jones's brother displays zero confidence in an investigation into the killing of his sister, he is not being cynical. He is shrewdly observing a government that executed a young man and sought to hide that fact from citizens. He is intelligently assessing a local government which, for two decades, ran a torture ring. What we have made of our police departments America, what we have ordered them to do, is a direct challenge to any usable definition of democracy. A state that allows its agents to kill, to beat, to tase, without any real sanction, has ceased to govern and has commenced to simply rule.

Name_____

Date_____Class_____

from *Labeling the Danger in Soda* (p. 374)
Tina Rosenberg

Read and analyze the following passage from "Labeling the Danger in Soda," using annotation to investigate how Rosenberg uses language and style to convey her meaning effectively.

Health warning labels on consumables are not new, and we can learn from how well they've worked. Alcoholic drink bottles carry a dense block of text, all in capital letters (which can be harder to read than lowercase) warning of the risk of birth defects, impaired driving and "health problems."

These labels are terrible, said Matthew L. Myers, president of the Campaign for Tobacco-Free Kids, who has been working on the issue of warning labels since 1981. "They're invisible, lengthy and confusing. People in ad agencies just roll their eyes. If you were going to write a warning label not to work, the traditional alcohol warning label fits that bill."

The other labeled product, of course, is tobacco. In 80 countries — and the number is growing — cigarette packs are covered with gross, full-colored pictures of gangrenous toes, cancerous lungs and rotted teeth, along with deathbed photos of cancer victims. In at least 50 countries, these photos cover half the front of the pack or more — in Thailand, its 85 percent of the pack front.

Hammond reviewed major studies and found graphic warnings to be highly effective at getting people to quit and at discouraging them from starting; the larger they were, the better they worked.

from *September 13, 2001: Hatred Is Unworthy of Us* (p. 380)
Leonard Pitts

Read and analyze the following passage from "September 13, 2001: Hatred Is Unworthy of Us," using annotation to investigate how Pitts uses language and style to convey his meaning effectively.

Every one of us, no one left out. We are not a nation that is only white or only Christian. We're a people of rainbow hues and multiple faiths.

If that heritage has taught us nothing else by now, it should have taught us this: It's ignorant to think you can judge a man's soul by looking at his face. Yes, I saw Arabs cheering our pain in the West Bank. I also saw them issuing condemnations in Washington.

Take it as a reminder: The enemy is not Arab people or the Muslim religion. The enemy is fanaticism, extremism, intolerance, hate. The madmen who commandeered those planes don't represent the followers of Islam any more than the madmen who blow up abortion clinics represent the followers of Christ.

Yes, we're angry. We're supposed to be angry. We have a right to be angry. But at the same time, we must be wary of the places to which we allow that anger to bring us.

If we let it deliver us to the doorstep of fanaticism, extremism, intolerance, hate, we might as well give up now. Because everything that matters has already been lost.

from *Hiroshima Speech* (p. 383)

Barack Obama

Read and analyze the following passage from "Hiroshima Speech," using annotation to investigate how Obama uses language and style to convey his meaning effectively.

Still, every act of aggression between nations, every act of terror and corruption and cruelty and oppression that we see around the world shows our work is never done. We may not be able to eliminate man's capacity to do evil, so nations and the alliances that we form must possess the means to defend ourselves. But among those nations like my own that hold nuclear stockpiles, we must have the courage to escape the logic of fear and pursue a world without them.

We may not realize this goal in my lifetime, but persistent effort can roll back the possibility of catastrophe. We can chart a course that leads to the destruction of these stockpiles. We can stop the spread to new nations and secure deadly materials from fanatics.

And yet that is not enough. For we see around the world today how even the crudest rifles and barrel bombs can serve up violence on a terrible scale. We must change our mind- set about war itself. To prevent conflict through diplomacy and strive to end conflicts after they've begun. To see our growing interdependence as a cause for peaceful cooperation and not violent competition. To define our nations not by our capacity to destroy but by what we build. And perhaps, above all, we must reimagine our connection to one another as members of one human race.

For this, too, is what makes our species unique. We're not bound by genetic code to repeat the mistakes of the past. We can learn. We can choose. We can tell our children a different story, one that describes a common humanity, one that makes war less likely and cruelty less easily accepted.

from *What's Wrong with Cinderella?* (p. 389)
Peggy Orenstein

Read and analyze the following passage from "What's Wrong with Cinderella?" using annotation to investigate how Orenstein uses language and style to convey her meaning effectively.

As a feminist mother — not to mention a nostalgic product of the Garanimals era — I have been taken by surprise by the princess craze and the girlie-girl culture that has risen around it. What happened to William wanting a doll and not dressing your cat in an apron? Whither Marlo Thomas? I watch my fellow mothers, women who once swore they'd never be dependent on a man, smile indulgently at daughters who warble "So This Is Love" or insist on being called Snow White. I wonder if they'd concede so readily to sons who begged for combat fatigues and mock AK-47s.

More to the point, when my own girl makes her daily beeline for the dress-up corner of her preschool classroom — something I'm convinced she does largely to torture me — I worry about what playing Little Mermaid is teaching her. I've spent much of my career writing about experiences that undermine girls' well-being, warning parents that a preoccupation with body and beauty (encouraged by films, TV, magazines and, yes, toys) is perilous to their daughters' mental and physical health. Am I now supposed to shrug and forget all that? If trafficking in stereotypes doesn't matter at 3, when does it matter? At 6? Eight? Thirteen?

On the other hand, maybe I'm still surfing a washed-out second wave of feminism in a third-wave world. Maybe princesses are in fact a sign of progress, an indication that girls can embrace their predilection for pink without compromising strength or ambition; that, at long last, they can "have it all." Or maybe it is even less complex than that: to mangle Freud, maybe a princess is sometimes just a princess. And, as my daughter wants to know, what's wrong with that?

from *I'm a Twelve-Year-Old Girl: Why Don't the Characters in My Apps Look Like Me?* (p. 399)
Madeline Messer

Read and analyze the following passage from "I'm a Twelve-Year-Old Girl: Why Don't the Characters in My Apps Look Like Me?" using annotation to investigate how Messer uses language and style to convey her meaning effectively.

I found that when an app did sell girl characters, it charged on average $7.53, which is a lot in the world of apps. After all, each of the apps I downloaded only cost an average of $0.26. In other words, girl characters cost about 29 times more than the cost of the apps themselves. Disney's "Temple Run Oz" charges $29.97 to become the only girl character. Sometimes there are small differences in being a boy or a girl — at one point in one of the Temple games, a boy receives a shield, whereas a girl gets a burst of speed — but nothing to warrant a huge price tag. And some of the girl characters, like the $9.99 "Emotika Diva" offered by the game "Super Running Fred," are not appealing.

These biases affect young girls like me. The lack of girl characters implies that girls are not equal to boys and they don't deserve characters that look like them. I am a girl; I prefer being a girl in these games. I do not want to pay to be a girl.

Not all apps have taken this route. "The Hunger Games" lets you choose between being a girl or boy for free. If I were an app maker, the ethical issue of charging for girl characters and not boy characters would be enough reason to change. But app-makers should eliminate this practice for a business reason too: If girls stop playing these games, then they also would stop making in-app purchases and stop watching the ads. If our character choices tell us these games aren't for us, eventually we'll put them down.

from *When I Saw Prince, I Saw a Vital New Black Masculinity* (p. 401)
Terryn Hall

Read and analyze the following passage from "When I Saw Prince, I Saw a Vital New Black Masculinity," using annotation to investigate how Hall uses language and style to convey her meaning effectively.

Prince did none of that. And yet he was just as – if not more – sexual than the hip-hop I enjoyed as a teenager. ... his music exposed me to a masculine sensuality that allowed a space for vulnerability, ambiguity and fluidity. All this acted as a counter-narrative to what I saw at home and in rap music.

When I was 19, I lucked my way into tickets at a Prince show in Los Angeles. Never before had I seen such energy, such masculinity, if you like, emanate from a stage. He had the energy of a man half his age and moved from instrument to instrument, playing each one masterfully. He sat on a stool with only a guitar and a microphone to sing his version of Chaka Khan's Sweet Thing, which was filled with as much tension and desire as the original.

Name_____

Date_____Class_____

from *Don't Ban Photos of Skinny Models* (p. 404)

Vanessa Friedman

**Read and analyze the following passage from "Don't Ban Photos of Skinny Models,"
using annotation to investigate how Friedman uses language and style to convey her
meaning effectively.**

The message in this case is that women, and young people, are not able to make such distinctions on their own. Yet that power — the ability of each individual to decide on her body for herself — is one we should be cultivating, not relinquishing.

To ban an ad depicting a specific body type is to demonize that type, labeling it publicly as bad. It also suggests that it is even possible to look at a woman, or a photo of a woman, and know whether she is healthy or unhealthy. That's a misguided idea, as Claire Mysko, chief executive of the National Eating Disorders Association, acknowledges: One individual can have a seemingly normal body mass index and still have a tortured relationship with food and her physical self; another can look almost bony, and be fine. You can't tell from the outside.

"The solution to body-shaming isn't to limit the number and kinds of bodies we are exposed to," said Peggy Drexler, assistant professor of psychology at Cornell University, and the author of "Our Fathers, Ourselves: Daughters, Fathers and the Changing American Family." "The more sorts of bodies young women see — fat, thin, short, tall — the better they understand that bodies come in all shapes and sizes, and that theirs fits in somewhere."

from *Gender Bias Without Borders* (p. 408)
Geena Davis Institute on Gender in the Media

Read and analyze the following passage from "Gender Bias Without Borders," using annotation to investigate how the Geena Davis Institute on Gender in the Media uses language and style to convey their meaning effectively.

Every speaking (i.e., utters one or more words discernibly on screen) or named character was evaluated in this investigation for demographics, sexualization, occupation and STEM careers. Our major findings from the investigation follow. Only significant and practical differences (5% or greater) are reported.

A total of 5,799 speaking or names characters on screen were evaluated, with 30.9% female and 69.1% male. This calculates into a gender ratio of 2.24 males to every one female. Turning to protagonists, only 23.3% of the films had a girl or woman as a lead or co lead driving the plot.

Further, 12 movies or 10% of the sample had a "balanced cast" or featured girls/women in 45%-54.9% of all speaking roles. Given that females represent 49.6% of the population worldwide, we might expect to see more girls and women on screen. If visibility is currency, then females have little to spend. This limited representation varies significantly by country, story genre, and content creator gender.

from *Toxic Masculinity Is Killing Men: The Roots of Male Trauma* (p. 414)
Kali Holloway

Read and analyze the following passage from "Toxic Masculinity Is Killing Men: The Roots of Male Trauma," using annotation to investigate how Holloway uses language and style to convey her meaning effectively.

We are all familiar with these recurring characters. They are fearless action heroes;... psychopaths in Grand Theft Auto; shlubby, housework-averse sitcom dads with inexplicably beautiful wives; bumbling stoner twentysomethings who still manage to [get] the hot girl in the end; and still, the impenetrable Superman. Even sensitive, loveable everyguy Paul Rudd somehow "mans up" before the credits roll in his films. Here, it seems important to mention a National Coalition on Television Violence study which finds that on average, 18-year-old American males have already witnessed some 26,000 murders on television, "almost all of them committed by men." Couple those numbers with violence in film and other media, and the numbers are likely astronomical.

The result of all this—the early denial of boy's feelings, and our collective insistence that they follow suit—is that boys are effectively cut off from their feelings and emotions, their deepest and most vulnerable selves. Historian Stephanie Coontz has labeled this effect the "masculine mystique1." It leaves little boys, and later, men, emotionally disembodied, afraid to show weakness and often unable to fully access, recognize or cope with their feelings.

from *How "Master of None" Subverts Stereotypical Masculinity by Totally Ignoring It*
(p. 416)
Jack O'Keefe

Read and analyze the following passage from "How 'Master of None' Subverts Stereotypical Masculinity by Totally Ignoring It," using annotation to investigate how O'Keefe uses language and style to convey his meaning effectively.

Many sitcoms rely on archetypes of masculinity to find humor. The guys of *The Big Bang Theory* are constantly trying to transcend their nerdiness to be closer to the male action heroes they grew up admiring. The entire run of *Two and a Half Men* relied on the fact that one of the men is a confident womanizer, and that the other is "soft." More nuanced sitcoms like *How I Met Your Mother*, the pinnacle of 21st-century rom-sitcoms, still played with the drastic ends of masculinity for humor. *HIMYM* featured a womanizing alpha-male personality (Barney), a sensitive man who has only ever been with one woman (Marshall), and an emotionally stunted man-child who thinks finding a wife will solve all of his problems (Ted, who is the worst). *Master of None* explores these aspects of masculinity as well, but not because three characters with these traits are all discussing their views. Instead, Dev has qualities of all these archetypes, which together create a fully-realized and conflicted character.

from _Let's Kill All the Mosquitoes_ (p. 421)
Daniel Engber

Read and analyze the following passage from "Let's Kill All the Mosquitoes," using annotation to investigate how Engber uses language and style to convey his meaning effectively.

In 2002, Alphey founded Oxitec, which would become the first company to deploy genetically modified mosquitoes as a weapon. Since 2010, the firm has performed field evaluations in Brazil, the Cayman Islands, and Panama. The treatment works like this: Oxitec employees drive a van around mosquito-ridden areas at five or 10 miles per hour. A bladeless fan propels genetically modified males out through a plastic tube, and then the bugs seek and interbreed with wild females. (At a test site in Brazil, Oxitec released 800,000 flies per week, for half a year.) According to the company's head of field operations, Andy McKemey, each of these field evaluations has resulted in at least a 90 percent decrease in the local population.

Officials in the U.S. would like to test the Oxitec approach. An incipient attempt in the Florida Keys, however, has run afoul of some locals, who worry over being guinea pigs in a Frankenfly experiment. Oxitec counters that its technique is both highly targeted (only one species of mosquito is affected) and self-limiting (if you stop releasing the GM mosquitoes, they quickly disappear from the ecosystem).

from *Why Online Harassment Is Still Ruining Lives—and How We Can Stop It* (p. 429)
Sarah Kessler

Read and analyze the following passage from "Why Online Harassment Is Still Ruining Lives—and How We Can Stop It," using annotation to investigate how Kessler uses language and style to convey her meaning effectively.

As [Twitter CEO Dick] Costolo noted, having a reputation as a place where women receive death threats is a business problem for technology companies that are striving to keep people engaged with their platforms and attract new users. But it's an even bigger problem for society. Imagine hundreds of people hurling slurs at you, urging you to kill yourself, and threatening to kill you. Or rape you, along with very specific descriptions of how they would like to do so–and your address. Your life would be disrupted, to say the least.

Over the past few months, I spoke to dozens of women who have been the targets of online harassment. One woman I spoke with about the online harassment she endured said she was so stricken with anxiety that her partner had to deliver medication to her in bed. Another was undergoing exposure therapy, during which she had been instructed to practice doing something she enjoyed–while facing an open laptop. Another had changed her name after an ex posted her nude photos all over the Internet. A game developer whose personal information had been published online had to call her father and explain why people were calling him to tell him she was a whore. Others talked about turning down prank pizza orders or worrying about a SWAT team showing up at their homes on the basis of fake 911 calls. At the very least, the harassment was a burden on their time and energy.

from *Advice to Youth* (p. 437)

Mark Twain

Read and analyze the following passage from "Advice to Youth," using annotation to investigate how Twain uses language and style to convey his meaning effectively.

Never handle firearms carelessly. The sorrow and suffering that have been caused through the innocent but heedless handling of firearms by the young! Only four days ago, right in the next farm house to the one where I am spending the summer, a grandmother, old and gray and sweet, one of the loveliest spirits in the land, was sitting at her work, when her young grandson crept in and got down an old, battered, rusty gun which had not been touched for many years and was supposed not to be loaded, and pointed it at her, laughing and threatening to shoot. In her fright she ran screaming and pleading toward the door on the other side of the room; but as she passed him he placed the gun almost against her very breast and pulled the trigger! He had supposed it was not loaded. And he was right—it wasn't. So there wasn't any harm done. It is the only case of that kind I ever heard of. Therefore, just the same, don't you meddle with old unloaded firearms; they are the most deadly and unerring things that have ever been created by man. You don't have to take any pains at all with them; you don't have to have a rest, you don't have to have any sights on the gun, you don't have to take aim, even. No, you just pick out a relative and bang away, and you are sure to get him. A youth who can't hit a cathedral at thirty yards with a Gatling gun in three quarters of an hour, can take up an old empty musket and bag his grandmother every time, at a hundred.

from *Letter from Delano* (p. 399)

Cesar Chavez

Read and analyze the following passage from "Letter from Delano," using annotation to investigate how Chavez uses language and style to convey his meaning effectively.

As your industry has experienced, our strikers here in Delano and those who represent us throughout the world are well trained for this struggle. They have been under the gun, they have been kicked and beaten and herded by dogs, they have been cursed and ridiculed, they have been stripped and chained and jailed, they have been sprayed with the poisons used in the vineyards; but they have been taught not to lie down and die nor to flee in shame, but to resist with every ounce of human endurance and spirit. To resist not with retaliation in kind but to overcome with love and compassion, with ingenuity and creativity, with hard work and longer hours, with stamina and patient tenacity, with truth and public appeal, with friends and allies, with nobility and discipline, with politics and law, and with prayer and fasting. They were not trained in a month or even a year; after all, this new harvest season will mark our fourth full year of strike and even now we continue to plan and prepare for the years to come. Time accomplishes for the poor what money does for the rich.

This is not to pretend that we have everywhere been successful enough or that we have not made mistakes. And while we do not belittle or underestimate our adversaries – for they are the rich and the powerful and they possess the land – we are not afraid nor do we cringe from the confrontation. We welcome it! We have planned for it! We know that our cause is just, that history is a story of social revolution, and that the poor shall inherit the land.

from _Remembrances for 100th Anniversary of Statue of Liberty_ (p. 542)

Concord Oral History Program

Read and analyze the following passage from "Remembrances for 100th Anniversary of Statue of Liberty," using annotation to investigate how language and style are used to convey meaning effectively.

Frances Faieta,
Elsinore Street.

I passed the Statue of Liberty twice in my life and was able to appreciate the great lady the second time around. In 1913, at age 3, I arrived from Pianella, Italy, with my mother and grandfather to join my father and uncle who worked as gardeners on the Higginson estate in Lincoln.

When my mother became homesick to see relatives in Italy, she returned with her 4 children in 1921. I was 11 years old then and it was a rough ocean voyage back. Living - conditions were primitive compared to the U.S.

Lucky for us my father realized the immigration laws were becoming stricter and he got us out in 1924 before the new immigration law went into effect. Otherwise we could have been stuck there.

On the boat over when the Statue of Liberty came into view, there was great excitement. Everyone was screaming and hollering, "Viva la Amerika, Viva la libertad!"

from *The Statue of Liberty Was Born a Muslim* (p. 549)
Michael Daly

Read and analyze the following passage from "The Statue of Liberty Was Born a Muslim," using annotation to investigate how Daly uses language and style to convey his meaning effectively.

Christie took a very different position two months ago, after the public was shocked by photos showing 3-year-old Aylan Kurdi dead on a Turkish beach, having drowned while he and his family were attempting to escape the horrors of Syria.

"We can't have that," Christie the presidential candidate said then of the dead child, also saying, "I'd sit down with our allies and figure out how we can help, because America is a compassionate country."

Too many of us have joined Christie in allowing the photos of the carnage in Paris to make us forget those images of little Aylan.

Never mind that, at the very most, only one of the Paris attackers was a Syrian refugee. The rest are confirmed to have been either French or Belgian.

Never mind that by allowing ourselves to be terrorized we are responding exactly how the terrorists want us to respond.

Never mind that this sort of reaction was the terrorists' primary purpose in murdering all those innocents.

As always, their ultimate goal is to cause us to respond in ways that make us less than we really are.

In the moments after the planes hit the Twin Towers on 9/11, we responded with what was best in us.

But in our subsequent grief and anger we ended up becoming so unlike ourselves that we engaged in torture.

We lost so much faith in our criminal justice system that we were afraid to haul the mastermind into court like any other murderer.

In another sign of our fear, the Statue of Liberty was closed to visitors for three years. The crown was closed for another eight.

Name_____

Date_____Class_____

from *Stephen King's Guide to Movie Snacks* (p. 620)
Stephen King

Read and analyze the following passage from "Stephen King's Guide to Movie Snacks," using annotation to investigate how King uses language and style to convey his meaning effectively.

I always start my order with the ritual drink — Diet Pepsi if possible, Coke Zero as a fallback, Diet Coke the court of last resort. A big diet cola sops up the calories and cholesterol contained in movie snack food just like a big old sponge soaks up water. This is a proven fact. One expert (me) believes a medium diet cola drink can lower your cholesterol by 20 points and absorb as much as one thousand empty calories. And if you say that's total crap, I would just point out I don't call it a ritual drink for nothing. Sometimes I add a strawberry smoothie with lots of whipped cream, but I'm always sure to take enough sips of my ritual drink to absolve me of those calories, too.

Name_____

Date_____Class_____

from *Why Teenage Girls Roll Their Eyes* (p. 630)

Lisa Damour

Read and analyze the following passage from "Why Teenage Girls Roll Their Eyes," using annotation to investigate how Damour uses language and style to convey her meaning effectively.

Adolescents usually hate being told what to do, and will reflexively resist even suggestions with which they agree. Imagine a girl who is planning to put on her warmest coat when her well-meaning mother urges her to bundle up. If the teenager is developing normally, not a cell in her body is inclined to respond with a sincere, "Great idea, Mom! I was just thinking the same thing." (And her mom might be stunned, or at least wonder what her daughter was up to, if she did.) But the girl still wants to be warm. Enter the eye roll! One spin around the socket while donning the coat and the girl advertises her resistance while doing as she intended all along.

Given that the drive for autonomy is a central force during adolescence, taking orders can be especially annoying for teenagers. So how should a girl respond when her parents say she can't go out for the evening until she unloads the dishwasher? She may see no point in fighting back, but still feel compelled to broadcast her objection. Again, ophthalmic calisthenics offer a useful solution. By rolling her eyes while putting away the plates, the girl establishes that she's an independent state electing to yield, for now, to the regional power.

from *A Theory of Fun for Game Design* (p. 633)
Raph Koster

Read and analyze the following passage from "A Theory of Fun for Game Design," using annotation to investigate how Koster uses language and style to convey his meaning effectively.

We shouldn't underestimate the brain's desire to learn. If you put a person in a sensory deprivation chamber, he or she will get very unhappy very quickly. The brain craves stimuli. At all times, the brain is casting about trying to learn something, trying to integrate information into its worldview. It is insatiable in that way.

This doesn't mean it necessarily craves new experiences--mostly, it just craves new data. New data is all it needs to flesh out a pattern. A new experience might force a whole new system on the brain, and often the brain doesn't like that. It's disruptive. The brain doesn't like to do more work than it has to. That's why we have the term "sensory overload,"* as an opposite to "sensory deprivation."

Games grow boring when they fail to unfold new niceties in the puzzles they present. But they have to navigate between the Scylla and Charybdis* of deprivation and overload, of excessive order and excessive chaos, of silence and noise.

This means that it's easy for the player to get bored before the end of the game. After all, people are really good at pattern-matching and dismissing noise and silence that doesn't fit the pattern they have in mind.

from *Earth without People* (p. 640)

Alan Weisman

Read and analyze the following passage from "Earth without People," using annotation to investigate how Weisman uses language and style to convey his meaning effectively.

As lightning rods rusted away, roof fires would leap among buildings into paneled offices filled with paper. Meanwhile, native Virginia creeper and poison ivy would claw at walls covered with lichens, which thrive in the absence of air pollution. Wherever foundations failed and buildings tumbled, lime from crushed concrete would raise soil pH, inviting buckthorn and birch. Black locust and autumn olive trees would fix nitrogen, allowing more goldenrods, sunflowers, and white snakeroot to move in along with apple trees, their seeds expelled by proliferating birds. Sweet carrots would quickly devolve to their wild form, unpalatable Queen Anne's lace, while broccoli, cabbage, brussels sprouts, and cauliflower would regress to the same unrecognizable broccoli ancestor.

Unless an earthquake strikes New York first, bridges spared yearly applications of road salt would last a few hundred years before their stays and bolts gave way (last to fall would be Hell Gate Arch, built for railroads and easily good for another thousand years). Coyotes would invade Central Park, and deer, bears, and finally wolves would follow. Ruins would echo the love song of frogs breeding in streams stocked with alewives, herring, and mussels dropped by seagulls. Missing, however, would be all fauna that have adapted to humans. The invincible cockroach, an insect that originated in the hot climes of Africa, would succumb in unheated buildings. Without garbage, rats would starve or serve as lunch for peregrine falcons and red-tailed hawks. Pigeons would genetically revert back to the rock doves from which they sprang.

from *My Daughter's Homework Is Killing Me* (p. 649)
Karl Taro Greenfeld

Read and analyze the following passage from "My Daughter's Homework Is Killing Me," using annotation to investigate how Greenfeld uses language and style to convey his meaning effectively.

The algebra is fast becoming my favorite part of this project. I may have picked an easy week, but something about combining like terms, inverting negative exponents, and then simplifying equations causes a tingle in a part of my brain that is usually dormant. Also, the work is finite: just 12 equations.

The Spanish, however, presents a completely different challenge. Here, Esmee shows me that we have to memorize the conjugations of the future tense of regular and irregular verbs, and she slides me a sheet with *tener*, *tendré*, *tendrás*, *tendrá*, *tendremos*, etc., multiplied by dozens of verbs. My daughter has done a commendable job memorizing the conjugations. But when I ask her what the verb *tener* means ("to have," if I recall), she repeats, "Memorization, not rationalization."

She doesn't know what the words mean.

I spend a few minutes looking over the material, attempting to memorize the list of verbs and conjugations. Then it takes me about half an hour to memorize the three most common conjugation patterns. I decide to skip the irregular verbs.

Esmee already worked on her Spanish this afternoon, so she goes right to the Humanities project, which she has been looking forward to. She calls her project "The Ten Secrets to Being the Only Sane Person in Your Family."
No. 6: Don't Listen to Anything Your Father Says.

from *Quiet: The Power of Introverts in a World that Can't Stop Talking* (p. 661)
Susan Cain

Read and analyze the following passage from "Quiet: The Power of Introverts in a World that Can't Stop Talking," using annotation to investigate how Cain uses language and style to convey her meaning effectively.

This is partly because we are all gloriously complex individuals, but also because there are so many different *kinds* of introverts and extroverts. Introversion and extroversion interact with our other personality traits and personal histories, producing wildly different kinds of people. So if you're an artistic American guy whose father wished you'd try out for the football team like your rough-and-tumble brothers, you'll be a very different kind of introvert from, say, a Finnish businesswoman whose parents were lighthouse keepers. (Finland is a famously introverted nation. Finnish joke: How can you tell if a Finn likes you? He's staring at your shoes instead of his own.)

Many introverts are also "highly sensitive," which sounds poetic, but is actually a technical term in psychology. If you are a sensitive sort, then you're more apt than the average person to feel pleasantly overwhelmed by Beethoven's "Moonlight Sonata" or a well-turned phrase or an act of extraordinary kindness. You may be quicker than others to feel sickened by violence and ugliness, and you likely have a very strong conscience. When you were a child you were probably called "shy," and to this day feel nervous when you're being evaluated, for example when giving a speech or on a first date. Later we'll examine why this seemingly unrelated collection of attributes tends to belong to the same person and why this person is often introverted. (No one knows exactly how many introverts are highly sensitive, but we know that 70 percent of sensitives are introverts, and the other 30 percent tend to report needing a lot of "down time.")

from *What Is Your Life's Blueprint?* (p. 670)
Martin Luther King Jr.

Read and analyze the following passage from "What Is Your Life's Blueprint?" using annotation to investigate how King uses language and style to convey his meaning effectively.

And when you discover what you're going to be in life, set out to do it as if God Almighty called you at this particular moment in history to do it. And just don't set out to do a good Negro job but do a good job that anybody could do. Don't set out to be just a good Negro doctor, a good Negro lawyer, a good Negro schoolteacher, a good Negro preacher, a good Negro barber or beautician, a good Negro skilled laborer. For if you set out to do that, you have already flunked your matriculation exam for entrance into the University of Integration. Set out to do a good job, and do that job so well that the living, the dead, or the unborn couldn't do it any better.

If it falls to your lot to be a street sweeper, sweep streets like Michelangelo painted pictures. Sweep streets like Beethoven composed music. Sweep streets like Leontyne Price sings before the Metropolitan Opera. And sweep streets like Shakespeare wrote poetry. Sweep streets so well that all the hosts of Heaven and Earth will have to pause and say, "Here lived a great street sweeper who swept his job well."

If you can't be a pine on the top of the hill, be a scrub in the valley. But be the best little scrub on the side of the hill. Be a bush if you can't be a tree. If you can't be a highway, just be a trail. If you can't be the sun, be a star. For it isn't by size that you win or you fail. Be the best of whatever you are.

Name_____

Date_____Class_____

from *The Politics of the Hoodie* (p. 677)
Troy Patterson

Read and analyze the following passage from "The Politics of the Hoodie," using annotation to investigate how Patterson uses language and style to convey his meaning effectively.

Like their peers in the suburbs, bundled up on BMX bikes or skateboarding in sweatshirts with the logo of Thrasher magazine, a generation of hip-hop kids found the hoodie suitable for the important adolescent work of taking up space and dramatizing the self. There was and is a theater of the hood: pulling it up with a flourish, tugging it down to settle in its energetic slouch. The hood frames a dirty look, obscures acne and anxiety, masks headphones in study hall, makes a cone of solitude that will suffice for an autonomous realm. And if, in its anti-surveillance capacity, the hood plays with the visual rhetoric of menace, it is heir to a tradition in teen dressing stretching back to the birth of the teenager, when he arrived fully formed in leather jacket and bluejeans. The cover of the WuTang Clan's first album catches the mood: Members of the group wear black hoodies and white masks, as if to abduct the listener into a fantasy of ninja stealth.

But this was just a prologue to an era in which the hoodie became at once an anodyne[1] style object and a subject of moral panic, its popularity and its selective stigmatization rising in proportion. A glance at almost any police blotter, or a recollection of the forensic sketch of the Unabomber, will confirm the hoodie as a wardrobe staple of the criminal class, and this makes it uniquely convenient as a proxy for racial profiling or any other exercise of enmity. The person itching to confirm a general bias against hiphop kids or crusty punks imputes crooked character to the clothing itself.

from *Labels, Clothing and Identity: Are You What You Wear?* (p. 684)
Michelle Parrinello-Cason

Read and analyze the following passage from "Labels, Clothing and Identity: Are You What You Wear?" using annotation to investigate how Parrinello-Cason uses language and style to convey her meaning effectively.

Looking back, I think that these clothing decisions walked the line between personal communication choice and being branded by someone else. Yes, I chose those clothes. Oh, man, did I choose those clothes. I spent hours seeking out the perfect pair of jeans from a thrift store to make myself look like I'd never put any thought into what pants I was wearing. I carefully selected the right black t-shirt with the right nonsensical slogan from Hot Topic and paid for it with cash I'd carefully saved from tutoring and babysitting. (Side note: I walked past a Hot Topic a few weeks ago in a mall and felt older than I thought possible). Those clothes were mine. I picked them out to send a particular message, and I owned that message.

Or did I? That message only had meaning as a rebuttal. Wearing those clothes only made sense because there were other clothes I was "supposed" to be wearing. If it wasn't perfectly clear that those baggy jeans and too-big t-shirts were "unacceptable," then I wouldn't have been wearing them.

from *Women Who Wear Pants: Still Somehow Controversial* (p. 688)

Nora Caplan-Bricker

Read and analyze the following passage from "Women Who Wear Pants: Still Somehow Controversial," using annotation to investigate how Caplan-Bricker uses language and style to convey her meaning effectively.

[P]ants walked right back into the political realm in the latter half of the 20th century. First, Rep. Charlotte Reid, a Republican from Illinois, caused a stir when she became the first woman in Congress to wear them on the chamber floor in 1969. The *Washington Post* reported at the time that Reid's colleagues were "incredulous"; one congressman gushed, "I was told there was a lady here in trousers, so I had to come over and see for myself." Washington has never inhabited fashion's cutting edge. The *Post* continues:

> Mrs. Reid said later she didn't think she would wear them again. "I am really quite serious about my service in the Congress and I wouldn't want to do anything that seemed facetious." She continued, "Neither would I want to do anything to take away from the femininity of the women in the House, even though I think pants are feminine-looking."

The legislative branch returned to the issue of women in pants in 1972, when it passed Title IX, prohibiting universities that receive federal funding from discriminating on the basis of sex—including in gender-specific dress codes. Two decades later, female senators finally followed suit in ditching their skirts. Until 1993, a rule in the upper chamber barred women from wearing pants on the floor, but when a small cadre of Democrats, including Barbara Mikulski of Maryland, started wearing trousers in protest, female Senate staff joined them, and the prohibition was abolished.

from *In Fashion, Cultural Appropriation Is Either Very Wrong or Very Right* (p. 695)
Jenni Avins

Read and analyze the following passage from "In Fashion, Cultural Appropriation Is Either Very Wrong or Very Right," using annotation to investigate how Avins uses language and style to convey her meaning effectively.

There are legitimate reasons to step carefully when dressing ourselves with the clothing, arts, artifacts, or ideas of other cultures. But please, let's banish the idea that appropriating elements from one another's cultures is in itself problematic.

Such borrowing is how we got treasures such as New York pizza and Japanese denim—not to mention how the West got democratic discourse, mathematics, and the calendar. Yet as wave upon wave of shrill accusations of cultural appropriation make their way through the Internet outrage cycle, the rhetoric ranges from earnest indignation to patronizing disrespect.

And as we watch artists and celebrities being pilloried and called racist, it's hard not to fear the reach of the cultural-appropriation police, who jealously track who "owns" what and instantly jump on transgressors.

In the 21st century, cultural appropriation—like globalization—isn't just inevitable; it's potentially positive. We have to stop guarding cultures and subcultures in efforts to preserve them. It's naïve, paternalistic, and counterproductive. Plus, it's just not how culture or creativity work. The exchange of ideas, styles, and traditions is one of the tenets and joys of a modern, multicultural society.

So how do we move past the finger pointing, and co-exist in a way that's both creatively open and culturally sensitive? In a word, carefully.

from *From Converse to Kanye: The Rise of Sneaker Culture* (p. 699)
Hugh Hart

Read and analyze the following passage from "From Converse to Kanye: The Rise of Sneaker Culture," using annotation to investigate how Hart uses language and style to convey his meaning effectively.

The role of sneaker as a high-status commodity originated in Victorian England, when members of the newly emergent middle class showed off their wealth and embraced the then-novel concept of "Leisure" by parading around the beach in costly rubber shoes designed to repel wet sand.

After cycling through a succession of materials and technologies geared toward enabling users to jump higher (Reebok Pumps) and run faster (Nike's Foamposite), 21st-century shoe design has now expanded to market style over athletic prowess. "Men take their biggest sartorial chances at the footwear level," Semmelhack says. "They wear larger shapes, embroidery and brilliant color they wouldn't feel comfortable with in other parts of their dress, so I think men's fashion is actually changing from the feet up. If you're wearing gold Christian Louboutin sneakers with spikes, you didn't buy them to play street ball. You're playing a different game. You're playing the game of fashion."

Name_____

Date_____Class_____

from _The Battle over Dress Codes_ (p. 702)

Peggy Orenstein

Read and analyze the following passage from "The Battle over Dress Codes," using annotation to investigate how Orenstein uses language and style to convey her meaning effectively.

Even so, while women are not responsible for male misbehavior, and while no amount of dress (or undress) will avert catcalls, cultural change can be glacial, and I have a child trying to wend her way safely through our city streets right now. I don't want to her to feel shame in her soon-to-be-emerging woman's body, but I also don't want her to be a target. Has maternal concern made me prudent or simply a prude?

More than that, taking on the right to bare arms (and legs, and cleavage and midriffs) as a feminist rallying cry seems suspiciously Orwellian. Fashions catering to girls emphasize body consciousness at the youngest ages — Gap offers "skinny jeans" for toddlers, Target hawks bikinis for infants. Good luck finding anything but those itty-bitty shorts for your 12-year-old. So even as I object to the policing of girls' sexuality, I'm concerned about the incessant drumbeat of self-objectification: the pressure young women face to view their bodies as the objects of others' desires.

In its landmark 2007 report on the sexualization of girlhood, the American Psychological Association linked self-objectification to poor self-esteem, depression, body dissatisfaction and compromised cognitive function. Meanwhile, a study published last year in the journal Psychological Science titled "Objects Don't Object," found that when college women were asked to merely think about a time when they'd been objectified, they became subsequently less supportive of equal rights.

Yet, for today's girls, sexy appearance has been firmly conflated with strong womanhood, and at ever younger (not to mention ever older) ages. Hence the rise of mani-pedi "spa" birthday parties for preschoolers; the heated-up cheers and dance routines of elementary school-age girls; the weeklong "slumber party camp" that promises to teach 9-year-olds "all the tricks of beauty."

from *How One Stupid Tweet Blew Up Justine Sacco's Life* (p. 707)
Jon Ronson

Read and analyze the following passage from "How One Stupid Tweet Blew Up Justine Sacco's Life," using annotation to investigate how Ronson uses language and style to convey his meaning effectively.

The furor over Sacco's tweet had become not just an ideological crusade against her perceived bigotry but also a form of idle entertainment. Her complete ignorance of her predicament for those 11 hours lent the episode both dramatic irony and a pleasing narrative arc. As Sacco's flight traversed the length of Africa, a hashtag began to trend worldwide: #HasJustineLandedYet. "Seriously. I just want to go home to go to bed, but everyone at the bar is SO into #HasJustineLandedYet. Can't look away. Can't leave" and "Right, is there no one in Cape Town going to the airport to tweet her arrival? Come on, Twitter! I'd like pictures #HasJustineLandedYet."

A Twitter user did indeed go to the airport to tweet her arrival. He took her photograph and posted it online. "Yup," he wrote, "@JustineSacco HAS in fact landed at Cape Town International. She's decided to wear sunnies as a disguise."

By the time Sacco had touched down, tens of thousands of angry tweets had been sent in response to her joke. Hannah, meanwhile, frantically deleted her friend's tweet and her account — Sacco didn't want to look — but it was far too late. "Sorry @JustineSacco," wrote one Twitter user, "your tweet lives on forever."

from *Men Explain Things to Me* (p. 716)

Rebecca Solnit

Read and analyze the following passage from "Men Explain Things to Me," using annotation to investigate how Solnit uses language and style to convey her meaning effectively.

I tend to believe that women acquired the status of human beings when these kinds of acts started to be taken seriously, when the big things that stop us and kill us were addressed legally from the mid-1970s on; well after, that is, my birth. And for anyone about to argue that workplace sexual intimidation isn't a life or death issue, remember that Marine Lance Corporal Maria Lauterbach, age 20, was apparently killed by her higher-ranking colleague last winter while she was waiting to testify that he raped her. The burned remains of her pregnant body were found in the fire pit in his backyard in December.

Being told that, categorically, he knows what he's talking about and she doesn't, however minor a part of any given conversation, perpetuates the ugliness of this world and holds back its light. After my book *Wanderlust* came out in 2000, I found myself better able to resist being bullied out of my own perceptions and interpretations. On two occasions around that time, I objected to the behavior of a man, only to be told that the incidents hadn't happened at all as I said, that I was subjective, delusional, overwrought, dishonest–in a nutshell, female.

Most of my life, I would have doubted myself and backed down. Having public standing as a writer of history helped me stand my ground, but few women get that boost, and billions of women must be out there on this six-billion-person planet being told that they are not reliable witnesses to their own lives, that the truth is not their property, now or ever. This goes way beyond Men Explaining Things, but it's part of the same archipelago of arrogance.

from *On Chicken Tenders Me* (p. 721)
Helen Rosner

Read and analyze the following passage from "On Chicken Tenders," using annotation to investigate how Rosner uses language and style to convey her meaning effectively.

Even the other kids' menu stalwarts have more history to them than the chicken tender, a relatively new addition to the gastronomic landscape that only reached deep-fryer ubiquity in the 1990s. (This itself is a fascinatingly rare phenomenon: when was the last time something truly novel hit the culinary zeitgeist that didn't have a trademark appended to it?) It takes more than one generation to develop the intricate root system of nostalgia that anchors the ballpark pastoral of hot dogs or nachos, the picket-fence vignette of fried bologna sandwiches, or the dusty-road Americana of a burger and an ice-cold Coke. Chicken tenders have no history, they have no metatext, they have no *terroir*.

This deliciousness without backstory was liberating for me when I was reviewing restaurants. I don't do much of that kind of writing anymore—for the most part, my meals are my own again—but I still need the kind of relief chicken tenders provide. It's exhilarating to be part of the food world as it rockets from fringe interest to massive cultural force, but there are times when I want to step off the ride, to make a food choice that doesn't double as a performance of my identity.

Name_____

Date_____Class_____

from _Black Bodies in Motion and Pain_ (p. 726)

Edwidge Danticat

Read and analyze the following passage from "Black Bodies in Motion and Pain," using annotation to investigate how Danticat uses language and style to convey her meaning effectively.

At the end of a week when nine men and women were brutally assassinated by a racist young man in Charleston, South Carolina, and the possibility of two hundred thousand Haitians and Dominicans of Haitian descent being expelled from the Dominican Republic1 suddenly became very real, I longed to be in the presence of Lawrence's migrants and survivors. I was yearning for their witness and fellowship, to borrow language from some of the churches that ended up being lifelines for the Great Migration's new arrivals. But what kept me glued to these dark silhouettes is how beautifully and heartbreakingly Lawrence captured black bodies in motion, in transit, in danger, and in pain. The bowed heads of the hungry and the curved backs of mourners helped the Great Migration to gain and keep its momentum, along with the promise of less abject poverty in the North, better educational opportunities, and the right to vote.

Human beings have been migrating since the beginning of time. We have always travelled from place to place looking for better opportunities, where they exist. We are not always welcomed, especially if we are viewed as different and dangerous, or if we end up, as the novelist Toni Morrison described in her Nobel lecture, on the edges of towns that cannot bear our company. Will we ever have a home in this place, or will we always be set adrift from the home we knew? Or the home we have never known.

Name_____

Date_____Class_____

from *On the Decay of Friendship* (p. 730)
Samuel Johnson

Read and analyze the following passage from "On the Decay of Friendship," using annotation to investigate how Johnson uses language and style to convey his meaning effectively.

Friendship is often destroyed by opposition of interest, not only by the ponderous and visible interest which the desire of wealth and greatness forms and maintains, but by a thousand secret and slight competitions, scarcely known to the mind upon which they operate. There is scarcely any man without some favorite trifle which he values above greater attainments, some desire of petty praise which he cannot patiently suffer to be frustrated. This minute ambition is sometimes crossed before it is known, and sometimes defeated by wanton petulance; but such attacks are seldom made without the loss of friendship; for whoever has once found the vulnerable part will always be feared, and the resentment will burn on in secret, of which shame hinders the discovery.

This, however, is a slow malignity, which a wise man will obviate as inconsistent with quiet, and a good man will repress as contrary to virtue; but human happiness is sometimes violated by some more sudden strokes.

A dispute begun in jest upon a subject which a moment before was on both parts regarded with careless indifference, is continued by the desire of conquest, till vanity kindles into rage, and opposition rankles into enmity. Against this hasty mischief, I know not what security can be obtained; men will be sometimes surprised into quarrels; and though they might both haste into reconciliation, as soon as their tumult had subsided, yet two minds will seldom be found together, which can at once subdue their discontent, or immediately enjoy the sweets of peace without remembering the wounds of the conflict.

from *By Any Other Name* (p. 770)
Santha Rama Rau

Read and analyze the following passage from "By Any Other Name," using annotation to investigate how Rau uses language and style to convey her meaning effectively.

I was very sleepy after lunch, because at home we always took a siesta. It was usually a pleasant time of day, with the bedroom darkened against the harsh afternoon sun, the drifting off into sleep with the sound of Mother's voice reading a story in one's mind, and, finally, the shrill, fussy voice of the ayah waking one for tea.

At school, we rested for a short time on low, folding cots on the veranda, and then we were expected to play games. During the hot part of the afternoon we played indoors, and after the shadows had begun to lengthen and the slight breeze of the evening had come up we moved outside to the wide courtyard.

I had never really grasped the system of competitive games. At home, whenever we played tag or guessing games, I was always allowed to "win"- "because," Mother used to tell Premila, "she is the youngest, and we have to allow for that." I had often heard her say it, and it seemed quite reasonable to me, but the result was that I had no clear idea of what "winning" meant.

When we played twos-and-threes that afternoon at school, in accordance with my training, I let one of the small English boys catch me, but was naturally rather puzzled when the other children did not return the courtesy. I ran about for what seemed like hours without ever catching anyone, until it was time for school to close. Much later I learned that my attitude was called "not being a good sport," and I stopped allowing myself to be caught, but it was not for years that I really learned the spirit of the thing.

from *Is Everyone Hanging Out without Me?* (p. 776)
Mindy Kaling

Read and analyze the following passage from "Is Everyone Hanging Out without Me?" using annotation to investigate how Kaling uses language and style to convey her meaning effectively.

We both lived by a weird code: Mavis and I might be friends on Saturday afternoon, but Friday nights and weekend sleepovers were for JLMP. If it sounds weird and compartmentalized, that's because it was. But I was used to compartmentalization. My entire teenage life was a highly organized map of activities: twenty minutes to shower and get ready for school, five-minute breakfast, forty-five-minute Latin class to thirty- minute lunch to forty-five-minute jazz band rehearsal, etc. Compartmentalizing friendships did not feel different to me. Mavis and I would say "hi" in the hallways, and we would nod at each other. Occasionally we would sit next to each other in study hall. But Mavis did not fit into my life as my school friend.

Then things started to change.

One Saturday night, I had JLMP over my house. They wanted to watch *Sleeping with the Enemy,* you know, the movie where Julia Roberts fakes her own death to avoid being married to her psycho husband? And I wanted to watch *Monty Python's Flying Circus* and show them the Ministry of Silly Walks, one of their funniest and most famous sketches. Mavis and I had watched it earlier that day several times in a row, trying to imitate the walks ourselves. I played it for them. No one laughed. Lauren said: "I don't get it." I played it again. Still no response to it. I couldn't believe it. The very same sketch that had made Mavis and me clutch our chests in diaphragm-hurting laughter had rendered my best friends bored and silent. I made the classic mistake of trying to explain why it was so funny, as though a great explanation would be the key to eliciting a huge laugh from them. Eventually Polly said, gently, "I guess it's funny in a random kind of way."

Name_____

Date_____Class_____

from *Yes, Chef* (p. 783)
Marcus Samuelsson

Read and analyze the following passage from "Yes, Chef," using annotation to investigate how Samuelsson uses language and style to convey his meaning effectively.

I don't know my mother's face, but I sometimes think I remember the sound of her breath. I was two when a tuberculosis epidemic hit Ethiopia. My mother was sick, I was sick, and my sister Fantaye was doing only slightly better than the two of us. We were all coughing up blood and my mother had seen enough in her young life to measure the ravages of that disease. She knew she had to do something. She put me on her back. It was all coming at her now: the fatigue and the fever; pieces of her lung splintering and mixing with her throw-up; the calcifications on her bones, where the disease had already spread. She and Fantaye walked more than seventy-five miles, my mother carrying me the whole way, under a hot sun, from our village to the hospital in Addis Ababa to get help. I don't know how many days they walked, or how sick my mother was by the time she got there. But I do know that when we arrived, there were thousands of people standing in the street, sick and dying, awaiting care. I do not know how my mother managed to get us through those lines and into that hospital. I do know that she never left that hospital and that perhaps it was only by the miracle of that henna cross that Fantaye and I got out alive.

Name_____
Date_____Class_____

from *My Father's Previous Life* (p. 788)
Monique Truong

Read and analyze the following passage from "My Father's Previous Life," using annotation to investigate how Truong uses language and style to convey her meaning effectively.

The girl was named Marie-Laure, my father said. She was my half sister, seven years older than me. She was "half" in that she was born to his first wife, and "half" in that her mother was Swiss and our father was Vietnamese. Every element of his story was unimagined, unexpected, and verging on the mythical. As he spoke, I thought of a Greek myth about the goddess Athena that I'd just learned, and how she was born fully formed from the head of her father, Zeus. My own father's story ended there. He clearly wasn't pleased to be confronted with a past that he'd kept deep inside his desk.

The photo of Marie-Laure held within it a world of adult emotions and fractured lives, which I was too young to inhabit or see. I understood right away, though, that the girl in the photo no longer existed. She was 18 by then, wearing her hair differently, no longer fond of that bright shade of yellow, and probably unrecognizable. Was it possible to miss someone you'd never met? The answer was yes; from the start, I heard the word "sister" and muted the "half."

from *You, Me, and the Sea* (p. 791)

Steven Hall

Read and analyze the following passage from "You, Me, and the Sea," using annotation to investigate how Hall uses language and style to convey his meaning effectively.

I lift it up and take the few steps to the water's edge, shark held out in front of me, then I carefully lower it into the sea. I release my grip and pull my hand back fast.

The shark darts away amongst the submerged rock pools. In less than a second, it's gone. I turn away, walk back up the beach.

It feels like something has been achieved, something great, something ridiculous, something not quite part of the real world - all of these things at once.

It's not until I get right back to the top of the beach that I realize I've made a mistake. I turn to look back at the place where I released the shark, and see a familiar black shape flipping and flopping on the sand.

The tide hasn't gone out. It's still *going* out.

All I'd managed to do was put the shark into another shallow, draining rock pool, so it could beach itself all over again. To save the shark's life, I'd have needed to actually wade out into the sea with it, past the rock pools, and let it go there.

I've underestimated the task. I've achieved nothing.

I set off back down the beach.

from *Music Lessons* (p. 796)
Sarah Vowell

Read and analyze the following passage from "Music Lessons," using annotation to investigate how Vowell uses language and style to convey her meaning effectively.

Once a week, the best band kids played with the orchestra. I played the bass drum in orchestra, which meant that I never got to play. My participation ratio was something like seventy-five measures of rest per one big bass wallop. This gave me plenty of time to contemplate the class warfare of the situation. Here's what I figured out: Orchestra kids wear tuxedos. Band kids wear tuxedo T-shirts.

The orchestra kids, with their brown woolens and Teutonic last names, had the well-scrubbed, dark blond aura of a Hitler Youth brigade. These were the sons and daughters of humanities professors. They took German. They played soccer. Dumping the fluorescent T-shirts of the band kids into the orchestra each week must have looked like tossing a handful of Skittles into a box of Swiss chocolates.

But nothing brings kids together like hate. The one thing the band kids and the orchestra kids had in common was a unified disgust for the chorus kids, who were, to us, merely drama geeks with access to four-part harmony. A shy violin player wasn't likely to haunt the halls between classes playing *Eine Kleine Nachtmnsik* any more than a band kid would blare "Land of 1000 Dances" on his tuba more than three inches outside the band room door. But that didn't stop the choir girls from making everyone temporarily forget their locker combinations thanks to an impromptu, uncalled-for burst from *Brigadoon.*

Andy Heap: chorus.

from *Hunger Makes Me a Modern Girl* (p. 803)
Carrie Brownstein

Read and analyze the following passage from "Hunger Makes Me a Modern Girl," using annotation to investigate how Brownstein uses language and style to convey her meaning effectively.

The ways that oddity and detachment intersected in the family might best be summed up in the story of the family dog. Buffy, a forty-pound golden retriever mix we adopted from the pound when I was six and my sister was three, had been smothered with love in her youth. Buffy, for whom we took a pet first-aid class in order to learn how to be responsible owners, who was the muse for my grade-school poetry exercises ("Buffy is fluffy!"), our sidekick for picnics and outings, on the sidelines for soccer games, and the subject most featured in my first roll of film-posing on my baby blanket and wearing sunglasses-after I was given a camera for my birthday. Buffy, who followed us around the cul-de-sacs while we engaged in dirt clod fights with the neighbor kids, and trotted after us while we rode Big Wheels and eventually bikes. Buffy, who suffered the sting of the archaic idea that you could punish a dog by smacking it on the nose with a rolled-up newspaper and whose tail was run over by my mother as she backed the car out of the driveway. And Buffy, turned back into a stray in her own home on account of the rest of us surrendering to emptiness, drifting away from anything we could call familiar, her skin itching and inflamed, covered with sores and bites, like tattoos, like skywriting, screaming with redness, as if to say *Please, please pet me!* But we didn't. When we decided to put her down, not because she was sick but because she was old and neglected—a remnant of a family we no longer recognized—my father asked my sister to do it. My sister was sixteen. She drove the dog to the vet one day after school by herself. No one else said good-bye.

from *La Gringuita* (p. 811)

Julia Alvarez

Read and analyze the following passage from "La Gringuita," using annotation to investigate how Alvarez uses language and style to convey her meaning effectively.

Like me, Dilita was a hybrid. Her parents had moved to Puerto Rico when she was three, and she had lived for some time with a relative in New York. But her revolutionary zeal had taken the turn of glamour girl rather than my New-England-hippy variety. In fact, Dilita looked just like the other Dominican girls. She had a teased hairdo; I let my long hair hang loose in a style I can only describe as "blowing in the wind." Dilita wore makeup; I did a little lipstick and maybe eyeliner if she would put it on for me. She wore outfits; I had peasant blouses, T-shirts, and blue jeans.

But in one key way, Dilita was more of a rebel than I was: she did exactly what she wanted without guilt or apology. She was in charge of her own destino, as she liked to say, and no one was going to talk her into giving that up. I was in awe of Dilita. She was the first "hyphenated" person I had ever met whom I considered successful, not tortured as a hybrid the way my sisters and I were.

Dilita managed to talk Utcho into letting me move into town with her and her young, married aunt, Carmen. Mamacán, as we called her, was liberal and light-hearted and gave us free rein to do what we wanted. "Just as long as you girls don't get in trouble!" Trouble came in one denomination, we knew, and neither of us were fools. When the matrons in town complained about our miniskirts or about our driving around with boys and no chaperons, Mamacán threw up her hands and said, "¡Pero si son americanas!" They're American girls!

Name_____
Date_____Class_____

from *Coming into Language* (p. 820)
Jimmy Santiago Baca

Read and analyze the following passage from "Coming into Language," using annotation to investigate how Baca uses language and style to convey his meaning effectively.

Through language I was free. I could respond, escape, indulge; embrace or reject earth or the cosmos. I was launched on an endless journey without boundaries or rules, in which I could salvage the floating fragments of my past, or be born anew in the spontaneous ignition of understanding some heretofore concealed aspect of myself. Each word steamed with the hot lava juices of my primordial making, and I crawled out of stanzas dripping with birth-blood, reborn and freed from the chaos of my life. The child in the dark room of my heart, who had never been able to find or reach the light switch, flicked it on now; and I found in the room a stranger, myself, who had waited so many years to speak again. My words struck in me lightning crackles of elation and thunderhead storms of grief.[...]

I withdrew even deeper into the world of language, cleaving the diamonds of verbs and nouns, plunging into the brilliant light of poetry's regenerative mystery. Words gave off rings of white energy, radar signals from powers beyond me that infused me with truth. I believed what I wrote, because I wrote what was true. My words did not come from books or textual formulas, but from a deep faith in the voice of my heart.

I had been steeped in self-loathing and rejected by everyone and everything-society, family, cons, God and demons. But now I had become as the burning ember floating in darkness that descends on a dry leaf and sets flame to forests. The word was the ember and the forest was my life...

from *Black Boy* (p. 823)
Richard Wright

Read and analyze the following passage from "Black Boy," using annotation to investigate how Wright uses language and style to convey his meaning effectively.

I ran across many words whose meanings I did not know, and I either looked them up in a dictionary or, before I had a chance to do that, encountered the word in a context that made its meaning clear. But what strange world was this? I concluded the book with the conviction that I had somehow overlooked something terribly important in life. I had once tried to write, had once reveled in feeling, had let my crude imagination roam, but the impulse to dream had been slowly beaten out of me by experience. Now it surged up again and I hungered for books, new ways of looking and seeing. It was not a matter of believing or disbelieving what I read, but of feeling something new, of being affected by something that made the look of the world different.

As dawn broke I ate my pork and beans, feeling dopey, sleepy. I went to work, but the mood of the book would not die; it lingered, coloring everything I saw, heard, did. I now felt that I knew what the white men were feeling. Merely because I had read a book that had spoken of how they lived and thought, I identified myself with that book. I felt vaguely guilty. Would I, filled with bookish notions, act in a manner that would make the whites dislike me?

from *Confessions of a Code Switcher* (p. 826)

Joshua Adams

Read and analyze the following passage from "Confessions of a Code Switcher," using annotation to investigate how Adams uses language and style to convey his meaning effectively.

From grade school to grad school, I've been both the accuser and the accused in the "talking white" witch trials. When I've said another Black person talks white, I never once meant to imply that I was equating being articulate to "whiteness" (or isolating it from blackness), though that is the conclusion most people reach. For me, it was an observation that they spoke in patterns more aligned with the ways I hear white people communicate (intonation, inflection, dialectics, phrases, hard consonants, types of slang, full pronunciations, etc.). I was policing them with the admittedly problematic assumption that, unlike me, they *weren't* code-switching. It was a subconscious "Wait.....why are you talking like that? There's no white people around."

It was also an ignorant assumption about engaging in Black cultural solidarity. This may be semantics, but I didn't assume all Black people talk the same, I just assumed all Black people don't talk like White people. Many of the patterns of the "bhaccent" ('talking black') stems from slavery. Newly captive Africans who were forced to learn English combined the foreign language with African speech patterns. Therefore on conscious and subconscious levels, I equated their lack of "blaccent" as assimilation (another problematic term) into "blanccent". I mistook their "why can't I be a Black person who talks educated?" as re-propagating the idea that talking "black" means talking dumb, not rebelling against it (since the antithesis is usually a condemnation of someone who talks "ghetto"). I couldn't understand if they sincerely rejected the equating intelligence to whiteness or if they used the way "uneducated" (Black) people talk as a stepping stone for their Exceptional Negroedom.

from *They're, Like, Way Ahead of the Linguistic Currrrve* (p. 830) Douglas Quenqua

Read and analyze the following passage from "They're, Like, Way Ahead of the Linguistic Currrrve," using annotation to investigate how Quenqua uses language and style to convey his meaning effectively.

A classic example of vocal fry, best described as a raspy or croaking sound injected (usually) at the end of a sentence, can be heard when Mae West says, "Why don't you come up sometime and see me," or, more recently on television, when Maya Rudolph mimics Maya Angelou on "Saturday Night Live."

Not surprisingly, gadflies in cyberspace were quick to pounce on the study — or, more specifically, on the girls and women who are frying their words. "Are they trying to sound like Kesha or Britney Spears?" teased The Huffington Post[2], naming two pop stars who employ vocal fry while singing, although the study made no mention of them. "Very interesteeeaaaaaaaaang," said Gawker.com[3], mocking the lazy, drawn-out affect.

Do not scoff, says Nassima Abdelli-Beruh, a speech scientist at Long Island University and an author of the study. "They use this as a tool to convey something," she said. "You quickly realize that for them, it is as a cue."

Other linguists not involved in the research also cautioned against forming negative judgments. "If women do something like uptalk or vocal fry, it's immediately interpreted as insecure, emotional or even stupid," said Carmen Fought, a professor of linguistics at Pitzer College in Claremont, Calif. "The truth is this: Young women take linguistic features and use them as power tools for building relationships."

from *The Seven Words I Cannot Say (Around My Children)* **(p. 833)**

Jessica Wolf

Read and analyze the following passage from "The Seven Words I Cannot Say (Around My Children)," using annotation to investigate how Wolf uses language and style to convey her meaning effectively.

A quick trip to Urban Dictionary provides several meanings for "Stife." My younger son and his friends employ its third definition: "Used to mean stingy in the very negative sense." I've done my due diligence, and in my view, that's my initiation fee. But to my boys, I'm barging up the ladder to the tree house, blatantly ignoring the sign that says Keep Out.

When my older son and his friends are together, listening to them talk is like trying to decipher the clicking of the Bantu. It's all delivered so fast – recognizable words cavorting with the unfamiliar – and there's not even a moment to ground myself in context clues. I think of it as a unique dialect, perhaps specific to our town – possibly even to our high school. I take in conversations as if they were pieces of music, having no real idea if they're complaining about finals or making plans to gather somewhere on a Saturday night. But their dialogue feels alive, and I love it.

from *The Art of Asking* (p. 837)

Amanda Palmer

Read and analyze the following passage from "The Art of Asking," using annotation to investigate how Palmer uses language and style to convey her meaning effectively.

In that moment, something seismic shifted. I'd been viewing my role on the street as a performance artist who would share the gift of her weird, arty impulses with the amenable public. I'd grown up an experimental theater kid, writing, directing, and acting in my own surreal and morbid plays on school stages. I wasn't an entertainer – I was making *art,* dammit. And though I wasn't afraid to disturb people, I never wanted to *hurt* them.

This interaction made me realize that working in The Street wasn't like working in the theater. The Street is different: nobody's buying a ticket, nobody's choosing to be there. On the street, artists succeed or fail by virtue of their raw ability to create a show in unexpected circumstances, to thoroughly entertain an audience that did not expect to be one, and to make random people *care* for a few minutes. The passersby are trusting you to give them something valuable in exchange for *their* time and attention, and (possibly) their dollars. Something skilled, unexpected, delightful, impressive, something moving. With few exceptions, they're not giving you a dollar to confront and disturb them.

That dad and his little girl didn't want *theater.*

They didn't want to be provoked.

They wanted to be entertained.

But they also wanted something more. They wanted *connection.*

It dawned on me, standing there in my white face paint and tutu, that I was effectively working in a service position: A strange combination of court jester, cocktail hostess, and minister. A strange, coin-operated jukebox of basic, kind, human encounters.

from *What I Talk about When I Talk about Running* (p. 872)

Haruki Marakami

Read and analyze the following passage from "What I Talk about When I Talk about Running," using annotation to investigate how Marakami uses language and style to convey his meaning effectively.

The river I'm talking about is the Charles River. People enjoy being around the river. Some take leisurely walks, walk their dogs, or bicycle or jog, while others enjoy rollerblading. (How such a dangerous pastime can be enjoyable, I frankly can't fathom.) As if pulled in by a magnet, people gather on the banks of the river.

Seeing a lot of water like that every day is probably an important thing for human beings. For human beings might be a bit of a generalization-but I do know it's important for one person: me. If I go for a time without seeing water, I feel like something's slowly draining out of me. It's probably like the feeling a music lover has when, for whatever reason, he's separated from music for a long time. The fact that I was raised near the sea might have something to do with it.

The surface of the water changes from day to day: the color, the shape of the waves, the speed of the current. Each season brings distinct changes to the plants and animals that surround the river. Clouds of all sizes show up and move on, and the surface of the river, lit by the sun, reflects these white shapes as they come and go, sometimes faithfully, sometimes distortedly. Whenever the seasons change, the direction of the wind fluctuates like someone threw a switch. And runners can detect each notch in the seasonal shift in the feel of the wind against our skin, its smell and direction. In the midst of this flow, I'm aware of myself as one tiny piece in the gigantic mosaic of nature. I'm just a replaceable natural phenomenon, like the water in the river that flows under the bridge toward the sea.

from *Boxcar—El Vagon* (p. 918)
Silvia Gonzalez S.

Read and analyze the following passage from "Boxcar—El Vagon," using annotation to investigate how Gonzalez S. uses language and style to convey her meaning effectively.

FRANCISCO We should confess our sins.

MANUEL The door will open. Trust me.

NOEL When?

FRANCISCO *Pesan. Pesan.* I like picking oranges the best. They smell so pretty.

Hermano, vamos a piscar narranjas. It's a very peaceful thing to do. I look at the strong branches. The leaves are bright green. The oranges are like candy holding on to very small stems. The orange tree is one of God's perfect trees.

MANUEL *Tranquilo, Francisco, tranquilo.*

FRANCISCO *Si. Tranguilo.*

[Francisco goes to his box and gets his rosary. He lies down and becomes still. Silence for a moment.]

MANUEL Noel.

[*He points to the hole.*]

NOEL It's your turn.

MANUEL It's for you.

NOEL No.

MANUEL *Andale.*

[Noel breathes through the hole.]

MANUEL [*cont'd*] In your anthropological studies, did they tell you about the migration of Mexico? If you studied cultures of the world, you may already know this for us *Mexicanos.* Well, actually this is the story of my wife's ancestors. My ancestry has Spanish, maybe some Italian and maybe even some German. Maybe that's why I'm so interested in anthropology. Always wanting to know how I came to be.

Dicen que her tribe needed to travel until they saw a sign. On their last journey, they spotted an eagle on a cactus devouring a serpent. That was it. That was the sign. That is where they placed their empire. And later *Españoles* came, and all the rest. Noel, we are all related in some way. It's true. It's what I believe. You're *mi hermano*.

[*Manuel takes the small knife and carves on the floor:*]

MANUEL [*cont'd*]

[*Slowly*] *Todos somos parientes.*

[*He looks at Noel*]

Es la verdad. Todos somos parientes.

from *The Tragedy of Romeo and Juliet* (p. 931)
William Shakespeare

Read and analyze the following passage from Act 1 of "The Tragedy of Romeo and Juliet," using annotation to investigate how Shakespeare uses language and style to convey his meaning effectively.

SAMSON Gregory, on my word, we'll not carry coals.

GREGORY No, for then we should be colliers.

SAMSON I mean, an we be in choler, we'll draw.

GREGORY Ay, while you live, draw your neck out of collar.

SAMSON I strike quickly, being moved.

GREGORY But thou art not quickly moved to strike.

SAMSON A dog of the house of Montague moves me.

GREGORY To move is to stir, and to be valiant is to stand. Therefore, if thou art moved, thou runn'st away.

SAMSON A dog of that house shall move me to stand. I will take the wall of any man or maid of Montagues.

GREGORY That shows thee a weak slave, for the weakest goes to the wall.

SAMSON 'Tis true, and therefore women, being the weaker vessels, are ever thrust to the wall. Therefore I will push Montague's men from the wall and thrust his maids to the wall.

GREGORY The quarrel is between our masters and us their men.

SAMSON 'Tis all one. I will show myself a tyrant: when I have fought with the men, I will be civil with the maids — I will cut off their heads.

GREGORY The heads of the maids?

SAMSON Ay, the heads of the maids, or their maiden heads. Take it in what sense thou wilt.

GREGORY They must take it in sense that feel it.

SAMSON Me they shall feel while I am able to stand, and 'tis known I am a pretty piece of flesh.

GREGORY 'Tis well thou art not fish; if thou hadst, thou hadst been Poor John. Draw thy tool. Here comes of the house of Montagues.

from *The Tragedy of Romeo and Juliet* (p. 931)
William Shakespeare

Read and analyze the following passage from Act 2 of "The Tragedy of Romeo and Juliet," using annotation to investigate how Shakespeare uses language and style to convey his meaning effectively.

MERCUTIO Where the devil should this Romeo be?

Came he not home tonight?

BENVOLIO Not to his father's. I spoke with his man.

MERCUTIO Why, that same pale hardhearted

wench, that Rosaline,

Torments him so that he will sure run mad.

BENVOLIO Tybalt, the kinsman to old Capulet,

Hath sent a letter to his father's house.

MERCUTIO A challenge, on my life.

BENVOLIO Romeo will answer it.

MERCUTIO Any man that can write may answer

a letter.

BENVOLIO Nay, he will answer the letter's master,

how he dares, being dared.

MERCUTIO Alas poor Romeo! He is already dead,

stabbed with a white wench's black eye, run

through the ear with a love song, the very pin

of his heart cleft with the blind bow-boy's

butt shaft. And is he a man to encounter

Tybalt?

BENVOLIO Why, what is Tybalt?

MERCUTIO More than prince of cats. O, he's

the courageous captain of compliments. He

fights as you sing prick song, keeps time,

distance, and proportion; he rests his minim

rests, one, two, and the third in your bosom.
The very butcher of a silk button, a duellist, a
duellist, a gentleman of the very first house, of
the first and second cause. Ah, the immortal
passado! The *punto reverso*! The *hay*!

BENVOLIO The what?

MERCUTIO The pox of such antic, lisping,
affecting phantasimes, these new tuners of
accent! "By Jesu, a very good blade! A new
tall man! A very good whore!" Why, is not this
a lamentable thing, grandsire, that we should
be thus afflicted with these strange flies, these
fashion-mongers, these pardon-me's, who
stand so much on the new form that they
cannot sit at ease on the old bench? O, their
bones, their bones!

from *The Tragedy of Romeo and Juliet*
(p. 931) William Shakespeare

Read and analyze the following passage from Act 3 of "The Tragedy of Romeo and Juliet," using annotation to investigate how Shakespeare uses language and style to convey his meaning effectively.

JULIET O serpent heart, hid with a flowering face!

Did ever dragon keep so fair a cave? Beautiful tyrant! Fiend angelical!

Dove-feathered raven! Wolvish-ravening lamb!

Despisèd substance of divinest show!

Just opposite to what thou justly seem'st,

A damnèd saint, an honorable villain!

O nature, what hadst thou to do in hell

When thou didst bower the spirit of a fiend

In mortal paradise of such sweet flesh?

Was ever book containing such vile matter

So fairly bound? O, that deceit should dwell

In such a gorgeous palace!

NURSE There's no trust,

No faith, no honesty in men; all perjured,

All forsworn, all naught, all dissemblers.

Ah, where's my man? Give me some aqua vitae.

These griefs, these woes, these sorrows make me old.

Shame come to Romeo!

JULIET Blistered be thy tongue

For such a wish! He was not born to shame.

Upon his brow shame is ashamed to sit;

For 'tis a throne where honor may be crowned

Sole monarch of the universal earth.

O, what a beast was I to chide at him!

NURSE Will you speak well of him that killed your cousin?

JULIET Shall I speak ill of him that is my husband?

       Ah, poor my lord, what tongue shall smooth thy name

       When I, thy three-hours wife, have mangled it?

       But wherefore, villain, didst thou kill my cousin?

       That villain cousin would have killed my husband.

       Back, foolish tears, back to your native spring!

       Your tributary drops belong to woe,

       Which you, mistaking, offer up to joy.

       My husband lives, that Tybalt would have slain,

       And Tybalt's dead, that would have slain my husband.

       All this is comfort. Wherefore weep I then?

       Some word there was, worser than Tybalt's death,

       That murdered me. I would forget it fain,

       But O, it presses to my memory

       Like damnèd guilty deeds to sinners' minds:

       "Tybalt is dead, and Romeo — banishèd."

       That "banishèd," that one word "banishèd,"

       Hath slain ten thousand Tybalts.

from *The Tragedy of Romeo and Juliet* (p. 931)

William Shakespeare

Read and analyze the following passage from Act 4 of "The Tragedy of Romeo and Juliet," using annotation to investigate how Shakespeare uses language and style to convey his meaning effectively.

JULIET O, bid me leap, rather than marry Paris,

    From off the battlements of any tower,

    Or walk in thievish ways, or bid me lurk

    Where serpents are; chain me with roaring bears,

    Or hide me nightly in a charnel house,

    O'ercovered quite with dead men's rattling bones,

    With reeky shanks and yellow chopless skulls;

    Or bid me go into a new-made grave

    And hide me with a dead man in his tomb —

    Things that, to hear them told, have made me tremble —

    And I will do it without fear or doubt,

    To live an unstained wife to my sweet love.

FRIAR LAURENCE Hold, then. Go home, be merry, give consent

    To marry Paris. Wednesday is tomorrow.

    Tomorrow night look that thou lie alone;

    Let not the Nurse lie with thee in thy chamber.

    Take thou this vial, being then in bed,

    [*Showing her a vial*]

    And this distilling liquor drink thou off,

    When presently through all thy veins shall run

    A cold and drowsy humor; for no pulse

    Shall keep his native progress, but surcease;

    No warmth, no breath shall testify thou livest;

    The roses in thy lips and cheeks shall fade

    To wanny ashes, thy eyes' windows fall

Like death when he shuts up the day of life;

Each part, deprived of supple government,

Shall, stiff and stark and cold, appear like death.

And in this borrowed likeness of shrunk death

Thou shalt continue two-and-forty hours,

And then awake as from a pleasant sleep.

from *The Tragedy of Romeo and Juliet* **(p. 931)**
William Shakespeare

Read and analyze the following passage from Act 5 of "The Tragedy of Romeo and Juliet," using annotation to investigate how Shakespeare uses language and style to convey his meaning effectively.

ROMEO [...] O, give me thy hand,

One writ with me in sour misfortune's book.

I'll bury thee in a triumphant grave.

[He opens the tomb.]

A grave? O, no! A lantern, slaughtered youth,

For here lies Juliet, and her beauty makes

This vault a feasting presence full of light.

Death, lie thou there, by a dead man interred.

[He lays Paris in the tomb.]

How oft when men are at the point of death

Have they been merry, which their keepers call

A lightening before death! O, how may I

Call this a lightening? O my love, my wife!

Death, that hath sucked the honey of thy breath,

Hath had no power yet upon thy beauty.

Thou art not conquered; beauty's ensign yet

Is crimson in thy lips and in thy cheeks,

And death's pale flag is not advancèd there.

Tybalt, liest thou there in thy bloody sheet?

O, what more favor can I do to thee

Than with that hand that cut thy youth in twain

To sunder his that was thine enemy?

Forgive me, cousin! Ah, dear Juliet,

Why art thou yet so fair? Shall I believe

That unsubstantial Death is amorous,

And that the lean abhorrèd monster keeps

Thee here in dark to be his paramour?

For fear of that I still will stay with thee

And never from this palace of dim night

Depart again. Here, here will I remain

With worms that are thy chambermaids. O, here

Will I set up my everlasting rest

And shake the yoke of inauspicious stars

From this world-wearied flesh. Eyes, look your last!

Arms, take your last embrace! And, lips, O you

The doors of breath, seal with a righteous kiss

A dateless bargain to engrossing death!

[He kisses Juliet.]

Come, bitter conduct, come, unsavory guide,

Thou desperate pilot, now at once run on

The dashing rocks thy seasick weary bark!

Here's to my love. *[He drinks.]* O true apothecary!

Thy drugs are quick. Thus with a kiss I die.

[He dies.]

from *The Social Conquest of Earth* (p. 1012)
E. O. Wilson

Read and analyze the following passage from "The Social Conquest of Earth," using annotation to investigate how Wilson uses language and style to convey his meaning effectively.

If groupist behavior is truly an instinct expressed by inherited prepared learning, we might expect to find signs of it even in very young children. And exactly this phenomenon has been discovered by cognitive psychologists. Newborn infants are most sensitive to the first sounds they hear, to their mother's face, and to the sounds of their native language. Later they look preferentially at persons who previously spoke their native language within their hearing. Preschool children tend to select native-language speakers as friends. The preferences begin before the comprehension of the meaning of speech and are displayed even when speech with different accents is fully comprehended.

The elementary drive to form and take deep pleasure from ingroup membership easily translates at a higher level into tribalism. People are prone to ethnocentrism. It is an uncomfortable fact that even when given a guilt-free choice, individuals prefer the company of others of the same race, nation, clan, and religion. They trust them more, relax with them better in business and social events, and prefer them more often than not as marriage partners. They are quicker to anger at evidence that an out-group is behaving unfairly or receiving undeserved rewards. And they grow hostile to any out-group encroaching upon the territory or resources of their in-group. Literature and history are strewn with accounts of what happens at the extreme [...].

from *Why We're Patriotic* (p. 1016)

Adam Piore

Read and analyze the following passage from "Why We're Patriotic," using annotation to investigate how Piore uses language and style to convey his meaning effectively.

Patriotism is an innate human sentiment. It is part of a deeper subconscious drive toward group formation and allegiance. It operates as much in one nation under God as it does in a football stadium. Group bonding is in our evolutionary history, our nature. According to some recent studies, the factors that make us patriotic are in our very genes.

But this allegiance—this blurring of the lines between individual and group—has a closely related flipside; it's not always a warm feeling of connection in the Cleveland-bound lounge car. Sometimes our instinct for group identification serves as a powerful wedge to single out those among us who are different. Sometimes what makes us feel connected is not a love of home and country but a common enemy.

That's why politicians so often invoke patriotism to demonize the other side, subtly implying that those who aren't with us, are against us. It's a partisan strategy, as predictable every election year as campaign buttons and patriotic bunting. When we identify as "Americans," or citizens of any country, there's something about a perceived threat, or slight to our nation, that works just as powerfully as a beautiful song to turn what might seem an intellectual idea into something emotional, raw, and subconscious. The instincts that drive patriotism, scientists explain, can express humanity's best side, and its worst.

from *People Like Us* (p. 1020)
David Brooks

Read and analyze the following passage from "People Like Us," using annotation to investigate how Brooks uses language and style to convey his meaning effectively.

It is a common complaint that every place is starting to look the same. But in the information age, the late writer James Chapin once told me, every place becomes more like itself. People are less often tied down to factories and mills, and they can search for places to live on the basis of cultural affinity. Once they find a town in which people share their values, they flock there, and reinforce whatever was distinctive about the town in the first place. Once Boulder, Colorado, became known as congenial to politically progressive mountain bikers, half the politically progressive mountain bikers in the country (it seems) moved there; they made the place so culturally pure that it has become practically a parody of itself.

But people love it. Make no mistake—we are increasing our happiness by segmenting off so rigorously. We are finding places where we are comfortable and where we feel we can flourish. But the choices we make toward that end lead to the very opposite of diversity.

The United States might be a diverse nation when considered as a whole, but block by block and institution by institution it is a relatively homogeneous nation.

Name_____

Date_____Class_____

from *Why Are All the Black Kids Sitting Together in the Cafeteria?* (p. 1024)
Beverly Daniel Tatum

Read and analyze the following passage from "Why Are All the Black Kids Sitting Together in the Cafeteria?" using annotation to investigate how Tatum uses language and style to convey her meaning effectively.

Why do Black youths, in particular, think about themselves in terms of race? Because that is how the rest of the world thinks of them. Our self-perceptions are shaped by the messages that we receive from those around us, and when young Black men and women enter adolescence, the racial content of those messages intensifies. A case in point: If you were to ask my ten-year-old son, David, to describe himself, he would tell you many things: that he is smart, that he likes to play computer games, that he has an older brother. Near the top of his list, he would likely mention that he is tall for his age. He would probably not mention that he is Black, though he certainly knows that he is. Why would he mention his height and not his racial group membership? When David meets new adults, one of the first questions they ask is "How old are you?" When David states his age, the inevitable reply is "Gee, you're tall for your age!" It happens so frequently that I once overheard David say to someone, "Don't say it, I know. I'm tall for my age." Height is salient for David because it is salient for others.

When David meets new adults, they don't say, "Gee, you're Black for your age!" If you are saying to yourself, of course they don't, think again. Imagine David at fifteen, six-foot-two, wearing the adolescent attire of the day, passing adults he doesn't know on the sidewalk. Do the women hold their purses a little tighter, maybe even cross the street to avoid him? Does he hear the sound of the automatic door locks on cars as he passes by? Is he being followed around by the security guards at the local mall? As he stops in town with his new bicycle, does a police officer hassle him, asking where he got it, implying that it might be stolen? Do strangers assume he plays basketball? Each of these experiences conveys a racial message. At ten, race is not yet salient for David, because it is not yet salient for society. But it will be.

from *Bringing Home the Wrong Race* (p. 1028)
Diane Farr

Read and analyze the following passage from "Bringing Home the Wrong Race," using annotation to investigate how Farr uses language and style to convey her meaning effectively.

What shocked me was less my peers' admissions of their parents' restrictions than their willingness to abide by them. Over the years, my mother and I had many heated discussions about her boundaries for love.

My parents only started seeing my perspective around the time I brought home my first black boyfriend, whom they liked despite themselves. Years later, when I became engaged to a Puerto Rican man, their prejudices had evaporated — so much so, in fact, that when our union did not last, my parents did not utter one ill word about his heritage or culture.

But these stories from my peers were different. They described boundaries set by parents who were mostly educated, progressive and democratic. Parents who taught their children that all people should be given the same opportunities in education, real estate, business and friendship, but who later, around the time their children hit puberty, started amending and tarnishing those values with an exception that went something along the lines of: "But you can't love one of them."

from *Sports, Politics, Tribe, Violence, and the Social Human Animal's Drive to Survive* (p. 1031)

David Ropeik

Read and analyze the following passage from "Sports, Politics, Tribe, Violence, and the Social Human Animal's Drive to Survive," using annotation to investigate how Ropeik uses language and style to convey his meaning effectively.

Sports are only less violent surrogates of precisely the same human need, to belong to a tribe that's doing well because as the tribe's chances go, so go yours. Think about the trappings of sports; the teams are your surrogate tribal warriors, wearing tribal uniforms, the battle grounds (stadia) decorated with tribal flags (banners) and tribal emblems (often fierce animals or warrior figures), the fans painting their faces in tribal/team colors and wearing tribal/team clothing, chanting tribal chants (team songs), fighting long- standing (tribal) rivalries. The warriors (your team) fight to defend YOUR territory (HOME field), and you root and cheer and do all sorts of superstitious stuff that you think will affect the outcome on a playing field you in fact have ZERO influence over, and your emotions and actual body chemistry go up, or down, depending on the outcomes.

And if everything goes as hoped, the season ends with a championship capped by huge civic rallies in which everyone chants and screams "WE won!" No. The *athletes* won. You *watched*. But it feels like YOU won, because you need to feel like your tribe is successful and dominant, because that literally makes you feel safer. And if your *team* lost you go out and trash the city like fans in Vancouver after the Stanley Cup loss last year, or countless other fans in countless other 'defeated' cities. Or, worse, you violently attack fans of the other team...the other tribe. It really is way more than just a game.

from *A Roz by Any Other Name* (p. 1036)
B. T. Ryback

Read and analyze the following passage from "A Roz by Any Other Name," using annotation to investigate how Ryback uses language and style to convey his meaning effectively.

STEFANO I have followed your graces from the masquerade, where I first laid eyes
     on such beauty.

ROSALIND [*To* VERA] Followed our graces? Chased our skirts is more likely.

STEFANO Your companion was in such an upset state, that it didn't seem
     appropriate to approach you at the time. When I saw you run into the house,
     I thought for sure I had lost you, until the light from yonder window broke
     upon the dew-kissed grass, betraying your secret counsel, leading me to the
     fair maiden of the house!

ROSALIND [*To* VERA] A likely story! Romeo must have put him up to this.

VERA Sir, as the light doth betray our counsel, so doth the wind betray your words,
     mis-delivering your compliments to the wrong ears. I am not the maiden of
     this house.

STEFANO Not you, miss. Your friend. The lustrous Rosalind.

     [*At this,* ROSALIND's *ears perk up. She inches forward.*]

ROSALIND Who was it, again, that did catch your eye?

STEFANO Rosalind was her name. Or so I was told. But if it is not, then lend me some
     parchment that I may write it down and tear it to bits, so that the name never
     resounds on my lips again.

ROSALIND No need for the parchment. My name is Rosalind.

STEFANO Can it truly be that I am beholding such beauty in my presence? That on
     yonder balcony, becrouched and hidden, lies the true object of my eyes'
     fancy.

VERA He's awful.

ROSALIND Shh. Let him finish.

STEFANO Oh, happy night that has brought me through forest, meadow, and a few

really wet areas that I'm not too sure about to your window's edge.

[STEFANO *pauses for a beat, and then lets out a shout of joy.*]

VERA What was that?

ROSALIND Excitement, I think.

from *The Treasures of the Gods* (p. 1089)

Neil Gaiman

Read and analyze the following passage from "The Treasures of the Gods," using annotation to investigate how Gaiman uses language and style to convey his meaning effectively.

"Sif's hair. My wife's golden hair. It was so beautiful. Why did you cut it off?"

A hundred expressions chased each other across Loki's face: cunning and shiftiness, truculence and confusion. Thor shook Loki hard. Loki looked down and did his best to appear ashamed. "It was funny. I was drunk."

Thor's brow lowered. "Sif's hair was her glory. People will think that her head was shaved for punishment. That she did something she should not have done, did it with someone she should not have."

"Well, yes. There is that," said Loki. "They *will* probably think that. And unfortunately, given that I took her hair from the roots, she will go through the rest of her life completely bald..."

"No, she won't." Thor looked up at Loki, whom he was now holding far above his head, with a face like thunder.

"I am afraid she will. But there are always hats and scarves..."

"She won't go through life bald," said Thor. "Because, Loki Laufey's son, if you do not put her hair back right now, I am going to break every single bone in your body. Each and every one of them. And if her hair does not grow properly, I will come back and break every bone in your body again. And again. If I do it every day, I'll soon get really good at it," he carried on, sounding slightly more cheerful.

"No!" said Loki. "I can't put her hair back. It doesn't work like that."

"Today" mused Thor, "it will probably take me about an hour to break every bone in your body. But I bet that with practice I could get it down to about fifteen minutes. It will be interesting to find out." He started to break his first bone.

"Dwarfs!" shrieked Loki.

from *The Odyssey* (p. 1099)

Homer

Read and analyze the following passage from Part 1 of "The Odyssey," using annotation to investigate how Homer uses language and style to convey his meaning effectively.

At this the beautiful nymph Kalypso smiled

and answered sweetly, laying her hand upon him:

"What a dog you are! And not for nothing learned,

having the wit to ask this thing of me!

My witness then be earth and sky

and dripping Styx that I swear by—

the gay gods cannot swear more seriously—

I have no further spells to work against you.

But what I shall devise, and what I tell you, will be the same as if your need were

    mine.

Fairness is all I think of. There are hearts

made of cold iron—but my heart is kind."[...]

"Son of Laërtês, versatile Odysseus,

after these years with me, you still desire

your old home? Even so, I wish you well.

If you could see it all, before you go—

all the adversity you face at sea—

you would stay here, and guard this house, and be

immortal—though you wanted her forever,

that bride for whom you pine each day.

Can I be less desirable than she is?

Less interesting? Less beautiful? Can mortals

compare with goddesses in grace and form?"

To this the strategist Odysseus answered:

"My lady goddess, here is no cause for anger.
My quiet Penélopê—how well I know—
would seem a shade before your majesty,
death and old age being unknown to you,
while she must die. Yet, it is true, each day
I long for home, long for the sight of home.
If any god has marked me out again
for shipwreck, my tough heart can undergo it.
What hardship have I not long since endured
at sea, in battle! Let the trial come."

Name_____

Date_____Class_____

from *The Odyssey* (p. 1099)

Homer

Read and analyze the following passage from Part 2 of "The Odyssey," using annotation to investigate how Homer uses language and style to convey his meaning effectively.

> And all this time,
> in travail, sobbing, gaining on the current,
> we rowed into the strait—Skylla to port
> and on our starboard beam Kharybdis, dire
> gorge of the salt sea tide. By heaven! when she
> vomited, all the sea was like a cauldron
> seething over intense fire, when the mixture
> suddenly heaves and rises.
> The shot spume
> soared to the landside heights, and fell like rain.
>
> But when she swallowed the sea water down
> we saw the funnel of the maelstrom, heard
> the rock bellowing all around, and dark
> sand raged on the bottom far below.
> My men all blanched against the gloom, our eyes
> were fixed upon that yawning mouth in fear
> of being devoured.
>
> Then Skylla made her strike,
> whisking six of my best men from the ship.
> I happened to glance aft at ship and oarsmen
> and caught sight of their arms and legs, dangling
> high overhead. Voices came down to me

in anguish, calling my name for the last time.
A man surfcasting on a point of rock
for bass or mackerel, whipping his long rod
to drop the sinker and the bait far out,
will hook a fish and rip it from the surface
to dangle wriggling through the air:
       so these
were borne aloft in spasms toward the cliff.

She ate them as they shrieked there, in her den,
in the dire grapple, reaching still for me—
and deathly pity ran me through
at that sight—far the worst I ever suffered,
questing the passes of the strange sea.
      We rowed on.
The Rocks were now behind; Kharybdis, too,
and Skylla dropped astern.

from *The Odyssey* (p.1099)
Homer

Read and analyze the following passage from Part 3 of "The Odyssey," using annotation to investigate how Homer uses language and style to convey his meaning effectively.

                    And Odysseus took his time,

turning the bow, tapping it, every inch,

for borings that termites might have made

while the master of the weapon was abroad.

The suitors were now watching him, and some

jested among themselves:

            "A bow lover!"

"Dealer in old bows!"

            "Maybe he has one like it at home!"

            "Or has an itch to make one for himself."

"See how he handles it, the sly old buzzard!"

And one disdainful suitor added this:

"May his fortune grow an inch for every inch he bends it!"

But the man skilled in all ways of contending,

satisfied by the great bow's look and heft,

like a musician, like a harper, when

with quiet hand upon his instrument

he draws between his thumb and forefinger

a sweet new string upon a peg: so effortlessly

Odysseus in one motion strung the bow.

Then slid his right hand down the cord and plucked it,

so the taut gut vibrating hummed and sang
a swallow's note.

       In the hushed hall it smote the suitors
and all their faces changed. Then Zeus thundered
overhead, one loud crack for a sign.
And Odysseus laughed within him that the son
of crooked-minded Kronos had flung that omen down.
He picked one ready arrow from his table
where it lay bare: the rest were waiting still
in the quiver for the young men's turn to come.
He nocked it, let it rest across the handgrip,
and drew the string and grooved butt of the arrow,
aiming from where he sat upon the stool.
       Now flashed
arrow from twanging bow clean as a whistle
through every socket ring, and grazed not one,
to thud with heavy brazen head beyond.

from *Heroic Acts to Protect the Word "Hero"* (p. 1137)

Linton Weeks

**Read and analyze the following passage from "Heroic Acts to Protect the Word 'Hero',"
using annotation to investigate how Weeks uses language and style to convey his
meaning effectively.**

      U.S. Army Gen. Norman Schwarzkopf once said that "it doesn't take a
hero to order men into battle. It takes a hero to be one of those men who goes
into battle."

      And the German writer Johann Wolfgang von Goethe said: "The hero
draws inspiration from the virtue of his ancestors."

      Our ancestral heroes first appeared in the oral storytelling tradition. They
were superhumans, almost gods, and the actions they took were mostly in the
best interest of humankind. The dictionary traces the word's meaning from "a
being of godlike prowess and beneficence" to "a warrior-chieftain of special
strength, courage or ability" during the Homeric period of ancient Greece.

      By the *Encyclopaedia Britannica* of 1911, the word had come to be
applied "generally to all who were distinguished from their fellows by superior
moral, physical or intellectual qualities."

from *Is Anybody Watching My Do-Gooding?* (p. 1141)

Katy Waldman

Read and analyze the following passage from "Is Anybody Watching My Do-Gooding?" using annotation to investigate how Waldman uses language and style to convey her meaning effectively.

The morbid, unspoken problem with studying real-life heroes is that they have a tendency to die. The three men who leapt in front of their girlfriends when a gunman opened fire in an Aurora, Colorado, movie theater can't tell us what they were thinking and feeling. Nor can the Sikh temple president who lost his life shielding worshippers from a skinhead's bullets. Nevertheless, a few papers shed some light.

In 2005, researchers ran personality tests on 80 Gentiles who risked their lives to shelter Jewish refugees during the Holocaust, as well as 73 bystanders. Two interesting commonalities arose among the "heroes": First, they were more likely to embrace, or at least tolerate, danger. Second, they were more likely to say they interacted frequently with friends and family. These findings expanded on a classic 1970 study of 37 Holocaust rescuers, in which researchers determined that the helping Gentiles were animated in part by "a spirit of adventurousness." (Related but more prosaic: Studies suggest that "sensation-seeking" is positively correlated with the willingness to give blood.) In 1984, scientists John P. Wilson and Richard Petruska determined that "high-esteem" college students—those who believed they were worthy and competent—more often rushed to aid an experimenter during a simulated explosion, while "high-safety" students, driven by a need for security and the desire to avoid anxiety, were less likely to lend a hand. In the realm of smaller, but still substantial, risk, 74 percent of kidney donors interviewed for a 1977 study said they put great faith and trust in people, compared with only 43 percent of non-donors.

from *Seeing through the Illusion of the Sports Hero* (p. 1146)
William Rhoden

Read and analyze the following passage from "Seeing through the Illusion of the Sports Hero," using annotation to investigate how Rhoden uses language and style to convey his meaning effectively.

Joe Paterno was revered at Penn State. He was admired and celebrated by journalists as the coach who did it the right way, who graduated his athletes and stressed character. But Paterno was fired for his role in the Jerry Sandusky child sexual-abuse scandal. The university's board of trustees determined that Paterno should have and could have done more to protect the children whom Sandusky abused. Will all the good that Paterno accomplished be buried with him, overshadowed by the scandal?

At the funeral of Julius Caesar[8] in Shakespeare's play, Mark Antony says, "The evil that men do lives after them; the good is oft interred with their bones."

But must this be?

Armstrong did overcome cancer and has, in fact, raised millions of dollars for cancer research. Paterno did in fact graduate players. Consider the public citizen who runs into a burning building and saves a family. Later we discover that the same citizen has been cited for domestic abuse. Should personal scandals negate the good deed? The lives are still saved.

Sport has no enduring worth unless attached to a set of higher values.

from *Joining the Military Doesn't Make You a Hero* (p. 1149)
Stephen Kinzer

Read and analyze the following passage from "Joining the Military Doesn't Make You a Hero," using annotation to investigate how Kinzer uses language and style to convey his meaning effectively.

To admire soldiers who have performed acts of bravery is fully justified. Not all combat heroes, however, are eager to stand before thousands of people and accept the honor they deserve. If we truly want to promote a positive form of hero-worship, we should not only abandon the idea that uniforms automatically transform ordinary people into giants. We should also recognize the other giants who protect and defend our society.

Our communities are full of everyday heroes. These are the nurses, schoolteachers, addiction counsellors, community organizers, social workers, coaches, probation officers, and other civilians who struggle to keep Americans from slipping toward despair, sickness, or violence. They guide people away from hopelessness and toward productive lives. Society collapses without these people. Yet we rarely give them the chance to acknowledge the gratitude of cheering multitudes. That honor is reserved for those whose individual merit may be limited to their choice — perhaps motivated by a variety of factors — to put on a uniform.

When soldiers were part of society, people recognized them as ordinary human beings. Now, with the emergence of the all-volunteer army, society has transferred the burden of war to a small, self-contained caste cut off from the American mainstream. This distance allows civilians to develop extravagant fantasies about soldiers that feed the militarist impulse. If we believe our soldiers are superheroes, it makes sense to send them to faraway battlefields to solve our perceived problems in the world. That is why, in this era of seemingly endless war, politicians, the defense industry, and even big-time sports compete with each other to promote hero-worship of soldiers and veterans.

Name_____

Date_____Class_____

from *Why Wonder Woman Is the Hero We Need Today* (p. 1152)

Emily Wanamaker

Read and analyze the following passage from "Why Wonder Woman Is the Hero We Need Today," using annotation to investigate how Wanamaker uses language and style to convey her meaning effectively.

However, as amazing as these messages of sisterhood and empowerment being spread by Wonder Woman are, it is perhaps Hannah's message that touches most closely on the importance of Wonder Woman in the world right now – not only as a feminist icon but also as a diplomat. One of the most iconic Wonder Woman quotes is as follows:

"We have a saying, my people, 'Don't kill if you can wound, don't wound if you can subdue, don't subdue if you can pacify, and don't raise your hand at all until you've first extended it.'"

Something that is often forgotten, but is an essential part of Wonder Woman's character, is that she was originally sent out of Themyscira not only to return officer Steve Trevor to the United States but also as an ambassador to the rest of the world from Themyscira, taking her Amazonian ideals of peace and love and spreading them throughout the world as much as she could manage. Additionally, part of the reasoning behind doing this was because the world was in chaos – Wonder Woman was introduced to the world just as the United States plunged into World War II, and as such, the world of man she was introduced to was, overall, an intensely divided place that had descended into war with no sign of stopping anytime soon.

from *Gilgamesh: A Verse Play* (p. 1158)
Yusef Komunyakaa and Chad Gracia

**Read and analyze the following passage from Part 1 of "Gilgamesh: A Verse Play,"
using annotation to investigate how Komunyakaa and Gracia uses language and style
to convey their meaning effectively.**

GILGAMESH If you do not bow

and step aside,

nothing but worms will live

in your skull by moonrise!

Gilgamesh attempts to shove past.

ENKIDU Because you are a king, Do you think—

CHORUS ONE Gilgamesh—

GILGAMESH Step aside! Bow to your king,

and step aside!

CHORUS ONE & TWO Enkidu—

GILGAMESH I am here to honor

my god-given birthright.

ENKIDU Is every virgin

yours to deflower?

CHORUS THREE Gilgamesh—

GILGAMESH Am I not the King of Uruk?

CHORUS ONE, TWO, & THREE Enkidu—

CHORUS THREE Somebody

pray for them!

ENKIDU One man does not birth

another man.

GILGAMESH I have killed men

twice your size.

Are you a fool?

ENKIDU I lived in the forest

and ran with the lion

and the wolf,

and I fear you.

GILGAMESH On your knees, you—

The Traveler exits.

CHORUS ONE Gilgamesh—

CHORUS ONE & TWO Enkidu—

GILGAMESH I am almost a god.

CHORUS THREE Gilgamesh—

CHORUS ONE, TWO, & THREE Enkidu—

ENKIDU How can you

be almost a god

and not yet a man?

GILGAMESH You are more animal

than man—

CHORUS ONE Where are the gods?

GILGAMESH But I shall still

make you bow down

like any other subject

under the blue skies of Uruk.

ENKIDU I am not bowing.

I am not running.

CHORUS TWO Two bulls locking horns.

ENKIDU I stand here.

I stand here.

GILGAMESH You stand here.

I am giving you a chance

to back down, to act—

CHORUS ONE Where are the gods?

ENKIDU I stand here

stock still.

GILGAMESH Bow down

and say you never

touched your king.

ENKIDU You are not a good king.

GILGAMESH Treason.

CHORUS ONE They are about to kill each other!

CHORUS TWO There is blood in the moon!

CHORUS ONE Where are the gods?

from *Gilgamesh: A Verse Play* (p. 1158)
Yusef Komunyakaa and Chad Gracia

Read and analyze the following passage from Part 2 of "Gilgamesh: A Verse Play," using annotation to investigate how Komunyakaa and Gracia uses language and style to convey their meaning effectively.

ENKIDU They have drawn my name

in the dirt and marked me down

for the underworld.

Enkidu is almost in tears.

GILGAMESH The fever is ravaging you,

my brother. Do not bow.

We must return to Uruk,

and build our gate.

ENKIDU May the termites grow

into a cloud

against Humbaba's forest.

May the Hunter

and the Woman of Red Sashes

who stole my soul

from the animals,

from my friends—

may those two

unbury the dead

in unending dreams.

GILGAMESH What is this?

Enkidu?

ENKIDU Humbaba's forbidden forest

that guarded evil down to the last mite

and the first prayer,

        I would now chop it down

        to a hill of splinters

        if I could raise my arm

        to swing an ax.

GILGAMESH We will stand together.

ENKIDU Shamash, old mantra

        of godhead and earthworms,

        I curse your heart

        for bringing me to this

        juncture, to this crook

        in the long road home.

GILGAMESH I am a king.

        I have never led

        an army to the brink,

        and death has never looked me

        in the eye.

ENKIDU Here you are, old friends

        from the forest, from the Steppe,

        you now linger again with me

        beside this deep,

        unlit door. This place that is

        no place. This echo from the dark

        where death and breath are the same

        sound rolling down from the hills,

        up to the edge of sky. Again,

        I taste the she-wolfs milk,

        and her howl is my cry

        at the edge of these woods.

        We are a drunken god's

        feverish deed and prank.

Activity 1: IDENTIFYING PASSIVE AND ACTIVE VOICE

In the following sentences, underline the complete subject and double-underline the verb or verb phrase. Then, identify whether the sentence is in the active voice or the passive voice.

Example: <u>The children</u> <u>were sitting</u> listlessly under the only tree on the playground. *Active*

1. According to scientists, bird populations are declining in North America.

2. The players were discouraged by a string of defeats.

3. After the accident, recommendations were made for improving safety at the intersection.

4. Servers are expected to report their tips.

5. The guidance counselor will be conducting a workshop on college applications this afternoon.

Activity 2: CHANGING PASSIVE VOICE TO ACTIVE VOICE

In each of the following sentences, change any passive-voice constructions to active voice.

Example: As I jogged around the lake at dawn, the attention of a stray dog was attracted by the sound of my footsteps.

Revision: *As I jogged around the lake at dawn, the sound of my footsteps attracted the attention of a stray dog.*

1. When the pigeons were startled by a barking dog, the whole flock ascended from the parking lot with loudly flapping wings.

2. The bridge was weakened by the rushing flood waters that came with the spring thaw.

3. Mistakes were admitted by the police officers during the press conference, but the crowd did not think the apology went far enough.

4. The dessert appeared after a spectacular banquet had been served by our hosts.

5. Free tickets were being given by the promoters to anyone who had a valid student ID.

Activity 3: REVISING A PARAGRAPH FOR MORE EFFECTIVE USE OF PASSIVE AND ACTIVE VOICE

The following paragraph, written for a general audience, includes some inappropriate use of the passive voice. Revise the paragraph to make more effective use of active voice. Not all sentences require revision; be prepared to explain why you decided to make any change.

Cats have long been seen as aloof and uninterested in human companionship. Even cat lovers may believe that cats are motivated more by a desire for food than by an interest in social interaction when they seek out human beings. But it has been suggested by several recent studies that cats do, in fact, bond with human companions. Cats domesticated themselves in prehistoric times—unlike dogs, who were intentionally domesticated by humans. Could it be that cats actually like to spend time with people, or that at least some cats like to be around some people some of the time? The answer given by scientists who study cats is a clear "yes." In one study, cats were brought to an unfamiliar place by their owners, and then the cats were left alone for a while to look around. When the owners returned, a majority of the cats acknowledged the familiar humans right away and then continued investigating the new space. It is believed that this behavior shows "secure attachment" in the same way that babies feel attached to caregivers. Other studies show that cats know their own names, even if they do not always come when they are called by humans, and that familiar humans are preferred over strangers by cats. Dog lovers may not be persuaded by such research that cats care about humans as much as dogs do. However, people who love cats will probably be happy to hear that affection for its owner can actually be felt by a cat and that the bond between human and cat can at least sometimes be mutual.

Activity 1: IDENTIFYING PROBLEMS WITH ADJECTIVES AND ADVERBS

In each of the following sentences, underline every adjective and double underline every adverb. If the sentence contains an error, identify the problem. If the sentence is correct, write *Correct*.

Example: The dog smelled <u>badly</u>, so we gave him a bath.

Problem: *An adjective should follow a linking verb like "smelled," but "badly" is an adverb.*

1. She felt terribly sick and performed poor on the test.

   PROBLEM: _____

   _____

2. My mother and father argue about which of the them does the most work around the house.

   PROBLEM: _____

   _____

3. The exhausted boy behaved badly in the grocery store.

PROBLEM: _____

_____

4. People who get a small amount of exercise are usually more healthier than people who sit all day.

PROBLEM: _____

5. The engine was running smooth until the car began to cross the desert at the hottest time of the day.

PROBLEM: _____

Activity 2: REVISING ADJECTIVE AND ADVERB ERRORS

Correct any adjective or adverb errors in the following sentences. If the sentence is correct as written, write *Correct*. Be prepared to explain why you made each revision.

Example: I could not have asked for a more better friend.

Revision: I could not have asked for a better friend.

1. July is one of the hotter months of the year in Chicago.

   REVISION: _____

   _____

2. We were glad we had camped out overnight to get tickets to the concert because the line was real long by morning.

   REVISION: _____

   _____

3. Both teams played poorly, and the result was one of the boringest games Karina had ever seen.

   REVISION: _____

   _____

4. Suddenly, the rain stopped, and a spectacularly beautiful double rainbow appeared.

REVISION: _____

_____

5. The cake looked delicious, but it tasted terribly.

REVISION: _____

Activity 3: REVISING A PARAGRAPH FOR ADJECTIVE AND ADVERB PROBLEMS

The following paragraph was written for a general audience and may include adjective and adverb problems. Revise the paragraph to correct any issues you identify.

Copenhagen, the capital of Denmark, tops many lists as the world's bestest city for riding

bicycles. More bicycles than cars cross the city each day, with near 40% of Copenhagen

residents biking regularly to work. Infrastructure in the capital city encourages biking.

Copenhagen is fairly flat, so bike riders do not face any real difficult hills or other obstacles. For

short trips, Copenhagen residents seem to feel badly about driving when they can bike instead.

For longer trips, however, cycling to work instead of driving has not always seemed like the best

option. Commuting by bike must be easy, or people will not do it. Therefore, planners have tried

to ensure that biking is the most fastest way to get to work, even for those who live outside

Copenhagen. Biking distances of more than three or four miles used to be difficulter than it is

now. But the towns surrounding Copenhagen have built bike superhighways separated from roads to encourage cyclists to ride to the capital. These bike superhighways, with well-maintained pavement and lights, allow even long-distance riders to bike safe in Denmark. When biking is the efficientest way to travel, who needs a car?

Activity 1: IDENTIFYING CAPITALIZATION ERRORS

In the following sentences, write *Missing* **if any required capitalization is missing,** *Unnecessary* **if there is unnecessary capitalization, or** *Correct* **if the sentence includes no errors in capitalization.**

Examples: Felicia and her Husband spent their Winter break in Alabama. *Unnecessary*

We went to grandma's house after school. *Missing*

1. When Spring comes, I want to see the Rocky Mountains.

2. During the depression, senator Huey Long of Louisiana introduced a program to limit individual wealth.

3. The committee meeting will be cancelled for the next two Tuesdays.

4. She is a Film major, but her favorite class last semester was Human Biology.

5. Harold would like to buy a new iphone next year, so he took a part-time job at Johnson's Garden Depot.

Activity 2: REVISING CAPITALIZATION ERRORS

Revise each of the following items to correct capitalization errors.

Example: The Washington state department of transportation operates Ferries from Seattle to Bainbridge Island.

Revision: The Washington State Department of Transportation operates ferries from Seattle to Bainbridge Island.

1. My father chose Hans Christian Andersen's Fairy Tale "the Little Mermaid" as a bedtime story because he was familiar with the Disney Movie.

    REVISION: _____

    _____

2. The doctor told Mrs. Sandoval that she should get a flu shot before the New Year.

    REVISION: _____

    _____

3. She studied spanish and art history before she decided to become a Librarian.

REVISION: _____

_____

4. Congress unanimously chose George Washington to lead the continental army during the American revolution, but as Commander-in-Chief he accepted no wages.

REVISION: _____

_____

5. The Empire state building has appeared in many films, including *King Kong* and *Sleepless In Seattle.*

REVISION: _____

_____

Activity 3: REVISING A PARAGRAPH FOR CAPITALIZATION

The following paragraph was written for a general audience and may include problems with capitalization. Revise the paragraph to correct any problems you find. Some sentences may not contain errors.

New York City has a number of statues of female figures, including Central Park's statue of Alice from *Through the looking glass.* However, of all the city's Public statues, only five feature women who actually lived. Visitors will find two of the five in Riverside Park along the Hudson river. One is a statue of Joan Of Arc, a french martyr who lived in the Fifteenth Century. The other is Eleanor Roosevelt, who was first lady of the United States throughout world war II. Bryant Park is home to a statue of Gertrude Stein, the Author of *the Autobiography of Alice B. Toklas.* The intersection of Broadway and 39th Street is known as Golda Meir square and features a bust of Meir, a woman raised in the American midwest who became Israel's first female Prime Minister in 1969. The fifth is a statue of Harriet Tubman, who escaped from slavery and helped dozens of others flee to Freedom. Fortunately, several new statues of women from History are planned. A statue featuring suffragists will include Elizabeth Cady Stanton and Susan B. Anthony, who fought for a woman's Right to Vote, and Sojourner Truth, whose speech "Ain't I a woman" noted that african american women needed the Vote as well. In addition, the "She built NYC" campaign is creating several new Monuments to pioneering women. If all goes well, New York City may soon have more statues of women to look up to.

Activity 1: IDENTIFYING COMMA SPLICES AND RUN-ONS

Underline every independent clause in the following examples. Identify any comma splices or run-ons. If a sentence is correct, write *Correct*.

Examples: <u>The squirrels in the park are fearless</u>, <u>one tried to steal my lunch</u>. *Comma splice*

Although they are fun to watch, <u>people should not feed them</u>. *Correct*

1. Vintage film posters can be expensive, but fans of old movies may be able to find moderately priced copies.
2. The chair was bright yellow, the color seemed appealing to me but revolting to my sister.
3. South of town is a reservoir where people swim in warm weather the water is cool and inviting.
4. She left her jacket in the cafeteria when she came back, it was gone.
5. Try to listen to him politely, ignore everything that he asks you to do.

Activity 2: REVISING COMMA SPLICES AND RUN-ONS

Rewrite each of the following items to eliminate the comma splices and run-ons. Revise each item in two different ways, using any of the methods discussed above for fixing comma splices and run-ons.

Example: The palm trees whipped back and forth a hurricane was coming.

REVISION 1: The palm trees whipped back and forth; a hurricane was coming.

REVISION 2: The palm trees whipped back and forth because a hurricane was coming.

1. In centuries past, people wore makeup to hide blemishes sometimes the makeup contained deadly ingredients, such as mercury or lead.

   REVISION 1: _____

   _____

   REVISION 2: _____

   _____

2. Every town in the county contributed a float to the annual parade, local high schools sent marching bands led by drum majors and baton twirlers.

   REVISION 1: _____

   _____

   REVISION 2: _____

   _____

3. Knowing how to cook is an important part of sticking to a budget if you have to buy prepared food, you will spend more money.

   REVISION 1: _____

REVISION 2: _____

_____

4. The house sat on a corner lot, when snow fell, Roberto had to shovel two sidewalks instead of one.

REVISION 1: _____

_____

REVISION 2: _____

_____

5. The setting sun lined up precisely between the tall buildings, a red-orange glow lit up both the sky and the faces of pedestrians.

REVISION 1: _____

_____

REVISION 2: _____

_____

Activity 3: REVISING A PARAGRAPH FOR COMMA SPLICES AND RUN-ONS

The following paragraph was written for a general audience and may include comma splices and run-ons. Revise the paragraph to correct any problems you find. Some sentences may not contain errors.

Knolling is a method of arranging objects, the arrangement places items in straight lines or at right angles to each other. The term "knolling" was invented by a janitor who worked for a furniture designer in the 1980s the janitor, Andrew Kromelow, liked to arrange and photograph his tools in clean lines and rows that reminded him of the company's Knoll furniture. Curators may use knolling to depict collections in intriguing ways. Museums display items such as pencils, flyswatters, and mobile phones using knolling visitors may find the patterns more interesting than any individual object. Knolling, sometimes called "flat lay," can also be a way to look at all the small parts that make up a whole for instance, some knollers have taken photos of all the items they are taking on a trip. Other knolling experiments include lining up many similar items by color, a photo of pieces of toast arranged each slice from untoasted to burned. Recently, some larger-scale knolling has made a splash on social media, with paramedics and firefighters lying on the ground at right angles next to their vehicles and gear the images are captured by drone. Viewers may think at first that these pictures show toys and dolls, they show life-sized equipment and real human beings. Many people find something very pleasing about the orderly arrangement of everyday objects, images of knolled items that are well organized and well photographed can attract a lot of attention online. Who knows those images may also inspire others to get knolling.

Activity 1: IDENTIFYING HOMOPHONE ERRORS

In the following sentences, underline any word that is incorrectly used. If the sentence contains no homophone errors, write *Correct*.

Example: If you eat at <u>there</u> restaurant, <u>you're</u> meal will be expensive but delicious.

1. The temperature this morning is much colder then yesterday, so remember too bundle up.

2. The coach told us to play as if we could not loose, but some of us could not accept his advise.

3. Patricia led the horse to it's stall.

4. The fishermen checked the weather forecast, wondering how their catch might be affected.

5. Anyone who's visiting the sight tomorrow must wear a hard hat.

Activity 2: REVISING HOMOPHONE ERRORS

Revise each of the following items to correct homophone errors.

Example: The man who's dog dug up our yard would not except responsibility for the damage.

Revision: The man whose dog dug up our yard would not accept responsibility for the damage.

1. The neighbors held one of there loud parties and invited everyone accept Thomas.

REVISION: _____

2. The site of my family waiting at the airport too meet me made me wonder weather moving away had been a good decision.

REVISION: _____

_____

3. A round-trip bus ticket is less expensive than two one-way tickets, but if my little brother looses it before the return journey, its not worth the cost.

REVISION: _____

_____

4. The pitcher through the ball wildly, and it past by the startled batter's ear.

REVISION: _____

_____

5. Your going to need you're wallet if you're planning to buy something to eat.

REVISION: _____

_____

Activity 3: REVISING A PARAGRAPH FOR HOMOPHONE ERRORS

A spellcheck found no problems with the following paragraph written for a student audience. Revise the paragraph to correct any homophone errors that you find. Some sentences may not contain errors.

You can find information online about almost any news story your interested in. However, its not always easy to tell weather what you've read is true. Their are different kinds of "fake news" and misinformation, and some are more harmful then others. Honest mistakes can be made buy anyone, including a professional journalist. Reputable news sources will publish corrections if material in they're publications turns out too be incorrect. At the other end of the spectrum is deliberate misinformation, which happens when an article is published by someone who's hole purpose is to trick you. Sometimes people create false stories for the money that advertising can bring; others want to influence people's beliefs or even make them loose faith in the idea of truth itself. If a story seems to outrageous to be true, it probably is, so the best advise is to investigate on your own. You should no that people are more likely to share information that confirms what they already believe. Never simply except that information is correct because you read it on a popular sight, because it has been shared widely, or because it tells a story you want to hear. A little research can help you find out the facts behind a story that might have lead you to believe a lie. To fight misinformation, do you're homework!

Activity 1: IDENTIFYING FRAGMENTS

Underline any fragments you find in the following examples. (Some items may not contain a fragment.)

Example: My favorite comedy series is too unconventional. <u>For my parents.</u>

1. If more people lived downtown. The streets would not be deserted at night. The neighborhood is eerily quiet after dark.

2. Corn on the cob is my favorite summer treat. When local corn is ripe in August, I eat it every day. Not even ice cream tastes better.

3. Although zombie movies are usually horror films. Zombies can appear in any genre. Even comedy films.

4. Every afternoon, the plaza is filled with skateboarders. Practicing their jumps. While tourists record every move on their phones.

5. Because the train station needed repair, the city decided to demolish it. Inspiring a campaign to save the classic building. It was over 150 years old.

6. As Mary began the last mile of the marathon, the sun came out. A rainbow crossed the sky. Looking up, she felt she might finish after all.

Activity 2: REVISING FRAGMENTS

Rewrite each of the following items to eliminate the sentence fragments. Revise each item in two different ways: (1) combine the fragment with a complete sentence, and (2) rewrite the fragment as a sentence of its own.

Example: After the music stopped. The crowd waited patiently, hoping for another song.

REVISION 1: After the music stopped, the crowd waited patiently, hoping for another song.

REVISION 2: The music stopped. The crowd waited patiently, hoping for another song.

1. Because Roberto needed to stop for gas. He realized he would be late to work that morning.

REVISION 1: _____

_____

REVISION 2: _____

_____

2. Creepy gargoyles staring down from the top of the cathedral. The statues are also spouts that move rainwater away from the building.

REVISION 1: _____

_____

REVISION 2: _____

_____

3. The jewel thieves were athletic as well as bold. Hopping over an iron fence and scaling the museum's walls.

REVISION 1: _____

_____

REVISION 2: _____

4. Annoyed by my constant questions. My sister marched into her room and slammed the door.

REVISION 1: _____

_____

REVISION 2: _____

_____

5. The players celebrated their historic victory. With the crowd's deafening cheers still ringing in their ears.

REVISION 1: _____

_____

REVISION 2: _____

_____

Activity 3: REVISING A PARAGRAPH FOR FRAGMENTS

The following paragraph was written for a general audience and may include fragments. Revise the paragraph to correct problems with fragments. (You may determine that some fragments are appropriate; if so, be prepared to explain why you made the choice not to revise them.)

In the late 19th century, the notorious Dalton Gang committed several train robberies in Oklahoma. Which made people compare the outlaws with other well-known thieves of the West. Such as Jesse and Frank James. According to contemporary sources. Bob Dalton was the mastermind of the gang, which included his brothers Grat and Emmett. Because Bob Dalton wished to outdo the James Gang. He created a plan to rob two banks in the town of Coffeyville, Kansas. On the same day in 1892. Unfortunately for the Daltons, news of their plan had leaked. In addition, the Dalton family had once lived near Coffeyville. Where Emmett had gone to school. Therefore, their faces were familiar to the townspeople. The daring daylight robbery went badly wrong for the outlaws. By the time the shooting had stopped. Bob and Grat and two other members of the gang had been killed, and Emmett, the youngest Dalton, was badly wounded. Having survived the Coffeyville robbery. Emmett served fourteen years in a Kansas penitentiary. Where he was described as a model prisoner. After his release, he and his wife went to California. Emmett later wrote a book. And made silent films about the Dalton Gang, even acting in one. Unlike his brother Bob, however. Emmett was not particularly interested in being famous. He ended up with a successful career in construction. Building houses in Hollywood.

Activity 1: IDENTIFYING PROBLEMS WITH MISPLACED AND DANGLING MODIFIERS

In each of the following sentences, underline the modifier. If it is misplaced, squinting, or dangling, identify the problem. If the sentence is correct, write *Correct*.

Example: <u>Cackling and flapping</u>, the henhouse erupted in a loud commotion. *Dangling*

1. Efficient and well-managed, the diner served a remarkable number of hungry local residents every morning.

2. Writing a summary quickly taught the students to look for main ideas.

3. Denying that the graffiti was mine, four cans of spray paint in my locker seemed to provide proof of guilt.

4. Two witnesses pointed out the suspect who had stolen the prize poodle in the police lineup.

5. Making a terrible screeching noise, Aunt Lucille noticed that the car's brakes were faulty.

Activity 2: REVISING MISPLACED AND DANGLING MODIFIERS

Correct misplaced, squinting, and dangling modifiers in the following sentences by revising each sentence in two different ways.

Example: After leaving an envelope hidden in the hollow tree, the secret of the neighborhood's most mysterious house was revealed.

REVISION 1: After the old man left an envelope hidden in the hollow tree, the secret of the neighborhood's most mysterious house was revealed.

REVISION 2: After leaving an envelope hidden in the hollow tree, the old man revealed the secret of the neighborhood's most mysterious house.

1. Covered in cat hair, guests avoided the sofa in the lobby of the quaint little inn.

   REVISION 1: _____

   _____

   REVISION 2: _____

   _____

2. The radio announcer proclaimed a great military victory over a crackling speaker.

   REVISION 1: _____

   _____

   REVISION 2: _____

   _____

3. Laughing often makes people feel more optimistic.

   REVISION 1: _____

REVISION 2: _____

_____

4. Carrying a bushel of rutabagas home from the farmer's market, an unexpected dinner was sure to follow.

REVISION 1: _____

_____

REVISION 2: _____

_____

Activity 3: REVISING A PARAGRAPH FOR MISPLACED AND DANGLING MODIFIERS

The following paragraph may include dangling and misplaced modifiers. Revise the paragraph to correct any issues you identify.

Advertising often makes a difference in the success of a product. Clever and memorable, products with great ads attract customers. Consider the billboards for Burma-Shave, a brand of shaving cream that dotted U.S. highways from 1927-1963. Americans' fondness for driving slowly resulted in the spread of billboard advertising. With a series of six or seven red billboards, each featuring one line of a comic rhyming poem, motorists waited for the punch line on the next-to-last billboard. The final sign always revealed the product name, "Burma-Shave." Increasingly famous, people driving along the highway loved the clever campaign. Proudly announcing, "If you/Don't know/Whose signs/These are/You can't have/Driven very far," motorists enjoyed being in on the joke. However, the days were numbered of Burma-Shave's success. Although showing no signs of being tired of the billboards, highways improved and cars went much faster. At fifty or sixty miles per hour, the distance needed between the billboards became too great. The Burma-Shave brand disappeared. Now in the Smithsonian Museum's collection, however, people will probably remember the Burma-Shave ad campaign better than they remember most modern billboard advertising.

Activity 1: IDENTIFYING PROBLEMS WITH PARALLELISM

In the following sentences, underline items that need to have parallel structures. If the structures are parallel, write Correct. If they are not parallel, write _Incorrect._

Examples: The soccer players in the park are wearing team jerseys <u>from Argentina</u>, <u>from Brazil</u>, and one player appears to support France. _Incorrect_

Either you give me my money back or I report you to the Better Business Bureau. _Correct_

1. We could not assemble the bicycle kit because it had a missing seat, broken spokes, and someone wrote terrible instructions.

2. The actors were prepared not only to say their lines but also gave a thrilling performance.

3. You have a good chance of getting the job thanks to your polished resume, flexible schedule, and retail experience.

4. Cooking for friends is more relaxing and less expensive than to go out for dinner.

5. After a week of trying out for the soccer team, Harry wanted to snack, sleep, and he planned to catch up on movies over the weekend.

Activity 2: REVISING PROBLEMS WITH PARALLELISM

Rewrite each of the following items to eliminate any problems with parallelism.

Example: Civilians who fly an American flag must either take it down at dusk or they should illuminate it.

Revision: Civilians who fly an American flag must either take it down at dusk or illuminate it.

1. Keeping succulent plants alive is easy if you follow simple guidelines: water them very rarely, provide indirect light, and the soil should be well drained.

REVISION: _____

_____

2. Before last weekend's hiking trip, we stocked up on high-energy snacks, reviewed the trail maps carefully, and we forgot to fill the car's gas tank.

REVISION: _____

_____

3. She could either keep working on the essay past midnight or she could get up before dawn to finish it.

REVISION: _____

4. Singing in the chorus, building sets with the stage crew, and costume design are good ways to participate in the drama club.

REVISION: _____

_____

5. Construction meant that pedestrians had to walk across a busy intersection, up an unpaved path, and go along a muddy ditch to get back to the sidewalk.

REVISION: _____

Activity 3: REVISING A PARAGRAPH FOR PROBLEMS WITH PARALLELISM

The following paragraph includes problems with parallelism. Revise any errors that you find. Some sentences may be correct as written.

Anyone who has ever wished either to reduce clutter or who does not want to take care of a large home might be interested in tiny house living. To be officially "tiny," a house must have an area of less than 400 square feet. Most tiny homes are not only small but also offer a lot of efficiency. Residents of tiny homes typically sleep in a loft space, own furniture that serves more than one purpose, and for entertaining, they go elsewhere. People who are attracted to life in tiny houses may be interested in living simply or to go off the grid. Living simply can be possible in a tiny house because it is usually less expensive to maintain one than the upkeep of an ordinary house. Nevertheless, much depends on whether the house is on a foundation or on wheels, whether or not the homeowner also owns the land, and on local regulations that the homeowner may have to comply with. As some tiny house residents have noted, living in a very small space is easier in a community than when the resident is isolated. In that case, a good way to test living in a tiny space in a vibrant community may be to live in an urban apartment.

Activity 1: IDENTIFYING PROBLEMS WITH PRONOUN-ANTECEDENT AGREEMENT

In each sentence, underline the pronoun, and double-underline the antecedent to which the pronoun refers. If there is a pronoun-antecedent agreement error or related issue in the sentence, briefly explain the problem. If there is no problem, write _None._

Example: Everyone waiting for an interview should leave his résumé at the desk.

Problem: _The pronoun is sexist; it does not agree in gender with the antecedent "everyone."_

1. Either the Santana sisters or Marcus should give their speech at the beginning of the ceremony.
PROBLEM: _____

_____

2. Can someone let me borrow his or her phone?
PROBLEM: _____

_____

3. The waiting crowd waved its hands and shouted wildly when the singer entered the hotel lobby.
PROBLEM: _____

_____

4. A soldier should obey his commanding officer at all times.
PROBLEM: _____

_____

5. Give the documents to Ms. D'Souza and the attaché when they arrive.

PROBLEM: _____

_____

Activity 2: REVISING PRONOUN-ANTECEDENT AGREEMENT ERRORS

Underline the pronoun and double-underline the antecedent in each of the following items. Then, rewrite each sentence in at least two different ways to correct problems with pronoun-antecedent agreement. Be ready to explain your choices.

Example: The <u>cat</u> and the <u>rabbits</u> ate <u>its</u> food in separate rooms.

Revision 1: *The cat and the rabbits ate their food in separate rooms.*

Revision 2: *The cat and the rabbits ate in separate rooms.*

1. A writer can create his own schedule, but flexibility is sometimes a mixed blessing.

REVISION 1: _____

_____

REVISION 2: _____

_____

2. Everyone should try to resolve their interpersonal problems through direct, open communication.

REVISION 1: _____

REVISION 2: _____

_____

3. Either cooking an elaborate meal or grabbing fast food can have their pros and cons.

REVISION 1: _____

_____

REVISION 2: _____

_____

4. The parliament has met their obligation to consider the law fairly.

REVISION 1: _____

_____

REVISION 2: _____

_____

Activity 3: REVISING A PARAGRAPH FOR PRONOUN-ANTECEDENT AGREEMENT ERRORS

The following paragraph, written for a general audience, includes pronoun-antecedent agreement errors and other related problems. Revise the paragraph to correct any problems you find. Some sentences may not contain any errors, and some sentences may contain pronouns that would disturb only some readers. If

you decide not to change a sentence, be ready to explain why.

Curling is a sport in which a team use their brooms to scrub an ice rink in order to make a big round rock slide smoothly to a target spot. But in addition to rocks and brooms, an unusual thing about curling is the fact that everyone who curls is supposed to be on their best behavior. The Curling Code of Ethics says that neither insults nor intimidation has their place in the sport. There are no referees to blow the whistle on a player who tries to hide their mistakes. Instead, someone who commits a foul by touching (or "burning") the curling stone is expected to say so, even if he knows that nobody else saw the foul. Both winners and losers are expected to show good sportsmanship and treat their opponents to a drink after the game ends. Curling may look odd, but anyone who treats honorable behavior as their sport's highest goal must be on the right track.

Activity 1: IDENTIFYING PRONOUN REFERENCE PROBLEMS

In each sentence, underline the pronoun. If the sentence contains a pronoun reference problem, describe the problem. If there is no problem, write *None*.

Example: Sonia told Maria that <u>she</u> should take a vacation.

Problem: *The pronoun "she" could refer to either Sonia or Maria.*

1. Ed's sister announced that he had bought the winning lottery ticket.

PROBLEM: _____

_____

2. They said on the radio that the storm will bypass this area.

PROBLEM: _____

_____

3. The twelve-story building had an elevator until it was condemned.

PROBLEM: _____

_____

4. The students played cards until midnight and watched a couple of horror movies afterward, which may not have been a good idea the night before the physics final.

PROBLEM: _____

_____

5. Three-year-old Sara put pretzels on a plate for her imaginary friend Sheela.

PROBLEM: _____

_____

Activity 2: REVISING PRONOUN REFERENCE PROBLEMS

Rewrite the following items to correct any problems with pronoun reference. If a sentence contains no error, write *Correct*.

Example: Donna called Olivia to say that her dog had escaped.

Revision: Donna found that her dog had escaped, so she called Olivia.

1. My brother's car is towed to the garage almost weekly, but he insists the car has many good years left.

REVISION: _____

_____

2. Neville whispered to Mr. Middlebury that he needed to leave the party immediately.

REVISION: _____

_____

3. During the kite-flying competition, enthusiastic kite handlers and onlookers cheered swooping and diving kites of all shapes and hues, which led to amazing photographs.

REVISION: _____

_____

4. Valerie enjoys traditional French cooking because she loves butter and cream, but her sister tells her that too much fat is unhealthy.

REVISION: _____

_____

5. The anchorwoman told every actress who came to the set that she needed a new contract.

REVISION: _____

_____

Activity 3: REVISING A PARAGRAPH FOR PRONOUN REFERENCE PROBLEMS

The following paragraph, written for a general audience, may include unclear or missing antecedents or other pronoun reference problems. Revise the paragraph to correct any problems you find. Some sentences may not contain any errors.

Tom Blake's name may not be famous everywhere, but he is widely known in the world of surfing. They claim on Wikipedia that Blake was "one of the most influential surfers in history" because of his revolutionary design changes to the traditional surfboard. Blake was born in Milwaukee, Wisconsin, in 1902. He grew up near Lake Superior and first heard of surfing from an educational film in high school, which may have influenced his later choices. In Detroit in 1920, Blake met Duke Kahanamoku, who had helped to popularize surfing around the world. Blake believed he had invited him to visit his native Hawaii. In the 1920s, Blake and Kahanamoku became friends, and he both learned to surf and also studied antique surfboards in a Honolulu museum. Blake's innovations included hollowing out and reinforcing the surfboards of the era, which were too heavy for many people to carry. But according to modern-day board designers, Blake's greatest contribution to surfing involved adding a fin to the traditional board's flat bottom so it could be maneuvered in the water. Previously, a surfer had to dip one foot in the water to turn, and that made performance surfing difficult. In inventing lightweight finned boards, Blake made surfing a more accessible sport.

Activity 1: Identifying inappropriate shifts in person and number

Determine whether each of the following sentences contains an inappropriate shift in person or number. If the sentence contains an inappropriate shift, explain the problem. If the sentence is correct as written, write *None.*

EXAMPLE:

We followed the recipe, but you could tell the results were going to be disastrous.

PROBLEM: *Inappropriate shift from first-person "We" to second-person "you"*

1. A person may be absolutely certain that there are no monsters under the bed, but I still have to check.

PROBLEM:_____

2. Everyone already knows too much about our family history in this town.

PROBLEM:_____

3. Finding the discipline to practice a difficult new skill is not easy, but anyone can learn new skills if you practice them hard enough.

PROBLEM:_____

4. When I start feeling restless during the long introduction, you get worried that the comedian will have trouble winning over the crowd.

PROBLEM:_____

5. Most of us on the student newspaper have their specialties, which include feature writing, opinion writing, and photography.

PROBLEM:_____

Activity 2: Revising inappropriate shifts in person and number

Revise each of the following sentences in two different ways to correct any inappropriate shifts in person and number.

EXAMPLE:

A vegetarian may have to explain to family members why you stopped eating meat.

REVISION 1: Vegetarians may have to explain to family members why they stopped eating meat.

REVISION 2: A vegetarian may have to explain the decision not to eat meat to family members.

1. One does not need to understand how and why dough rises if they want to bake bread.

REVISION 1: _____

REVISION 2: _____

2. For someone to be accepted to West Point, you have to demonstrate leadership skills and excellent academic qualifications.

REVISION 1: _____

REVISION 2: _____

3. As the child of immigrant parents, you felt like a cultural interpreter.

REVISION 1: _____

REVISION 2: _____

4. We were willing to wait overnight in the ticket line, but you weren't allowed to put chairs or sleeping bags on the sidewalk.

REVISION 1: _____

REVISION 2: _____

Activity 3: Editing a paragraph for inappropriate shifts in person and number

Edit the following paragraph, written for a student audience, to revise any inappropriate shifts in person and number. If you decide that some shifts are acceptable, be ready to explain your reasoning.

Anyone who has studied a foreign language knows that you can rarely translate idioms literally. Those who create word-for-word translations will find that his or her results may sound comical—and may be very difficult to understand. For instance, most of us would not think twice about using an English expression like "It's raining cats and dogs" if you needed to indicate heavy rain. But if someone translates the literal words into another language, a listener may think they are trying to be confusing. A Portuguese-English phrase book published in 1855 by a man who spoke no English used a Portuguese-French phrase book and a French-English dictionary to create famously terrible translations. Even for readers who spoke no Portuguese, one was likely to find the English phrases mystifying and hilarious. Humorist Mark Twain said that the book was "perfect." People might agree that many expressions from the book, like "to craunch the marmoset," have a certain flair, even if you have no idea what they mean.

Activity 1: Identifying inappropriate shifts in verb tense

In each of the following sentences, underline all the verbs and verb phrases. If the sentence contains an inappropriate shift in tense, write *Shift*; if it is correct as written, write *Correct.*

EXAMPLES:

Every August, the Perseid meteor shower <u>fills</u> the sky with light, so astronomers <u>hope</u> the weather <u>will be</u> clear. *Correct*

Startled, we <u>leaped</u> from our sleeping bags, and then we <u>race</u> away from the terrifying sound as fast as we <u>can move</u>. *Shift*

1. If you worked nearby, you would be able to spend less time traveling to the job.
2. As the morning sun's rays broke over the horizon, the vampire races toward home.
3. My dog Pickles escapes the yard and roams the neighborhood, but the little boy next door found him and brought him home.
4. When movie versions of Shakespeare's *Hamlet* are made, the actor who plays Hamlet was often forty years old, even though the play's hero was a college student.
5. The witness answered the defense attorney's questions without hesitation, but suddenly, during the cross-examination, he freezes.

Activity 2: Revising inappropriate shifts in verb tense

Revise each of the following sentences to correct any inappropriate shifts in verb tense. If the sentence is correct as written, write *Correct.*

EXAMPLE:

open
Kittens' eyes ~~opened~~ a few days after birth, and they start exploring their surroundings in
three to four weeks.

1. A rainy gust from the storm blew the screen door open, and the children and their
babysitter spend the next half hour moving several very startled tiny tree frogs back
outdoors.

2. Most of the chocolate in Vivian's bag of Halloween candy had disappeared, but when she
accused her sister of eating it, their mother admitted responsibility.

3. Marjane Satrapi's graphic novel *Persepolis* explored the author's rebellious youth when
she was growing up in Iran in the 1980s.

4. According to psychological research, unskilled people often greatly overestimate their
own abilities, a cognitive bias that was called the Dunning-Kruger effect.

5. The teenagers in town followed a long tradition of driving up and down Main Street on
Saturday nights because there are few other entertainment options.

Activity 3: Editing a paragraph for inappropriate shifts in verb tense

Edit the following paragraph to revise any inappropriate shifts in verb tense.

Is advertising as a profession doomed? This may seem like a strange question in an era
when ads appeared everywhere. However, research suggests that the field of advertising
had changed. Advertisers today have to contend with a constantly growing and changing

number of platforms, from print to television to digital, and each required different kinds of advertising. For example, social media ads often appeared in the corner of a screen for just a few seconds, while television ads last thirty seconds or longer and aim to attract a viewer's full attention. Perhaps an even bigger problem for advertisers today, however, was that more people than ever before dislike ads so much that they are sometimes willing to pay more to avoid them. If social media users could pay a small fee never again to see ads about weird tricks to lose abdominal fat, will they do it?

Activity 1: Identifying subject-verb agreement errors

Underline the simple subject or subjects of every clause in the following examples, and double-underline the verbs. Put any dependent clause in parentheses. Finally, mark any sentence that contains a subject-verb agreement error with *SV*; if the sentence is correct, write C.

EXAMPLES:

In the sparrow's nest <u>was</u> two cowbird <u>eggs</u>. *SV*

The baby <u>birds</u> (<u>that</u> <u>hatch</u> from those eggs) <u>will be</u> much bigger than sparrows. *C*

1. A bag of marbles were given to each child at the birthday party.

2. There was no fingerprints anywhere on the museum cases that the jewel thieves had opened.

3. Neither of the specials that the waiter described sound good to me.

4. He and everyone who works at the school is planning ways to raise funds for the choir tour.

5. The bundle of letters, which was kept in a box in the writer's attic, is a discovery that has thrilled scholars.

Activity 2: Revising subject-verb agreement errors

Rewrite the following items to correct any subject-verb agreement errors. If a sentence contains no error, write "Correct."

EXAMPLE:

Bat populations in many parts of the country has been affected by a deadly disease called white-nose syndrome.

Revision: Bat populations in many parts of the country have been affected by a deadly disease called white-nose syndrome.

1. Everyone in these hills have a story to tell about the way life used to be.

2. Was the rooster and the cat squabbling in the yard this morning?

3. The first joke does not even make Miss Stanton smile, but the final series of anecdotes causes her to laugh so hard that tears come to her eyes.

4. At the county courthouse is clerks waiting impatiently for the judge to arrive.

5. There is a couple of methods that may help you get rid of hiccups, but nothing is certain to work.

Activity 3: Revising a paragraph for subject-verb agreement

The following paragraph, written for a general audience, may include subject-verb agreement errors. Revise the paragraph to correct any problems you find. Some sentences may not contain any errors.

In the early 1930s, making a living by farming in some parts of the Great Plains were first difficult and then impossible. Native prairie grasses with deep roots that had once held the soil in place was uprooted over time so that farmers could plant food crops such as wheat. Then the rain stopped falling. In the resulting "Dust Bowl" conditions, strong winds picked up the dry soil and blew it around in "black blizzards" that was unstoppable and made the land barren. As a result, there was soon few surviving farms in the hardest-hit counties in the Texas and Oklahoma panhandles. Many families lost everything and was forced to move away from their farms. However, in the Dust Bowl region nowadays is many farms and ranches. Is a repeat of the 1930s conditions possible? According to scientists, the biggest problem for farmers remain a severe drought. Dry topsoil is simply more likely to blow away. But irrigation systems are in place in the region now that was unknown in the Dust Bowl era. In addition, the crops planted on an Oklahoma farm today has the ability to thrive on less water. Finally, thanks to the volunteers of the Depression-era Civilian Conservation Corps, who planted millions of trees in the 1930s, the Great Plains are now more resistant to the forces of soil erosion and destructive, unstoppable winds.

Activity 1: Identifying nonstandard verb forms

In the following examples, underline the complete verb in every clause. Double underline any verb forms that are nonstandard. Some sentence may not include any nonstandard forms.

EXAMPLE:

My mother <u>was</u> angry that we <u><u>had drank</u></u> all the milk.

1. After the cattle had went to the watering hole, they stood calmly under the elm trees.

2. Her father asked why she had not wrote her aunt to thank her for the gift.

3. He throwed dozens of wild pitches, but the manager let him stay in the game.

4. The cat lay in the sun until the day grew warm, and then it went under a chair.

5. Before the car alarm started to go off, a garbage truck had drove down the street, and the workers had tossed each empty metal can back to the curb with a loud clang.

Activity 2: Revising verbs

Revise each of the following items to correct any verb forms that are not standard. Some sentences may not require any correction.

EXAMPLE:

As I set the envelopes on the table, I seen a car coming up the driveway.

As I set the envelopes on the table, I saw a car coming up the driveway.

1. We thought we had overcame our nervousness before leaving for the party, but the moment we walked in the door, our anxiety returned.

2. Marie has rode competitively in equestrian events since she was nine years old.

3. The film suggested that if aliens had taken over the planet, few humans would have been able to tell the difference.

4. Sergio lay the tablecloth on the table and then sat the china dishes carefully on it.

5. Before Mark announced that he needed more volunteers, Fauzia had rose to say that she wanted to participate.

Activity 3: Revising verbs in a paragraph

The following paragraph, written for a general audience, includes verb form errors. Revise the paragraph to correct problems with verb forms. Some sentences may not contain any errors.

Many people enjoy crafting because they can create heirlooms and gifts out of items they have maked. Craft projects take time and effort, and a lot of crafters who have began with good intentions end up never finishing a project. Sometimes these people carry the project with them through life. Shannon Downey, who enjoys embroidery, has boughten unfinished sewing projects at estate sales and finished them for crafters who have past away. When she came across an unfinished quilt with hexagonal pieces representing all fifty states, she knowed she had to complete it. The quilter, Rita Smith, had died at 99. The hexagons had state birds and flowers drew on them, but only two had been stitched. Downey asked crafters from her Instagram feed to volunteer to help. Her request had took off. More than a thousand people had soon wrote to Downey offering to embroider a hexagon for the #RitasQuilt project. Downey embroiders, but she does not quilt, so she founded thirty quilters prepared to stitch the embroidered pieces together. "Humans are amazing. Community can be built anywhere," she wrote in an Instagram post. Many people following #RitasQuilt have spoke up to say that the project proves that "social media can be used for good."